IT'LL RAIN SOMEDAY...

ALWAYS DOES

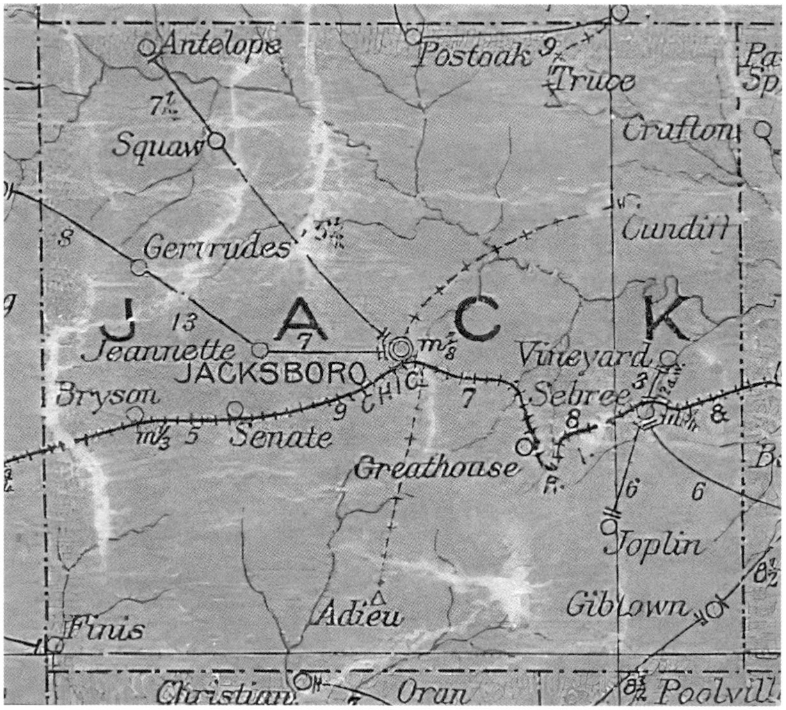

Antique map of Jack County circa 1900. Shows Greathouse location.
Photo courtesy of Lynelle Cherryhomes.

IT'LL RAIN SOMEDAY... ALWAYS DOES

A Historical Narrative

CAROL DURHAM HENDERSON

TCU Press
Fort Worth, Texas

Library of Congress Cataloging-in-Publication Data

Names: Henderson, Carol, author.
Title: It'll rain someday . . . always does : a historical narrative / Carol Henderson.
Description: Fort Worth : TCU Press, [2021] | Summary: "Leaving behind a potato-digging dirt farm, a good mother, 6 siblings and the memory of an abusive father, at the age of sixteen Thomas Henry Cherryhomes pointed his horse west toward Amarillo. Joining other cowpokes he rode the Chisholm Trail, where he learned the skill of driving a hard bargain and found his calling: He would become a cattle rancher. Enduring 'hell and high water' and more than a few nightmares, he made that dream come true. Pushing through the nineteenth into the twentieth century, his exploits left a story for the ages. Drawn from tattered hand-written letters, family lore and legend, this family history tells of a ranch still owned by his descendants one hundred years later"-- Provided by publisher.
Identifiers: LCCN 2021021317 | ISBN 9780875657912 (cloth)
Subjects: LCSH: Cherryhomes, Thomas Henry, 1860-1943. | Farmers--Texas--Jack County--Biography. | Ranchers--Texas--Jack County--Biography. | Ranch life--Texas--Jack County--History. | Family farms--Texas--Jack County--History. | Jack County (Tex.)--Biography.
Classification: LCC F392.J22 H46 2021 | DDC 976.4/54406092 [B]--dc23
LC record available at https://lccn.loc.gov/2021021317

TCU Press

TCU Box 298300
Fort Worth, Texas 76129

To order books: 1.800.826.8911

Design by Bill Brammer

Landscape of My Father

By Julia Kennedy Kirkland

He smiled then, knowing there were clouds snagged in his hair
Slate mountain streams reflected in his eyes,
Desert grit silted between his toes.
Rocky crags formed in the rifts of his knuckles
The hoof beats of a stag echoed in his pulse,
A blue-gold arid sunrise spread wide across his heart,
The harsh cry of all creation sounded
A wild orchestra in his soul.
This was his salvation.
This, his benediction.
This, his home.

**Poem printed with permission from Julia Kennedy Kirkland*

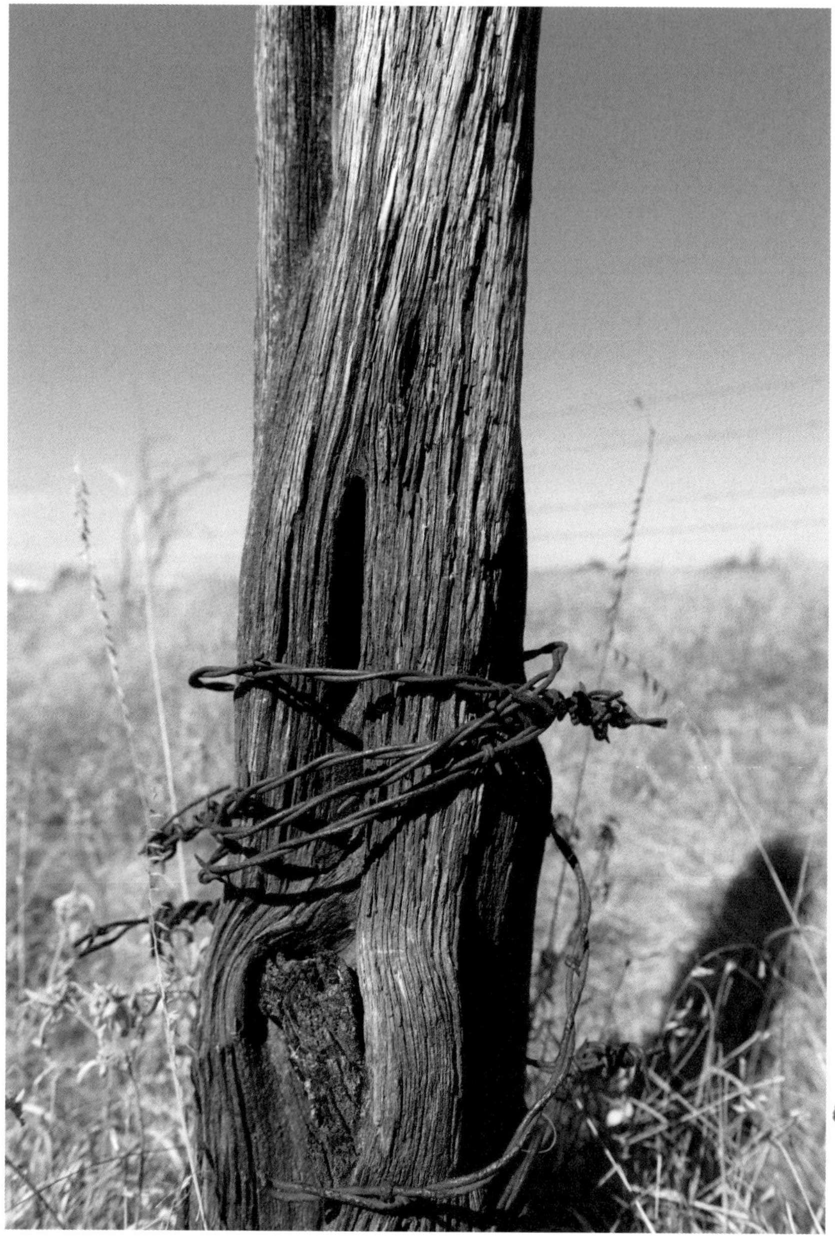

Photo by Jeremy Enlow.

INTRODUCTION

He might have come striding off the pages of a Faulkner novel and been named Thomas Sutpen. In fact, his name was Thomas. Thomas Henry Cherryhomes. And he was my great-grandfather. And much like the fictitious Thomas, my great-grandfather was innately smart and tough as nails.

Born in 1860, on a dirt farm near the bustling town of Austin, Texas, T. H. Cherryhomes had a front-row seat to the gaudy mix of Southern mores and Wild West realities: the Texas frontier. A blend of myth and remembrance and reality, this story is based on family lore, hundred-year-old photographs, and dusty handwritten letters. Thomas Henry Cherryhomes's tale is one of success, pride, deep tragedy, and deep love of family and land.

Tackling life with the bravado of a shrewd gambler, my ancestor's accomplishments creased the edges of Texas folklore. From a hardscrabble, potato-digging, dirt-farming youth, T. H.'s hard work and shrewd business sense led him to live the life of a successful ranch owner who raised prized shorthorn cattle, well-bred hound dogs, outstanding paint horses, and no small amount of hell—when he saw the need to raise it. He was destined to become one of the few brave nineteenth-century pioneers to settle the rich promising land called Texas, and a hundred years later, T. H.'s descendants continue to revere his name, operate his original ranch lands, and experience his shadow presence.

When he was young, his six siblings, by turns, admired, cajoled, and feared him. His children and grandchildren loved and respected him, and even when his tall shadow proved a difficult place to stand, they freely admitted that

T. H. Cherryhomes was the bravest, shrewdest, and most fair-minded man they would ever know.

Learning the skill of making a good trade, honing that skill to a fine edge, when T. H. was fourteen or so, he made a trade that would forever change the direction of his life. Following a long drawn-out bartering session, he made a trade for a very good knife. Sometime later, he traded that very good knife for a better-than-good hunting dog. And with that hunting dog, T. H. tracked, killed, and skinned enough wildlife to earn enough money to buy a very good young horse.

And on that horse, he rode West and away from his family farm. Reaching the Chisholm Trail a few months later, he joined other cowpokes as they trailed cattle to Kansas and back to Texas. With that experience under his belt, he learned how to buy and sell cattle of his own and save his money. In 1890, when he was thirty years old, he bought over a thousand acres of Jack County, Texas. Establishing himself as a ranch owner that other ranchers kept their eyes on, he was a born leader, innately bright, and with an affable personality. Before his death in 1943, the T. H. Cherryhomes ranch comprised thirty-five thousand acres, and my great-grandfather owned the largest amount of land in Jack County.

The original ranch lands continue to be owned and operated by his direct descendants. The Texas Department of Agriculture has recognized the ranch as a Family Land Heritage Ranch.

My own personal love of that land, my sense of Texas history, and familial loyalty demand that I tell the story of that unique man who was my ancestor. Both a historical narrative and an epic personal journey, T. H. Cherryhomes's story is a tale whose time has come.

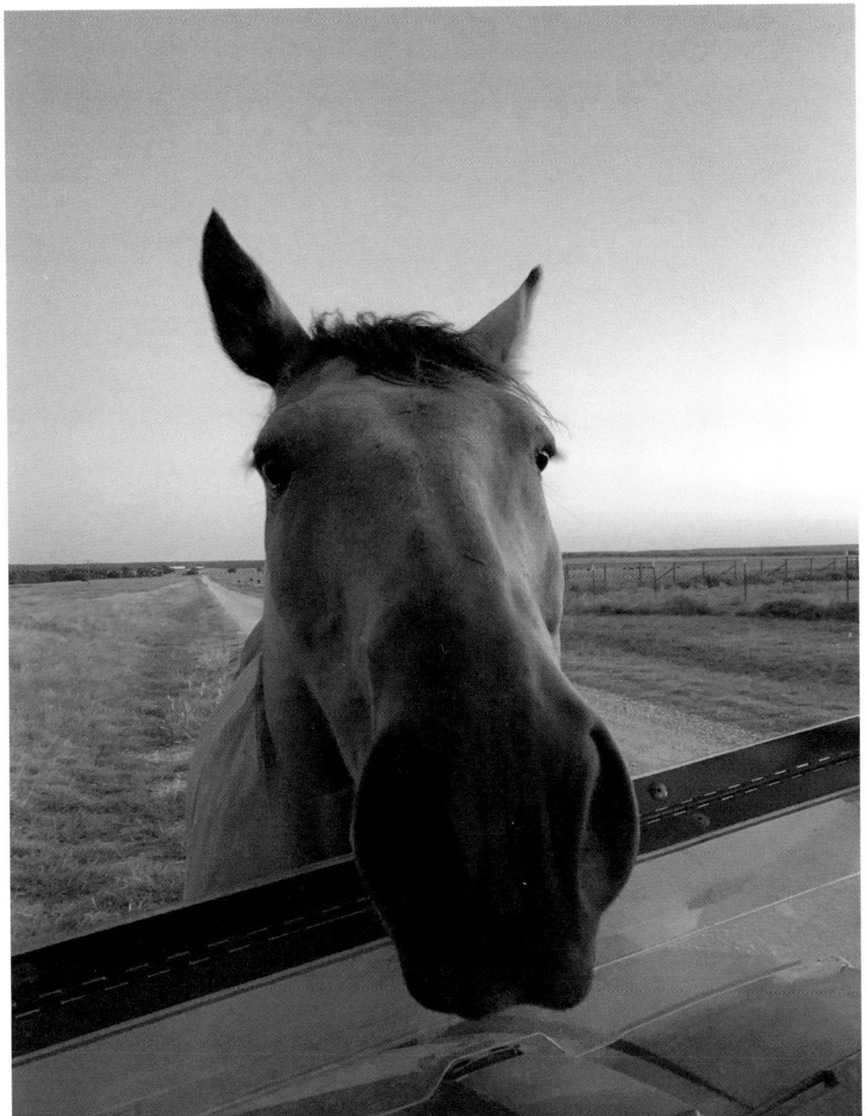

Photo by Jeremy Enlow.

CHAPTER 1

In 1859, a family named Cherryhomes, living in the Shenandoah Valley of Virginia, heard rumors about the new state of Texas. It was told that laws there were lax, the land wide open for settlers, and free-spirited folks were eager to move there. The gossip had it that the state was big enough for outlaws on the run and farmers eager for land, for reprobates and churchgoers: there was room for all. The gossip carried more than a hint of excitement, independence, devil-may-care attitudes. And even though the Kiowa and Comanche Indians were still a problem in some places, and Billy the Kid continued to terrorize the imaginations of the not-so-brave-at-heart, the newness of it, the opportunities, and the sheer vastness of the land sounded larger and livelier than anything folks could imagine, and many a restless young man was tempted to pull up stakes and head West.

One such man in particular, a nineteen-year-old, black-haired, handsome father of two, apprenticed to a blacksmith, had been falsely accused of murder. The offspring of ancestors who had lived in in the Shenandoah Valley for over two hundred years, Henry Smith Cherryhomes began to grow more and more restless and fearful and filled with indignation. His own mother-in-law had proclaimed to any and all who would listen that her daughter's rambunctious husband, with his fiery temper, was a murderer. Henry had never liked his in-laws, so the feeling was mutual. And the gossip being fueled by his kin fairly stuck in his craw. Mortified and angry, his agitation reaching a fever pitch, Henry threw a cussin', wall-eyed fit and yelled to his pretty young

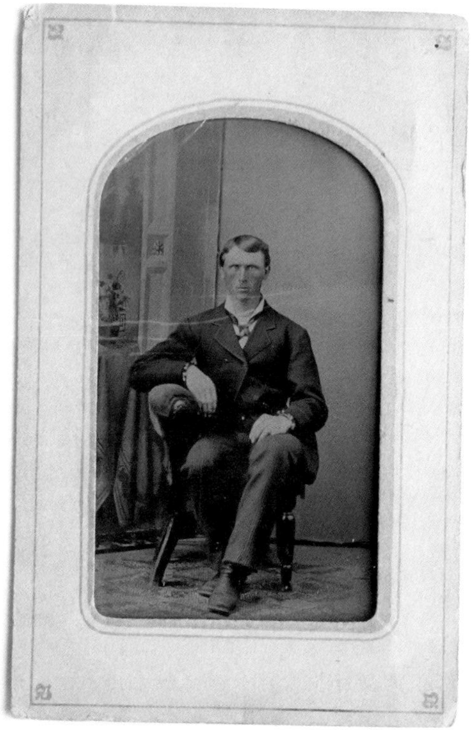

Young Henry Smith Cherryhomes, father of T. H., circa 1860.
Family collection.

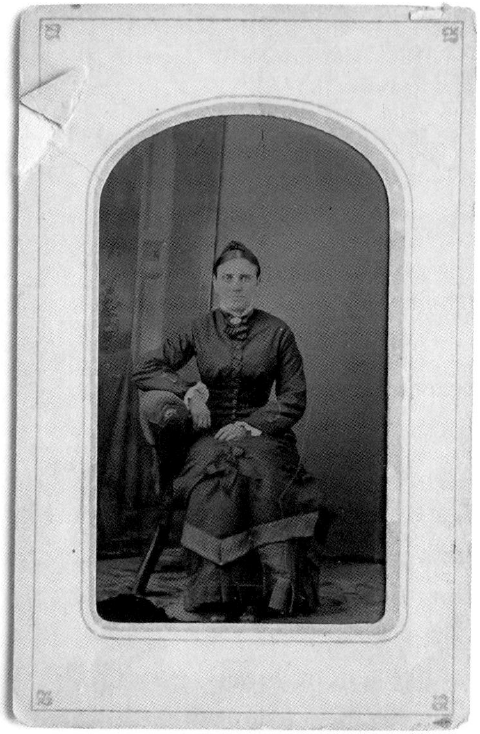

Young Narcissa Stanley Cherryhomes, mother of T. H., circa 1860.
Family collection.

wife, with the unlikely name of Narcissa, "'I god! I'm leavin' this hell hole, had enough of the lies. Never killed any man. Sick of your family and their high and mighty ways. Goin' to Texas with or without you . . . I'm a goin'."

Narcissa, weeping in confusion, torn between her family and her Henry, pleaded with him to stay. Face the charges. Prove his innocence.

But she knew her chances of changing his mind were slight. Henry, always with a burr under his saddle, was often on the lookout for excitement, never content. But a murderer he was not. And he would not hang around the valley while his name was being dragged through the mud and his Cherryhomes family humiliated.

Tradition be damned, never mind how long his ancestors had lived there, never mind the summer evenings spent playing and singing bluegrass music, never mind that he was a trained smithy and had promise of a decent future—at least he thought he did until the murder charges popped up. He was leaving Virginia and that was by gawd that.

Narcissa, blindly in love with the loud-talking braggadocio, dried her tears, turned away from her mother's warnings and pleas, packed up her little family's few belongings, and helped load the wooden covered wagon that would be her home for the following three months. Shaken and sad and scared, but certain that another baby was on the way, she and her two little girls padded the wagon floor with quilts, gathered up the cast iron cooking pot, the beef jerky, and a change of clothes, and told Henry she was ready when he was.

Three long bumpy months later, months spent sleeping under the stars or tossing and turning on the miserable hardness of the wagon floor . . . months creating stories to tell the children and singing songs to lull them to sleep, the little family pushed its way through the Piney Woods of East Texas and came to a stop in Washington County, Texas.

Their visits around the campfires of fellow travelers along the way had been filled with wild and wooly stories about the new state of Texas. In one particular area, close to the town of Austin, everything was said to be new with promise, and the fresh air carried shouts of eager settlers snatching up the land . . . land that was there for the takin'.

When, to Henry's delight, he found a clearing close to Austin, he shouted that they had reached their destination. And a fine-looking piece of land it was: a few partially cleared acres with a creek, just right for his little family. He assured Narcissa that all would be well, that he would find work somewhere. So it was, that with not much more than a crude tent, an iron kettle,

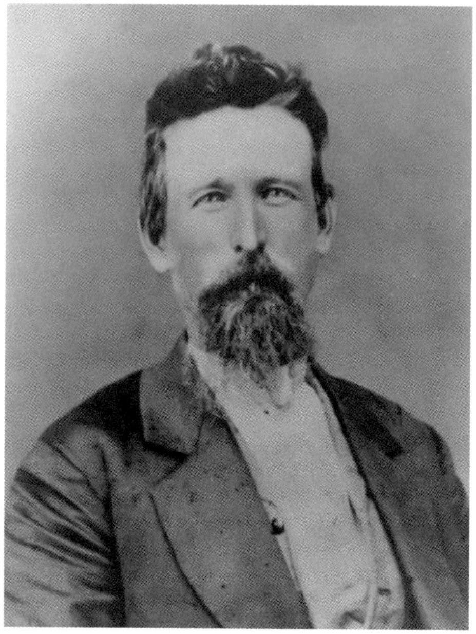

Henry Smith Cherryhomes, father of T. H., circa 1881.
Family collection.

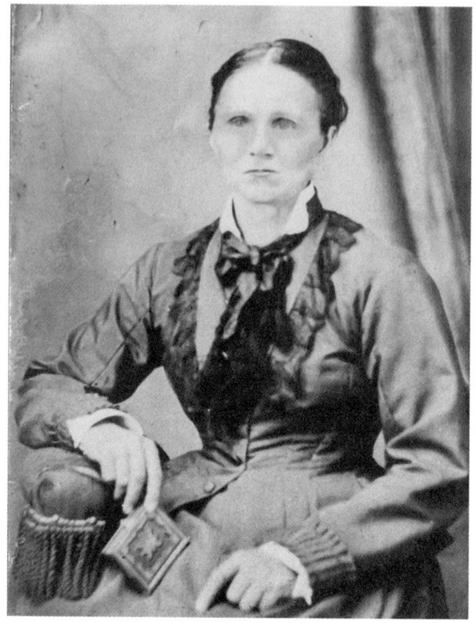

Narcissa Stanley Cherryhomes, mother of T. H., circa 1881.
Family collection.

a campfire, a few quilts, and a Bible, the little family made do. The one-room log cabin would come later.

Narcissa, pregnant and intimidated, put on an almost-hopeful face and assured the girls they had found their perfect new home. And they must get a garden planted before the hot summer set in. Meanwhile, Henry, declaring he would not be gone long, walked to the edge of the booming town of Austin and a day later found work in a small dry goods store. Even though work as a smithy was available, the store with its supply of liquor and other goods was more to his liking. In fact, he thrived. Telling tall tales, drinking whiskey on the dusty wooden front porch of the little establishment, making small talk with any man who made eye contact, yes, it suited him just fine.

Reminded by passersby that the iron framework on the new capital building was going up, he considered working there where the pay was a good deal better. And he tried his hand at that for a time. But for the most part, he much preferred playing the role of cutup while glad-handing customers in the dry goods store. After all, his future seemed wide open and the newness, mixed with no small amounts of liquor, made his head spin with excitement. The Texas state census in 1860 listed Henry Cherryhomes as "Peddler second class."

Meanwhile, in her rare quiet moments, Narcissa remembered her mother's warnings to "never marry that itchy twitchy man." But there she was, hundreds and hundreds of miles away from home, and despite it all, she was still wildly in love with her husband.

July 1860 arrived with heat and mosquitos and horse flies, and by the fourth day of that month, it was time for her baby to be born. Alerting Henry, who happened to be within shouting distance that day, telling him to fetch the nearest neighbor women, the young woman from Virginia gave birth to her new son—her first baby to be born in Texas. Offering whiskey to the neighbor menfolk and shouting a loud hooray when told he was the father of a baby boy, Henry declared that he would name the baby Thomas Henry. Topping off the excitement, Henry received word that he had been cleared of the murder charges; another man had confessed. Giddy and happy and a little bit drunk, Henry hugged his wife and swore to always be the upstanding husband and father he was meant to be. Narcissa, happy and tired, told the girls to call the baby T. H. Thomas Henry sounded like much too big a name for a tiny baby. Besides, in her mind, there was only one Henry Cherryhomes, and he was her husband.

And so it was that my great grandfather, T. H. Cherryhomes entered the dusty, dangerous, exciting world of the Texas frontier.

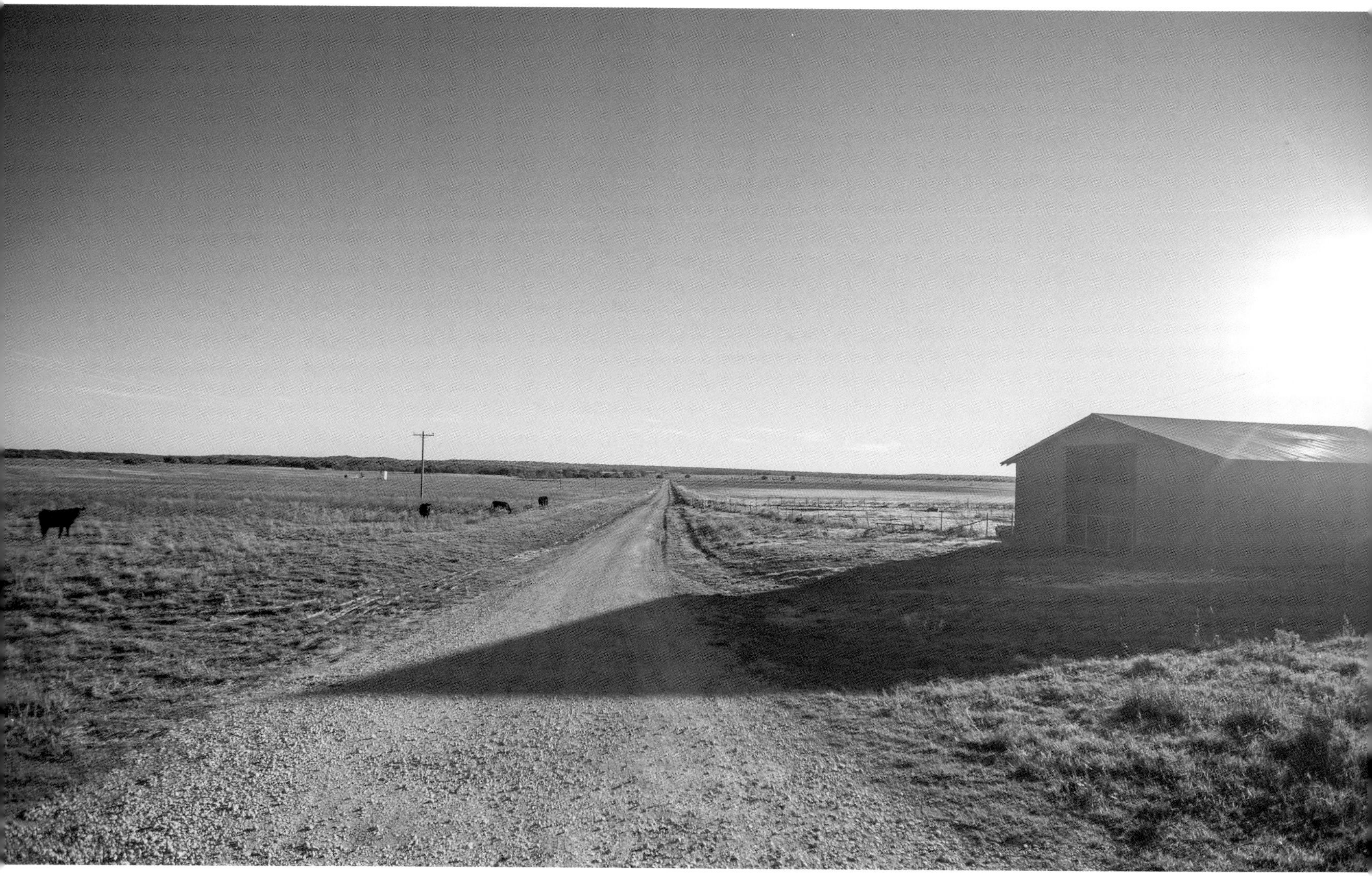

Glass Hollow Road leading to the heart of the ranch. Photo by Jeremy Enlow.

CHAPTER 2

History tells us that the bloody Civil War, the War between the States, ended in 1865. But what history books do not always make clear is this: in 1869, on the Texas frontier, bad blood between families, friends, and neighbors lingered on, and often arguments were settled with fist fights, shoot-outs, or hangings. Perhaps it was one such argument that caused Henry Cherryhomes to decide to leave the town of Austin. Maybe it was the ever-present Ku Klux Klan popping up here and there, waving their own brand of terror, threats, and fear. Whatever the cause, after living in Washington County for almost nine years, making friends, and putting down roots of a sort, Henry announced to his wife they were moving. And just when the green beans in her garden were ready to pick, just when she drew an easy breath thinking that their little two-room house might be enlarged, and just when her neighbors had become close friends. *Why?* Narcissa wondered. *Where?*

"Movin' north to Cooke County," Henry declared. He had that look in his eyes, that quickness in his step, and that itchy twitchy way of talking and moving around. Narcissa knew better than to ask too many questions or put up too much protest. She told the children to bundle up their belongings and half-listened as the older girls begged her to promise she would tell them stories and sing them songs "like you did when we bounced along in the old covered wagon on our way to Texas." While in fact she had no idea where Cooke County was or how long it might take to get there, she knew Henry was standing firm. They were moving.

Eight-year-old T. H. took the news in stride. Accustomed to hard work, he looked forward to a break in his daily routine, and the prospect of a new adventure sounded exciting. What he did not know, and what his Pa did not expect, was that the move would land them smack in the middle of civil unrest, old grudges, lawlessness, and murder.

Before the start of the war, Cooke County had voted in favor of secession. But the vote was close. And in 1869 many folks in that part of the state continued to believe that all Rebels were traitors and should be shot, while others, glad the war had mostly ended, still believed that the Rebels were on the side of right and the Unionists were just flat wrong. Trouble lingered like rancid-smelling air.

Secret societies organized with the sole intent of getting rid of the Confederate holdouts, remained active. "Those damned rebel rascals about town (and there were a good many of them) have a large quantity of ammunition and we Union men intend to have it and damned soon" (Ephraim Childs, *Gainesville Citizen*, 1862).

Settling on a small hardscrabble farm near Gainesville, Henry's family and every other newcomer were met with sharp-eyed suspicion. Local citizens always gave strangers the once-over and questions were asked: "Come here from Austin, did ya? Hear that part of the state has its own vigilante laws." "Family in Virginia? Guess that makes you a Rebel for sure." "Take our advice, you newcomers best take a care who you buddy up to." "Anybody tell you about the day when vigilantes hung forty Union sympathizers? Yup, not so long ago. Right over yonder in that bunch of oak trees."

Changing the subject to exaggerated stories about his past successes, Henry claimed to have owned a prosperous dry goods store and left Austin only to increase his land holdings.

But the whispered speculations and sideways glances refused to go away, and Narcissa, alarmed and wary when Henry, never one to keep his mouth shut, announced to the new neighbors that he was a proud Confederate, Hell, he fought in the war . . . Took a bullet . . . Wounded . . . Damned near died. Narcissa knew the truth: Henry had enlisted, saw no active duty, and a few months later was discharged due to a "general weakness." "Oh Lord," she sighed. No telling what wild story he would come up with next.

Henry's bragging about his farming skills and how he was going to make the new farm one of the biggest and most successful in north Texas did not win new friends for the family. The reality was in plain sight: Henry's attempts at farming left him little to brag about. The whole farm was a hit-or-miss enterprise. The evidence was there for all to see. "Plain as the nose on your face." Potatoes planted too late in the year, corn infested with worms, turnips dry and not fit to eat. Farm chores bored him, crop failures left him frustrated and angry, and the incessant needs of his growing family made him irritable and fractious. And then there was Narcissa, who seemed to always be pregnant and complaining about one thing and the other. "Damnation, woman. I'll drink corn liquor if I want to . . . and not you or nobody else is goin' to stop me. Now where is that lazy T. H.? It's time to milk the cows and he knows it. I'm of a mind to give him a thrashin' when he shows up, just see if I don't."

Shaking heads in amazement, snickering behind his back, the neighbors pretended to listen while Henry bragged how well his farm was getting along and how proud he was. But secretly, he knew the move had been a mistake, and knowing that only made him miserable and cranky. And in his misery, Henry needed someone to blame, someone to heap with scorn.

T. H. was his favorite target.

"Slop them hogs, boy. Mend the chicken yard fence and be quick about it. Hungry, ya say? Well, pull a peach off yonder tree, but don't be takin' more than two. Gotta sell what you and the damned birds don't eat. Now you git on and do what I tell ya."

Life on the new farm was anything but pastoral, and Narcissa, back aching and tired, met most days with a scowl and her own bad tempers. Yes, the new house was bigger. Yes, it had a front porch and two rocking chairs, but why? Why on earth had she fallen in love with a man who jumped around like a fart in a hot skillet and smelled twice as bad?

And to top all her other misery—a husband who left home for weeks at a time, a new baby on the way, suspicious neighbors, and few friends—violence rang out all around the countryside. Feeling the fear and uncertainty, she was horrified to learn that T. H. had witnessed at least three separate hangings. Struggling to steel themselves against Henry's irrational and erratic ways, the entire family heard the echoing sounds of Sunday preachers hollering about hellfire and damnation at prayer meetings as they turned sour with cruel words and gossip. Then when a local Methodist minister was murdered by vigilantes in search of a scapegoat, it seemed to T. H. and his siblings and his Ma that not one person in their world was safe.

Time did little to improve the family plight. Henry continued to leave home for weeks at a time. It was 1872, seven children filled the small log cabin, and all who could walk and talk were given chores, biscuits, and fierce expectations.

T. H., twelve years old, hardworking and smart as a whip, made decisions for the farm when his Pa was gone. His only escape was riding the bay horse to town for supplies or to a neighbor's farm to barter for food or work tools.

CHAPTER 3

Working in the fields, trading and bartering with the neighbors, saving his meager earnings, T. H. was keeping busy. It was the best way he knew to put Pa's hateful ways out of his mind. In fact, he was right proud of his bartering skills. Then came the day when he traded a good sharp pocketknife for a bright-eyed, smart-looking dog. Well, he fairly strutted on his way home to show off his new prize, but only to his Ma and sisters. Pa would raise a stink about another mouth to feed. T. H. was certain that his sister would make over that dog and treat him like a pet, slipping food scraps past Ma's sharp-eyed glances. T. H. had big plans for that hunting dog.

And it had to be admitted . . . T. H. looked forward to the days when Pa left the farm. Experience had taught him that when Henry was away, the chores did not seem so hard or the days so long. T. H. liked going on nighttime hunts . . . raccoons and wolves and who knew what other furry critters his hound dog could scare up. Everything he shot wore a furry pelt. And there was a cash market for those pelts. He would sell those pelts, make extra money, put that money in his hidey-hole, and save it for a rainy day. Swearing to himself that he would spend his savings only on things necessary to his family. And, to no one's surprise who knew T. H., the more he bartered, the better his trading skills became. He became not just good, but exceptional at making a good trade.

There was one long hot day in early summer when T.H. had spent from daylight to dusk hoeing the cotton patch, thinking sundown could come none too soon. Hot and sweaty and tired, he walked toward the water well, hoping for a cool drink of water. Chickens were scratching the dry ground hunting for bugs, the milk cow was in her pen, announcing she was ready to be milked, and the flea-bitten hound dog was dozing on the front stoop. But something didn't seem right. Something was missing. Something didn't look right. Glancing at the corral, there was one horse where there should be two. He frowned. The bay, the horse he favored and had come to think of as his, the quick to run, easy-gaited gelding, was gone.

"Hey Pa. Where's my horse?" Henry, cranky as usual, busy cussing a long-eared mule, frowned and looked up. "Sold him. Bought more peach trees. Now, you git on and dig deep and plant them trees. Water 'em good now." Many years later, telling this story to his young nephew, T.H. halted, his eyes clouding at the painful memory. "Yessir, losing that horse sorely hurt my pride." That horse had been his companion, his escape from the deadly hard work. To make matters worse, "Once I got the damned trees planted, Pa made me water them, twice a day." That meant filling two five-gallon buckets with water, toting them up a tall hill, emptying each bucket on a skinny little sapling, and repeating the whole ordeal until all five of the hateful new trees had been soaked.

Repeating this story to his nephew, T. H. was once again filled with hurt feelings and grief. He had been betrayed. No two ways about it.

That horse represented more to his dreary life than he could put into words. Freedom. Glimpses of happiness. That bay horse carried him away from the grinding chores, taking him round the county where he made friends and earned a little money.

Many days Pa got bleary-eyed drunk. And when he did, it signaled he was about to leave for days or weeks or months—or it might mean that someone was about to get a whippin'. The family all hoped he would be gone by sundown on those drunk days. No one would miss him or his unreasonable demands. "You young 'uns better do what I say. All of you will get a whippin' if you don't." When he pointed to the cat-o'-nine-tails whip, an evil looking thing, snatching it from a hook beside the open barn door, and shaking it in the general direction of the children, fear struck at the core of his family. The girls began to cry and the boys scattered like a flock of scared chickens.

But when Pa was gone, T. H. liked helping neighbors when they needed an extra hand. "Taters ready to dig, T. H. Got a minute or two to help? How 'bout tomorrow evenin' before sundown? Make it worth your time—two bits, maybe three?" And as the hidey-hole gradually filled, he made a far-fetched plan: Down the road from his house where the closest neighbor lived, he saw a good-looking sorrel stud horse, and that got him to thinkin' maybe, just maybe. Time would tell, but deep down inside T. H. believed that horse was going to be his.

And that hound dog? That dog loved to hunt, and when T. H. grabbed the old shotgun, it was hard to tell who was the most excited, the boy or the dog. With coons and rabbits and squirrels thick as thieves around the countryside, well, he was a pretty good shot, and furry pelts were selling at decent prices, so it wasn't long until he had a good amount of money stashed away. All the while T. H. dreamed his dreams of leaving the hardscrabble farm.

At sixteen, six feet tall, and strong as an ox, he knew in his bones that he was done with bending over to take a whippin' from his Pa. T. H. knew the Bible said to honor your Ma and Pa, but he was done with the whippings. "It ain't right that a man's family has to be scared of its own Pa . . . just not right."

Narcissa and the children tried to please Henry, who had developed a full-blown contempt for small children along with a giant-sized craving for the whiskey jug. And almost any time he reached for the jug, everyone went on high alert. "Lord help us. Someone's gonna get a whippin', sure as shootin'."

The older girls whispered to the eager ears of neighbors that their Pa was mean. There was no pleasin' him. Relatives and friends muttered among themselves, "It's that wife of his," said the menfolks. "Complaining all the damned time . . . drive any man to drink." "Not her fault," said the women. "That man is an awful load. More chillun than they can feed. If it wasn't for that oldest boy of hers, don't know what she'd do. Henry shows up once in a blue moon. She gits pregnant, then he leaves . . . an awful load, I tell ya, married to a devil, poor thing."

* * *

One unusually hot day, in late September 1877, when the army worms had invaded their small wheat field and Henry was in an especially black temper, muttering to himself and blaming everything in sight for his bad luck, he and T. H. were out by the barn working on this and that when T. H. called out, "Where's the hammer, Pa?" Henry, red-faced and sweat rolling into his eyes, glaring with hatred at a broken axle on the old wooden wagon, mumbled to himself, "What does that snot-nosed boy want now?" Mean eyes looking up, Henry snarled, "Can't you see I'm busy? There you are a loafin' and lookin' like you need somethin'. This here wagon's a wreck and whose fault is it? Not mine, I tell you. Git yourself over here and make yourself useful before I take a whip to you."

T. H., stopping in mid-stride, stood stock still. Years of abuse and neglect rolled over him. Taking a big deep breath, he knew, without a shadow of a doubt, he knew he would not listen to one more cussin', would not take one more whippin' or one more threat. Squaring his broad shoulders, pulling his tall lean body up to its full six feet and two inches, clinching his fists, blue eyes narrowing into slits of anger, T. H. began a slow menacing walk in the direction of his Pa.

Astonished to see his sixteen-year-old son approaching him with the look of a grown man who had been wronged, Henry briefly wondered when that boy had grown so tall. Sensing danger, eyes darting around looking for the whip, Henry startled at the sound of a man's deep hard voice coming out of the mouth of his son. "Pa." The sound flew at Henry like a fast moving bullet. "Don't be reachin' for that whip. That there broke wagon is wore out and it's nobody's fault, but you're mad and fixin' to blame me and you're plannin' on using that whip, but you're wrong. Not today, not ever again. You and your meanness and your liquored-up breath and shouts of do this and do that, no sir-ree. You. Need. To. Leave. Now. Git your sorry self outta here and don't come back."

Silence. Silence as big as all outdoors filled the space between father and son, and for a split second, Henry thought one more time about reaching for the whip where it leaned, just out of his reach, against a scrubby mesquite tree. Squinting at the low-hanging sun, throwing a hateful glare in the general direction of the boy who had dared stand up to him, Henry kicked at a rock, turned away, and stomped toward the open door of the barn. Ducking his head, yanking off his sweat stained straw hat, slapping it in a fury against his dirty pant leg, he stopped. Gawd Dammit. He had been outmatched and outsmarted by his own son. But so what? So what if he was? Clomping into the darkness of the dusty barn, his shaky hands reaching for his saddle and bridle, Henry made his decision. With quickening steps, he turned to the open barn door, headed to the corral, threw the reins around the neck of the big grey gelding, saddled him, and mounted up.

Henry gave the excited horse a hard kick with the heels of his run-down boots and snarled at T. H. where he stood watching with leery eyes, "Heh. You're just a chip off the old block. Time will tell just how big and tough you are, you little good for nuthin'."

Kicking the horse into a fast trot, thinking how that boy did not know one thing about the hardness of life, not one thing at all, Henry urged the horse toward a dusty dirt road that headed east. Narcissa, hearing the ruckus, stepped out onto the front porch in time to see the backside of a grey horse, kicking up dust and carrying away her husband and the father of her children.

The news spread fast, and hearing about the uproar, the neighbors all had strong opinions. The menfolk, slowly shaking their heads, hawked and spit, narrowed their eyes, and muttered, ". . . be damned . . . T. H. kicked out his own Pa. A gawd damned shame." "Yup. He was a quick one with the belt and cuss words, guess ever-body knew about his tom-cattin' around, but by gawd."

The womenfolk agreed it was about time that awful excuse for a husband was gone. They had listened with eager ears to Henry's girls and their weeping complaints about the meanness of their Pa. And that poor wife of his, married to a cantankerous drunk. "Good riddance."

And Narcissa? It's a good bet that she was more relieved than sad. Perhaps in the following days she looked at her two-year-old baby and sighed, "Thank God and all the saints I won't ever have to get pregnant again. But, oh Lord, what will the neighbors say?"

While the rowdy, still handsome, still arrogant, and hot-tempered Henry rode away from home and family, did he even give them a second thought? Not if court records are to be believed. Kicked out of one nest, he headed to a softer one, one he began feathering months before. In the nearby town of Paradise, he knew a young lady. Heading her way, knowing she would be glad to take him in, he made a plan of his own. And, for many many years, that was the last anyone in his family heard of him. Henry S. Cherryhomes, kicked out of his home, turned his back on wife and family. Changing his name to Holmes, he married again, and moved to Missouri, where he lived out his long life.

CHAPTER 4

When their Pa left home, the Cherryhomes bunch, Ma and all the children, looked more and more to the sixteen-, almost seventeen-year-old T. H. as the head of their family. To the girls, even the older one, he had become a stranger. As far as the boys were concerned, when T. H. said "jump," they did. But T. H. had other plans. And on the nights when he and the hound dog were especially lucky and brought home fox and rabbits and even a wolf or two, he knew that his savings amounted to almost enough to buy himself a horse. A horse of his own. A horse to take him away from the miserable farm and the boredom of its incessant needs.

Still angry at his Pa, when the work days were slow due to rain or cold, he brooded over many things, but his mind always came back to how his own Pa had sold the best horse they had, the horse that belonged to him. It just wasn't right. What he could not know and didn't dare to hope for was this: Many years later, perhaps motivated by that memory, and still holding a grudge against his Pa, T. H. would own a large herd of forty or more horses.

One day when T. H. was alone and counting his savings, he had maybe his best idea ever.

Down the road from the farm, a man owned a three-year-old colt just ready for breaking. One thing led to the other, and soon T. H. was getting paid two bits a week to help break that horse. Getting paid for breaking a horse he already thought of as his own was a daydream come true.

Working with the horse came easy to him, and the colt, with its gentle nature, obliged him. Within a couple of weeks, T. H. had him trained to the bridle, bit, and saddle. "How much you take for that colt?" he asked the owner.

Smiling and cutting off a plug of tobacco with his rusty pocket knife, the bearded man, whom T. H. had known for six years, mumbled a few words, signaling the start of a give-and-take conversation that would eventually lead to a trade.

Acting as though he had been bested in the trade, when he knew he had not, T. H. handed over the cash money and reminded the older man that the trade included the reins, the saddle blanket, and "that ole wore out saddle bag you got over yonder."

Riding that horse home to the Cherryhomes farm, humming a tuneless song, grinning in spite of himself, T. H. sat tall in the saddle and allowed a wave of pride to roll over him.

* * *

Hearing from friends and family that she was better off with Henry gone gave Narcissa hope. After all, she was smart and strong and prided herself in having a good deal of courage. She had birthed seven babies, often in the worst of circumstances. She had taught each of them to read and write, and she would soon teach the two-year-old—that chore was going to start as soon as he could talk. Her older girls gave her strength and comfort, and it wasn't as though she was totally alone. The three-room wooden house was still full of children, friends, and neighbors, and everyone she knew had offered to help if she needed anything, anything at all.

All thing considered, Narcissa had settled into her new way of life very well. And when T. H. asked her to sit on the porch with him late one September afternoon because he wanted to talk to her for a spell, she wasn't surprised. Her oldest son had been quieter than usual, keeping to himself more and more. She knew something was nagging at him and she was glad, not only to rest for a minute or two, but glad to have a chance to hear what he had on his mind.

Settling into two rocking chairs on the shady front porch, mother and son sat in silence until, clearing his throat, T. H. leaned forward and stopped rocking. "Ma. Been thinkin'," he began. "There's no future for me here on this little farm. The dust has settled from Pa's leavin', and well, maybe it's time for me to leave too. Not for good. I'll be back. But with the girls to help out and the little ones growing like weeds, and they already help out with the chores . . . well, I don't think you need me here like you did before Pa left."

Narcissa nodded her head while listening to her son's earnest voice. A soft smile worked its way across her thin lips, but Narcissa had little to say. She knew—deep down inside she knew—it was time for him to find his own way. When he began telling her a few stories about the cattle trail drives, adding "Why, there's a trail not far from the farm, headed west to catch up with the big trails in Amarillo," she knew and nodded her approval.

A woman of few words, Narcissa stood up, wiped her hands on the front of her ever-present, red-checked apron, and said, "If that's what you think you oughta do, then do it." Turning her back to the rocking chairs and her son, she opened the creaking screen door and stepped into the house saying, "Almost supper time. Mouths to feed." And that was that.

In two days' time, T. H. had gathered his meager belongings, finished repairing the chicken-yard fence, checked the hand pump at the water well and oiled it just for good measure, inspected his horse's hooves, and knew his horse was ready to hit the road. Nickering as though he understood a big adventure was about to happen, the horse shook his mane and turned back to the oat bin.

After a restless night, T. H. dressed, walked to the water well, and pumped enough water to splash his face and clear his mind. He saddled the horse and returned to the house where coffee was now boiling, and family was stirring. Although hugging was not an everyday thing to do, T. H. gave his sisters a brief arm around their shoulders, and turned to Ma just as she swiped a tear from her cheek. "Here, you take these biscuits and beef jerky," she said. "You're doin' the right thing."

Tossing a few words of advice in the general direction of his little brothers, T. H. turned to the back door, pulled it open, and stepped outside. He put the cloth-wrapped food in his saddle bags, tied a rolled-up quilt behind the saddle, and checked his Colt .45 revolver one more time, just for luck. His future waited, and he was ready.

Riding away from his hardscrabble life, his Ma, and his siblings was not as hard as he had thought it might be. And that sureness was made firm when he stopped in front of a farmhouse fifty miles or so to the west of his family farm, dismounted, and walked up to the front door. An elderly gray-haired man answered his knock. "Yes," he told T. H., "could use some farm help for a few days, maybe a month. Pay ya ten maybe twelve dollars for thirty days' work."

After two months and twenty-six dollars—the farmer had been extra generous—T. H. said it was time to move on. *Good riddance to farm work*, he thought. *I might slop hogs, break horses, chop wood, but be damned if I would ever walk behind a mule-pulled Georgia plow risking life and limb on the fickle crops and north Texas weather ever again.*

My great-grandfather was more than ready for trail drives. The trail bosses were ready for him and every strong young man that wanted to sign on. Experience didn't matter; strength and determination did, and T. H. had a big supply of both. He could almost hear the cattle calls, the whoops and whistles and shouts of the drovers. They were out there a few miles to the west. It was Amarillo where the real action lay, and he couldn't wait. He was eager to see the countryside and eager to see the big city in Kansas. He could not wait.

After ten days of pushing his horse to the limit by day, sleeping on the ground by night, eating up most of his food rations, and slapping at flies and the last of fall's grasshoppers, T. H. finally reached West Texas. He was amazed at how the land flattened out, and there was something on the horizon, more than a cluster of hills and different from a stand of trees. . . . Amarillo. The town popped up out of nowhere, and in a few more hours he was riding down its dusty streets and having himself a cool drink from the water trough at the horse stable. With just enough cash to pay for feed and

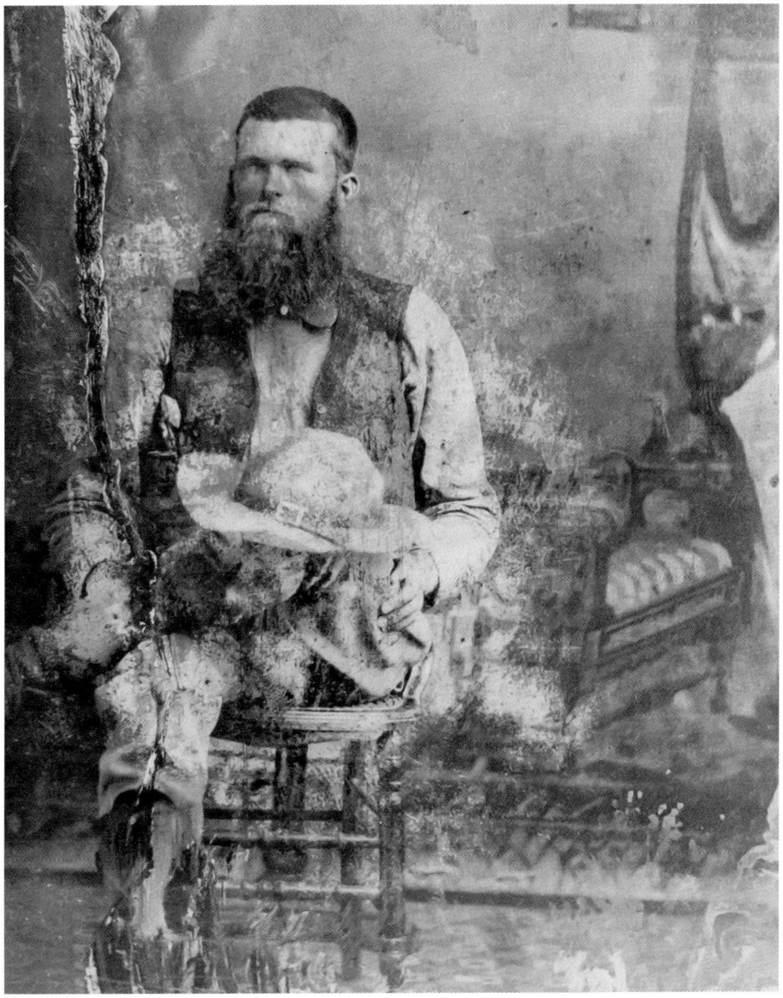

Young T. H. Cherryhomes, age eighteen. Family collection.

board, he left his horse for a couple of nights.

Setting out on foot, he began asking questions and hoping for the right answers. Luck was with him. The first trail boss he stopped to talk to was in a hiring mood, and hearing he had his own horse, seeing that he was fit and strong, the trail boss thought, "Yep, he looks about right." Hired on the spot, my great-grandfather grinned from ear to ear, which was a big display of emotion from that well-contained young man.

CHAPTER 5

"There are moments when you stand on the brink of a new experience and understand that you have no choice about it. Either you walk into the experience or you turn away from it, but you know that no matter what you choose, you will have altered your life in a permanent way."

—DENNIS COVINGTON
Salvation on Sand Mountain

Camped just outside the town of Amarillo, the herd of longhorns milled and bawled, and T. H., mounted on his well-fed, rested horse, rode up to the chuck wagon an hour before daylight. The year was 1877, and in the months that followed, that happy young cowpoke would absorb a lifetime's worth of information.

Although it's not known how large the herd was when T. H. set out on his first drive, it has been said that a smart trail boss, ten cowboys, a wrangler, and a cook could "trail 2,500 cattle three months at a cost of sixty to seventy-five cents a head" (TSHAonline.org/handbook/articles/syc02). Perhaps that statement is an exaggeration, but it is known that a drive to Kansas from Texas could take anywhere from twenty-five to one hundred days.

Because the drives are so important to the history of the West, the economy of the country at large, and to the overreaching education of my ancestor, a bit of additional information is needed for this story.

The work of moving large herds of longhorn cattle required strength, smarts, and courage. The men riding at the tail end of the herd, referred to as drovers, ate dust and foul smells from daylight to dark. Rattlesnakes and wolves were a constant threat, and the rattle of the creaky cook wagon, with its clanking pots and pans, did little to calm the fractious cattle. Each brute, weighing five hundred pounds or more, with pointed horns longer than the beast was tall, was quick to anger, easily startled, and always a threat to the unsuspecting cowboy.

Trailing in single file, a bawling, ornery herd of one thousand head might stretch out for two miles while they kicked up a regular storm of dirt and noise. Every cowboy had to have a quick eye and decisive mind. The men riding on either side of the trailing cattle were called wranglers. Staying alert and cracking the whip at an ill-tempered steer was required. A matter of life or death. An angry longhorn turning on a wrangler and his horse could end the life of both in short order. A steer or a cowboy with wanderlust was a threat to all.

Riding the trails was not ever for the fainthearted. Dangers ranged from poisonous insect bites and thickets of thorny brush to snake bites, but T. H. had lived his seventeen years in dangerous times and dangerous places. He could and would handle anything that came his way.

Watching as bucking horses seemed determined to break the neck of any cowboy, T. H. never admitted to having been thrown himself. He commiserated with the best of the riders over shared saddle sores and blistered hands. The infamous, unpredictable weather threw up its own challenges. Riding north, even on a mild day, cowboys often faced forty-mile-per-hour winds blowing everything from dirt and dead tree leaves to small rocks. Fresh drinking water was not always available, and the beating sun took its toll on men and animals alike.

Wagon drivers hauling supplies of food and extra saddles might run over an unseen snake or two. It's not commonly known in today's world, but snakes could wrap themselves around the wooden spokes of a wagon wheel and before the driver noticed, fling itself into the lap or onto the leg of the wagon driver or his passenger. Or, frightening as it may seem, the wagon wheel might flip a snake into the back of the wagon where it could hide under tarps, surprising the unsuspecting hand as it reached to uncover pots, pans, and food, striking fear and poison in all directions. The cowboys soon learned that when a stopped chuck wagon driver let loose with streams of cussin', spittin', and threats, it was a sure sign that a slithering snake had been discovered hiding in a sack of dried beans.

Along with the rest of the cowboys, T. H. learned to keep his eyes open, mouth shut, and ears on alert. No man or horse dared lull into an easy rhythm for long. A sharp gust of wind might slam a buggy-sized tumbleweed into a lead animal, making it wild eyed with fear. Lightning strikes hitting nearby trees caused all hell to break loose. And stampeding cattle were a horror often causing a horse to stumble over unseen boulders, its rider to fall into certain death.

Wearing wool shirts, heavy-duty britches, broadbrimmed hats, and high-topped and high-heeled boots, the men were dressed for work, not pleasure, and few if any of them had a change of clothes. Why the high heels? Flat-soled boots could easily slip and a man's foot become stuck in the stirrup. No cowboy wanted that to happen. He had to be sure-footed, firmly seated, and quick-witted. A surprised and hissing snake could cause a horse to jump backwards, buck, and rear, leaving the rider flat on his backside watching his horse run away. But being left flat on his butt was preferable to having a foot caught in the stirrup of a runaway horse. The risk of a man being dragged to his death was very real.

Chuck wagon. The word conjures up images of old-time Western movies. But the food the cook dished out deserves a mention rarely commented on in the Hollywood versions of trail drives. Lunch and supper mainly consisted of beans, cornmeal, sowbelly, and biscuits. An occasional pot of "Sonofabitch Stew" was guaranteed on the rare occasions when a beef was killed for the crew to eat, made from a concoction of animal parts not always eaten, such as brains, tongue, liver, kidneys, lungs, and marrow and gut. One old crusty

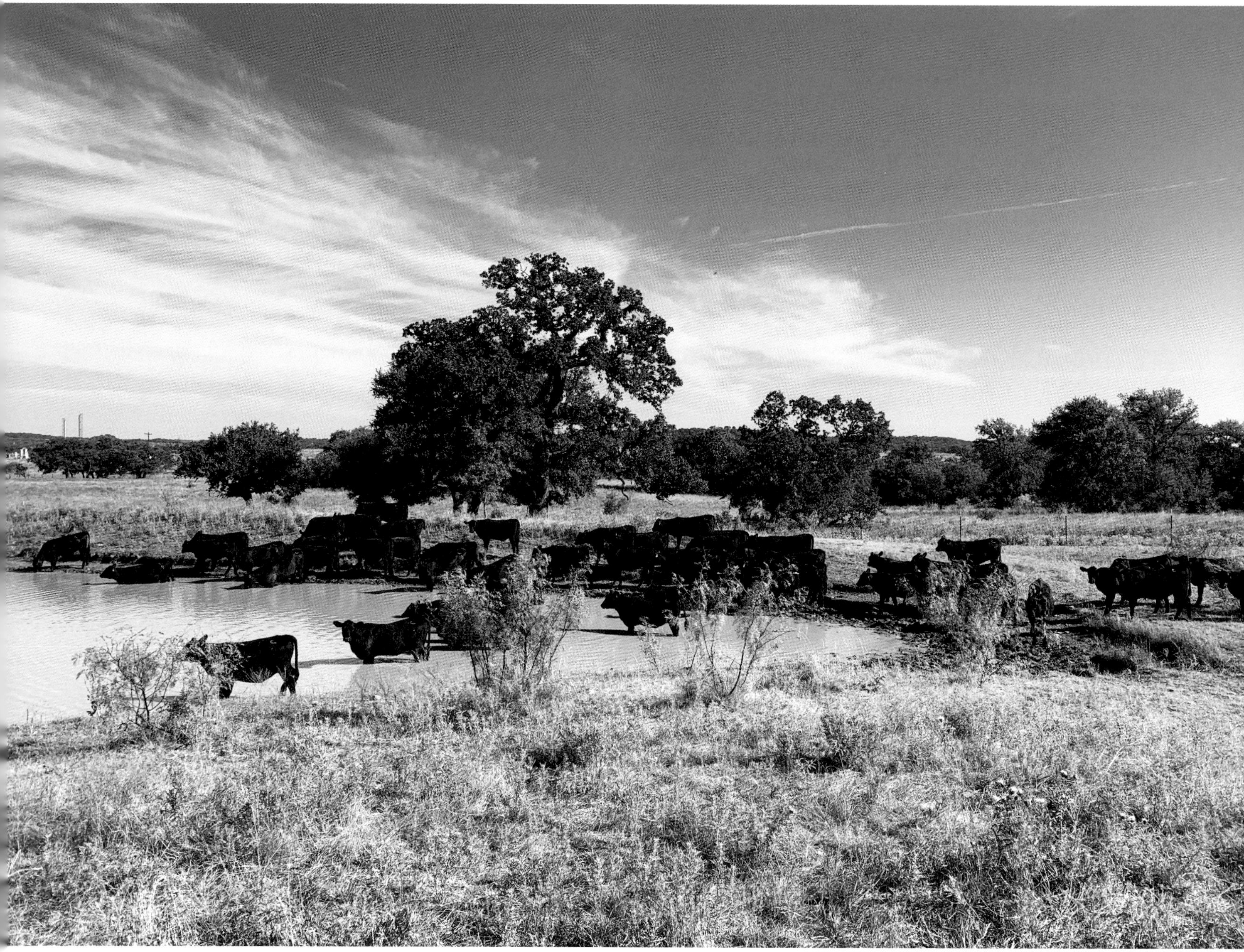

cook is supposed to have said, “throw in ever’thin’ but the hair, hide, and holler.”

Ready before sunup, the Arbuckles coffee was boiled to perfection by throwing a fistful of coffee into a pot of boiling water and boiling it until thick. It was said to be ready when the cook threw in a horseshoe and the horseshoe didn’t sink.

Ingenuity and strength saw the cowboys through the worst of times, and in hard days and good days T. H. proved to be a reliable, smart, and good hired hand. Even on the worst of days, when rain poured, lightning strikes spooked the cattle, and static electricity danced between their horns, and when he slept under the dark night air and the coyotes crept too close for comfort, T. H. felt a freedom he had never known. A freedom to be his own man—and the best was yet to come.

OPPOSITE
Looking for water, 2020.
Photo by Jeremy Enlow.

CHAPTER 6

Like a sharp-eyed hound dog with a good nose for the hunt, T. H. watched and learned. When cattle buyers rode though the herds, separating the keepers from the rejects, the young man took note. Listening to the sounds of the bartering and haggling traders, he recognized the banter. T. H. mused to himself that the cattle trading business sounded a lot like trading small potatoes for big ones, and he learned how to do that when he was ten. He became convinced that the trading wasn't as hard as it might look. He talked to the trail boss, and soon T. H. began buying and selling a few head of steers for himself. While it wasn't easy money, he made a profit on most trades, and it was just downright fun to do it.

He had an accurate eye for good cattle and his know-how with making a trade did not go unnoticed. Turning a profit even on the slowest of trade days, his knack for sorting through a herd of twenty or more steers and picking out the top ten in a matter of minutes was above average. Soon the more experienced buyers began talking: "Damn. That kid knows what he's doin'." "How old is he anyhow? Trades almost like an old-timer." And more than one old-time trader dropped hints to T. H., offering him extra work and better pay, serious money.

One man in particular, Alexander O'Farrell, caught wind of the talk around the cow camp, hearing about a young cowboy, new to the trail but smart as a whip, who seemed born to be an all-around cattle man. O'Farrell walked up to T. H. one day and almost out of the blue started talking business. Flattered and more than a little surprised, T. H. listened to O'Farrell's offer. If the young man would come to work for him, and him alone, buying and selling cattle, he would give him a precent of each sale. Plus $1.50 each day he worked. Saying he needed replacement stock, the older man told T. H. he wanted him to go to the Fort Worth Stockyards to buy steers. "Money is not a problem. I'll back you up." After making the deal, he wanted the cattle trailed to his land in West Texas, close to Wichita Falls, about 110 miles or more from Fort Worth.

Keeping a straight face, hoping to hide his surprise and eagerness, T. H. said he would think about the offer. And he did, all night long. Market price might drop the day the cattle got delivered to the sale. He might get outsmarted making a trade. But why not . . . why not give it a try? He knew his way around Fort Worth and the stockyards, knew the territory between there and Wichita Falls. Some of the trail was within spittin' distance to the old farm and his ma. There was no way he could refuse the offer.

Sunup found T. H. holding a tin cup full of boiling hot coffee, his eyes scanning the crew until he spotted O'Farrell. Hesitating only a few seconds, he walked toward the man with a determined stride. "Mornin', Sir," T. H. said. "Been thinkin'. Just one question. When do you want me to start?" And with that, a handshake, and thin-lipped smiles, T. H. Cherryhomes was on his way to realizing a dream.

It's not known how many years my great-grandfather worked for Alexander O'Farrell, the West Texas landowner, but it is certain that the two men were successful. T. H., buying and selling cattle of his own and making money for his employer, while along the trails he shouted "hallo" to familiar faces, reacquainting himself with old neighbors and friends and a few relatives. Stopping at times, shooting the breeze when time allowed, he heard the gossip of the day, and when he casually asked how things were going at the Earhart place in Jack County, a place where his married older sister lived, he heard that the place might be for sale. Something new to think about.

He liked that part of the country: good cattle grazin' land, nice folks, people he could relate to. He could imagine himself putting down roots on Jack

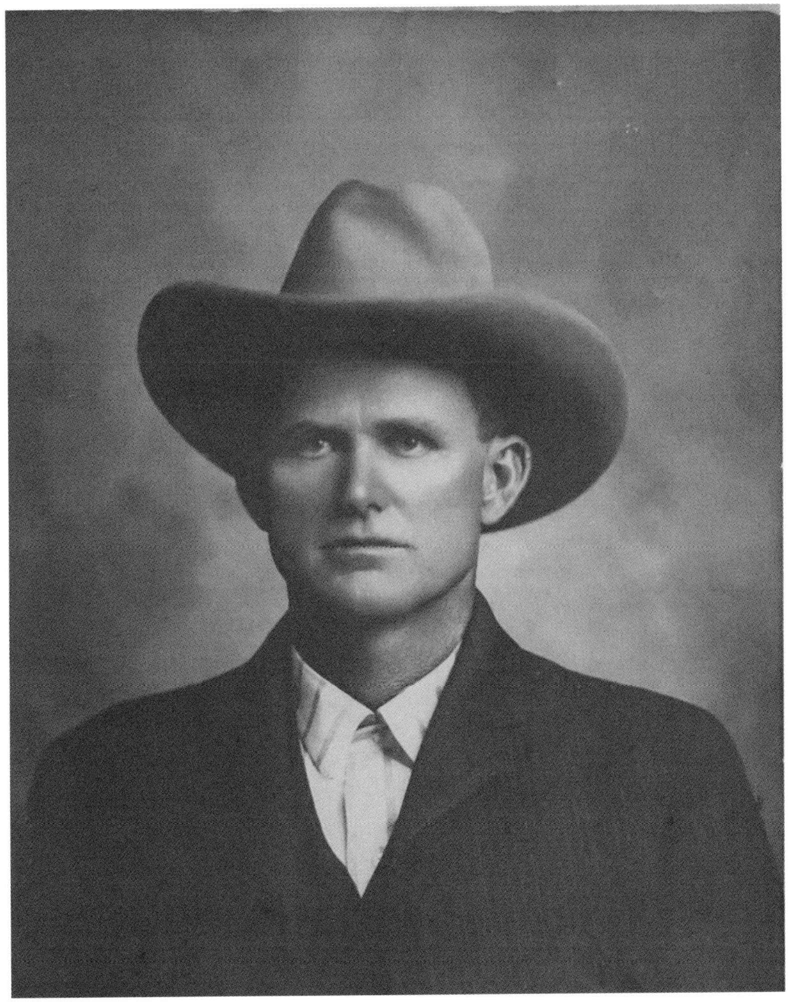

T. H. Cherryhomes, age twenty-one.
Family collection.

County land and making a fine go of his life in the meantime. His hard-won experience had earned him a first-rate education—he was well schooled in the art of buying and selling cattle, showmanship, managing his money, and doing business with a wide range of men from cowhands to ranch owners. And one thing he knew for certain: he could make a go of it as a ranch owner, and being a ranch owner seemed a damned sight better than being a ranch hand.

And so it was that in 1890, T. H. met with the owners of the Earhart land, located in the northeast corner of Jack County. Late one afternoon, the two men talked about the weather ("Shore could use some rain") and Texas politics ("That governor Sul Ross, well he's an OK kind of man. Hate to see him leave that office. Man of the people."). Accustomed to economy of words, they briefly talked about cattle markets and the pros and cons of such a risky business. Then, standing to leave, T. H. extended his hand to the owner of the ranch and offered a few more words. "If you ever get the notion to sell off some of this place, I'd like to talk to you about it." Turning to leave, T. H. tipped his hat and stepped out the door into the twilight.

"Let's talk about your idea tomorrow," the owner said. With a smart nod of his head, my ancestor agreed, and in his heart he knew the deal was as good as made. He was thirty years old, ready to settle down, and with the purchase of that one thousand-plus acres of Jack County land, Thomas Henry Cherryhomes planted his feet and swore to be the best he could be at his new way of life.

CHAPTER 7

The year T. H. turned twenty-two, he started to grow tired of cowhands and family speculating about his busy life, knowing that his aunties frowned and gossiped about how he was still a bachelor and should marry, settle down, have some children, and quit his restless ways. While T. H. was not one to be pushed into any decision, he did know a pretty girl living in Jack County. In fact, her brother had married T. H.'s older sister, and it wasn't such a leap to think of that girl as his wife.

Sarah Alice Berry came from a long line of intelligent and resourceful women. Her mother came to Texas in a covered wagon with a nest egg of $1,200 tied around her tiny waist and a shotgun at her side. Tales of Julia Anne Berry killing snakes with one hand and gathering up her brood of children with the other shined in stories told at family dinners. And Sallie (Sarah Alice), daughter of that brave lady from Tennessee and the young woman who caught T. H.'s eye, would make a good wife; he was sure of it.

A hand-tinted photo of Sallie as a young woman shows a petite girl, with long brown hair and big brown eyes looking directly into the camera. Primly posed, wearing a blue frock and a straw hat trimmed with pink and blue flowers, at first glance, Sallie looked the picture of a delicate Southern Belle. But a closer inspection shows a woman with straight-backed resolve and determination—a woman who was her own person.

T. H., at six-feet-three-inches tall, with sandy colored hair, sharp blue eyes, square jaw, and high cheekbones, knew what he wanted and didn't hesitate for long to court young Sallie. Amiable unless riled, soft-spoken, and

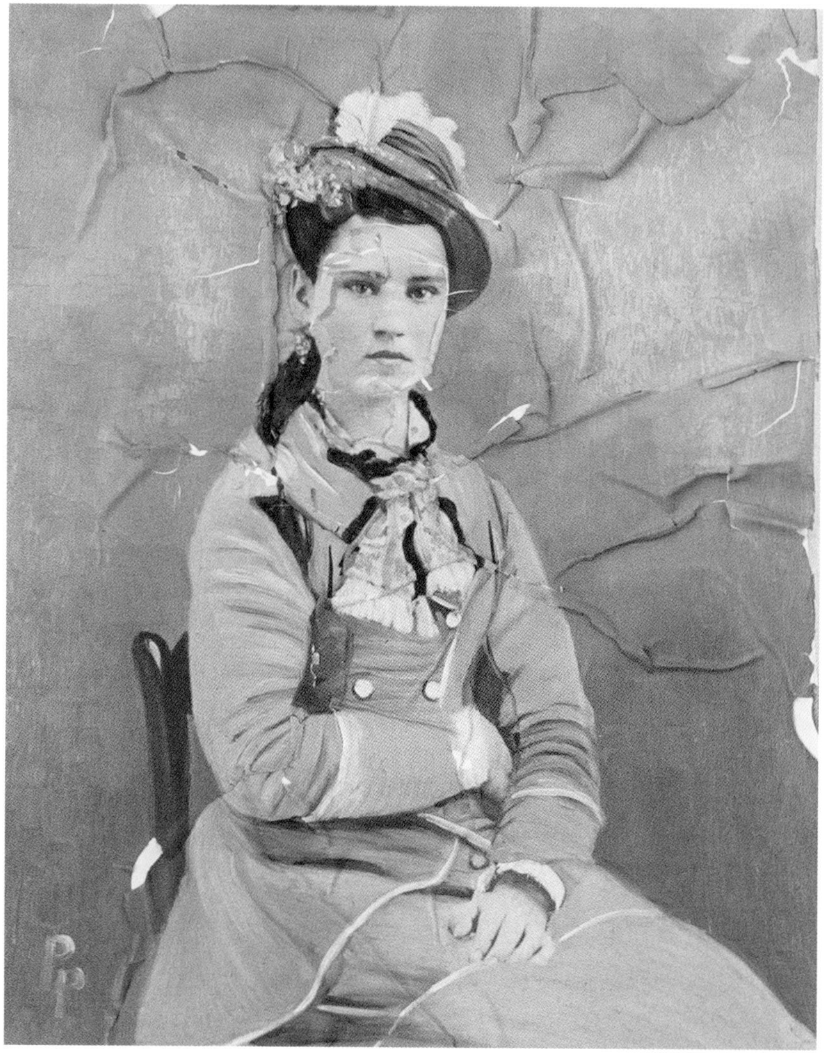

Sarah Alice Berry. Portrait taken prior to marriage to T. H. Cherryhomes. Family collection.

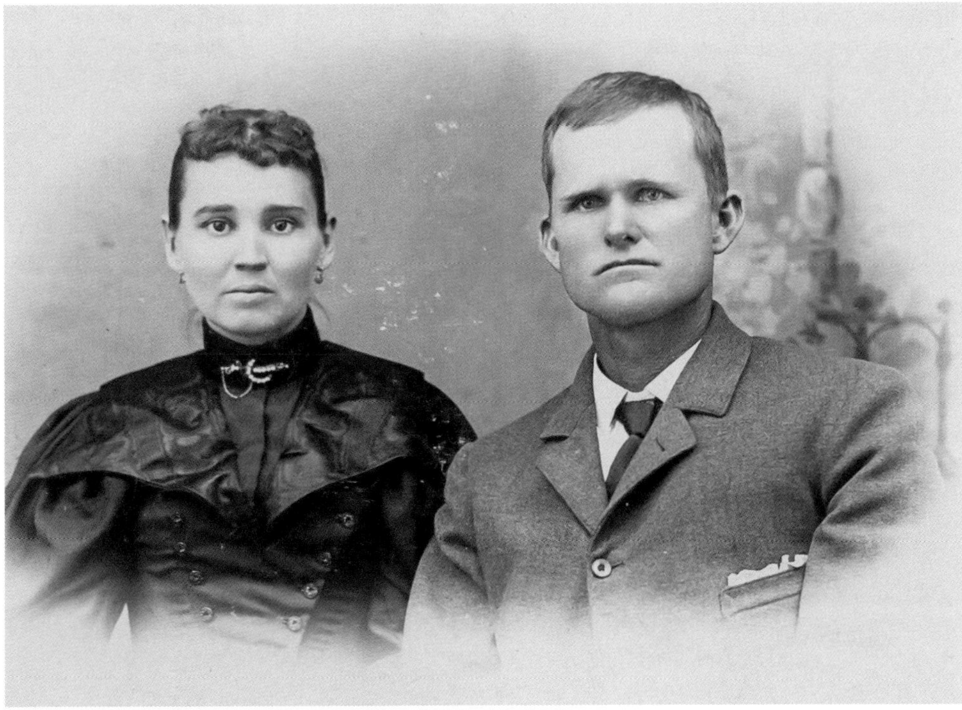

Sarah Alice Berry Cherryhomes and T. H. Cherryhomes: newlyweds. Family collection.

handsome, T. H. and the hardworking, intelligent young lady, Sarah Alice Berry, made a handsome couple. On the day they married, in 1883, their future looked bright—everyone said so.

T. H. and Sallie spent the first year of the marriage buying and selling steers, working, and loving the Jack County land. Sometime within the first year of their marriage, their daughter was born. Bertha Cherryhomes would prove to be the light of their lives, calm and steady. And if the couple was disappointed that their first born was not a boy, they never showed it. Sallie was happy to have a girl to walk through life with. T. H., the idol of his older

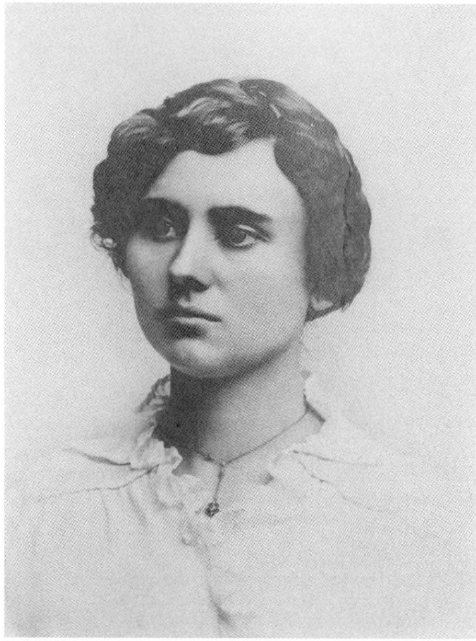

Bertha Cherryhomes, daughter of T.H. and Sallie. Family collection.

sisters, knew that his life was good, and the new baby was welcome. Beaming with pride and confidence, T. H. began making plans for his daughter's future, all the while imagining how she would grow to be an educated and genteel pride of his family.

And as predicted, three years later, little Bertha was a joy to behold. Quiet and calm and beautiful, she owned a grace and charm unusual for a young one. "'At little girl is somethin'. Look at that smile. And smart. Why, Sallie says she already loves books and stories and never causes a minute's problem."

With another baby on the way, Sallie leaned on little Bertha for help. "Be a good girl and gather the eggs for me. I'll make us a good custard and you can lick the bowl while it bakes."

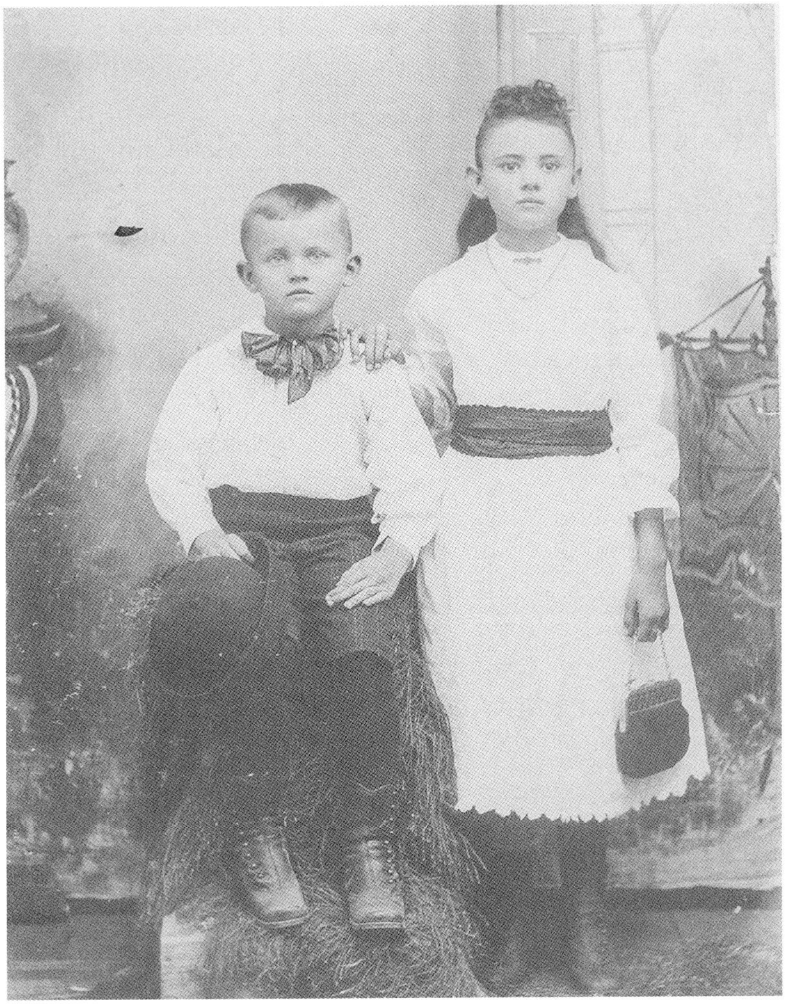

Bertha and Thomas Roy Cherryhomes, children of T. H. and Sallie Cherryhomes.
Family collection.

In the heat of summer of 1886, Sallie took to her bed; the neighbors were called; and T. H., stomping dirt from his boots, came into the farmhouse kitchen with excitement jumping all over him. "It's time, is it? Sallie ready to have that baby. You can fetch me when he gets here." Certain that the new baby was a boy, the anxious father slammed the kitchen door and walked to the barn. Pouring oats into the feed bins, swatting at a pesky wasp, sweating in the dusty tack room, he managed to stay busy and close to the house.

"T. H.!" someone shouted. "He's here. Cute as a button." And with that T. H. had the answer to his unspoken prayer. Baby Thomas Roy had arrived. A son—a son to carry the Cherryhomes name. A girl and now a boy. *The perfect family*, he thought. Looking up at the cloudless blue sky, the young man who would become my great-grandfather stood tall and proud and spoke a loud "yes" to his future.

From the outset, the baby boy had a personality in stark contrast to his big sister's. Where Bertha had been a quiet baby, Roy, fretful and cranky, kept his mother on the run. And often it was little Bertha who calmed and crooned and soothed the new arrival. And in the years to follow, the personality differences would become greater even while the bond between sister and brother grew stronger.

CHAPTER 8

Walking on his land, riding horseback over its ridges and down its rocky hills, T. H. felt a contentment he had never known. He had his wife of eight years, Sarah Alice Berry, whom everyone called Sallie, his young daughter, Bertha, born in 1883, and a son, born in 1886, to carry on his name and his love of the land and cattle. A son he named Thomas Roy. And now this land, where almost fresh-looking arrowheads poked through the sandy river-bottom land, and other remains of Kiowa campgrounds lined hills and valleys. Where the West Fork of the Trinity River rolled along with its belly full of catfish and crappie and water snakes. A river with water for his cattle, fish for the taking, and green winter grass. An unfamiliar sensation swept over him—it must surely be happiness. There was no other word for it. T. H. allowed himself to relish the new feeling and, in case there was a God somewhere up in that blue sky, he threw up a quiet "thank you" in his general direction.

But it was time to get busy. Idle hands, devil's workshop. His mother's words echoed in the back of his mind, warning that the hay needed cuttin' and the hen house needed a good mucking and where was that new hired hand and what was he up to?

My great-grandfather was living a new kind of busy life, listening to his children laugh, play, and cry. A man not given to much in the way of reverie, T. H. smiled as he kicked his paint horse into a long lope and headed home, where Sallie was sure to have hot cornbread waiting and, if he was lucky, a big mess of fried catfish with fresh tomatoes for lunch.

Belly full and midsummer breeze sliding through the backyard oak trees, T. H., picking his teeth with the point of his ever-sharp pocketknife, stood in the shade and pondered. He would call this land the River Ranch. Seemed about right. That settled in his mind while he remembered that a nearby piece of land called SunnyBrook Farm was for sale. He might just ride on over there and take a good long look-see. As he mounted his horse and headed west, T. H. thought, that SunnyBrook place had folks livin' on it. And maybe, just maybe, they would stay on and work for him when he took over the place. Once again, his mind jumped ahead of the what-ifs and settled on the notion of owning that place. In fact the day would come, a day in the near future, when he would buy up more and more land, and if the owners seemed interested in selling but didn't want to move away, he'd sweeten the deal by offering to pay them for staying put and working for him. And so it happened that agreements were struck, families were not uprooted, and they earned a living wage working for T. H. And it was an agreement that worked well for many years. Even today, the now-fenced pastures on which folks had once built cabins and lived and worked continue to be known by those old family names. And, of course, he bought SunnyBrook Farm.

As T. H. rode along home, thoughts of his still-pretty wife meandered through his mind. A tiny girl, all right, but her looks were deceiving. She was determined and tough. He had known her and her family for a long time. Allie, his sister, had married Sallie's brother, making their children double first cousins or some such thing. Sallie's mother settled in Chico, close to T. H.'s River Ranch. So it's no surprise that his Sallie was strong and fully in charge of her own mind. He had seen those brown eyes of hers snap and crackle with anger while she held her tongue as long as her iron will would allow. Yep, a woman to be reckoned with for sure. Even when T. H. let loose with a string of cuss words, stomp and spit and glare, Sallie could handle him, and did.

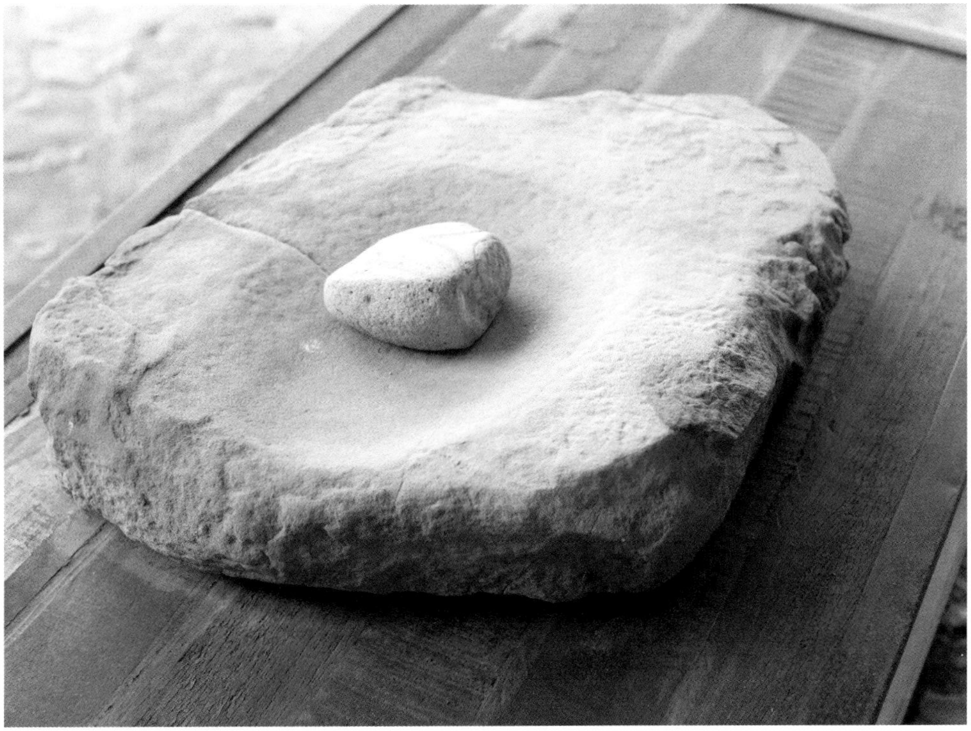

Native American Metate (grinding stone) found on River Ranch. Family collection.

The public faces and speech of the young couple was formal and reserved, as was the custom of the day. In the presence of others, Sallie referred to T. H. as "Mr. Cherryhomes," but everyday life was much less than formal. Days were filled with hard work and demands. This was a couple who had lived and would continue to live in an intimate relationship with the land. Well acquainted with nature and its random ways, they and their ancestors had ridden cattle trails, traveled in covered wagons, and slept on the ground. An undercurrent of wildness continued to run below the surface of their uncharted lives. An intense relationship with the land and the elements influenced every inch of their beings. The hardiest of pioneers survived and prospered. The frail did not. And in nineteenth-century Texas, the Cherryhomes family were among the last of the pioneers.

CHAPTER 9

The sun came up and the sun went down, and life for the young family was consistent and busy. Ranch hands worked in dust or mud, depending on the season. Sallie tended to the children and their skinned knees and chigger bites, while smiling at their giggles and laughs and hands full of wildflowers. Stepping into her role of wife, mother, and head caretaker, Sallie knew that the stability of her family life depended on her soft voice and determined will. Sallie's life was never dull: in addition to taking care of the children, she orchestrated the feeding of family, hound dogs, and chickens, inspected the fresh hen eggs, took charge of the garden, and did the washing and the ironing.

Aware that the ranch—T. H. called it the River Ranch, because the West Fork of the Trinity River ran smack through the middle of it—was thriving, Sallie watched and approved when, in 1889, T. H. bought over a thousand acres of Jack County land. And when she heard that more land was for sale, the so-called SunnyBrook Farm, she expected that her husband was on his way to being a full-fledged ranch owner. T. H. had his dreams of the future. Sallie knew and was not the least surprised to hear him muse about buying more cattle, more land, planting corn and wheat, and on and on. Acreage to the south and to the north nudged at his imagination. "If that prairie land could be bought, just think how this ranch might expand," he would say.

And while his ranching business thrived, Sallie quietly claimed her own well-deserved pride in their success. A success due to the partnership of a man and woman who were determined to make the best out of every day and every opportunity.

White's Prairie, Bean's Prairie, the Greathouse land. Dreaming big. Planning with care. In time, the dreams would come true.

T. H. spent his days calculating with bankers and trusted family, borrowing money, selling cattle to pay off the loans, and orchestrating ranch land and cattle and hired hands and harvest time. T. H. hardly noticed when his children began to look like grown-up people. But never mind, the day would come when they might all kick back and with children educated and prosperity in sight, T. H. and Sallie could smile in the knowing that all was well in their happy lives.

But, as will happen, fate had other plans.

When Bertha was eleven years old, her parents each wrote notes to her with their wishes for her promising future. Notes for her to keep, to reflect on when she was a grown woman with children of her own.

From her father, these words of advice written in elaborate penmanship:

12-7-94
Dear Bertha,
In all things great and small things, be as thorough as you can.
Is the wishes of your Father.
THC

By contrast, Sallie's pen wrote in a tight and measured script. A note that would prove to be an eerie foretelling:

Dear Bertha,
Desire not to live long, but well.
How long we live, not years but actions tell.
Your Mother,
S.A.C.
Cundiff Texas
January 9th, 1894

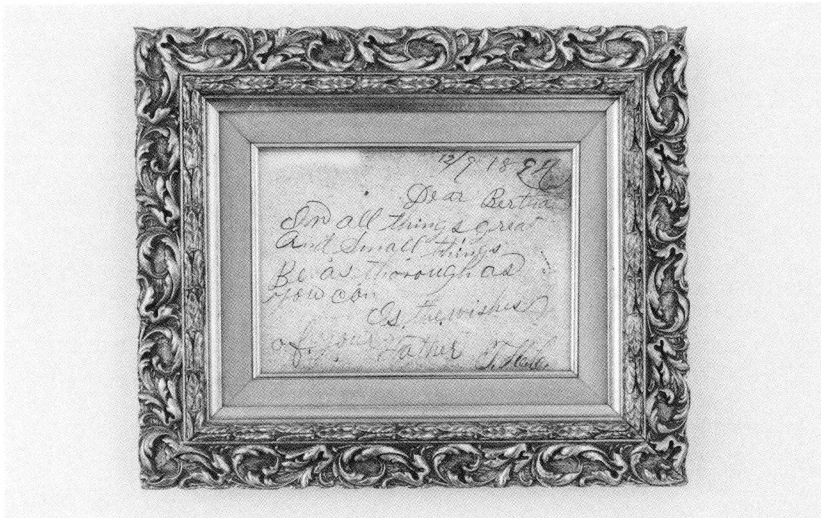

Dear Bertha
In all things great
And small things
Be as thorough as
you can
Is the wishes
of your Father

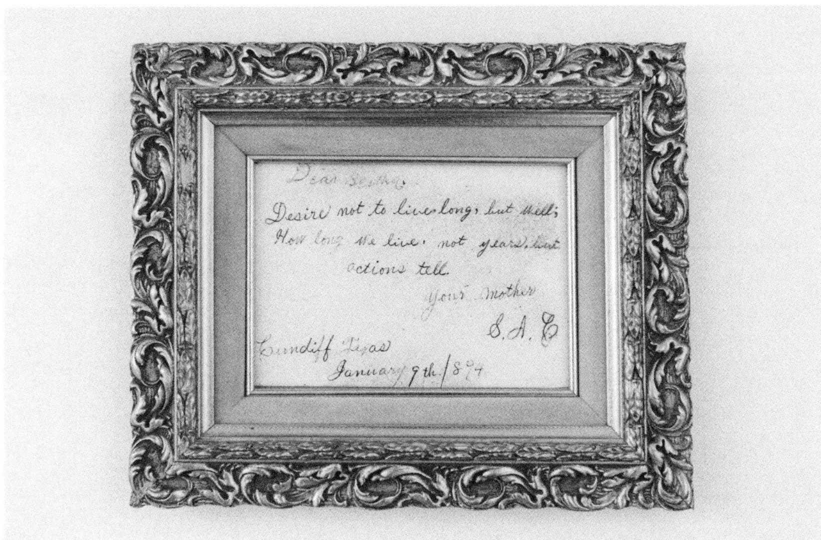

Dear Bertha
Desire not to live long, but well;
How long we live, not years, but
actions tell.
Your mother
S. A. C.
Cundiff Texas
January 9th/1894

T. H. and Sallie's notes for Bertha, written in 1894. Family collection.

At the age of sixteen, Bertha, ever the apple of her father's eye, smart and eager for life, was sent to Fort Worth to enroll in Draughon School of Business. Living with relatives, she earned a certificate of graduation and returned to the ranch where T. H. needed her to sit herself down at his handmade oak desk, get out the ledgers, and keep the books updated and current. Filling the unmarked pages with numbers and details, Bertha did as she was asked. The Cherryhomes ranch was growing, and her help was needed. She fielded questions such as "How many head of cattle did we ship last year at this time?" "Where is that dad damned account of the feed bill?" "Hell's fire, we need to plant more acres of corn next year." If Bertha ever objected to her new and growing responsibilities, there was no mention of it. The profit and loss columns became her new domain.

Reaching an unusual level of importance in the community of ranchers and farmers where patriarchy ruled the day, Bertha sat in on business meetings at T. H.'s home office and took notes at meetings with the local banking lenders. Known for dependability and quiet strength of character, at the age of twenty, she held an unusual prominence for a woman of the day.

Relatives and friends held her in awe and respect. A local Red Cross group, organized at the beginning of the First World War, took pride in her membership. The local chapter of the Eastern Star welcomed her membership. Worshipping in the Jacksboro Methodist Church with her mother and aunties, while her father, a sometimes Baptist, went about daily business even on Sundays, Bertha's name and involvement lent the groups a certain status . . . not that she ever flaunted her family's name even as it grew in importance. Bertha remained calm, polite, and reserved and did not shirk from hard work and fundraising for the community.

She knew the family rules and never thought to break them. Family business matters were private and never to be discussed with outsiders. Whether about the ranch profit and loss or speculations about who voted for which political candidate, the "family talk" did not leave the house.

While Bertha studied in Fort Worth, T. H. bought a two-story Victorian house on Live Oak Street inside the city limits of Jacksboro, with a big kitchen, dining room, living room, office, and two downstairs bedrooms. Bertha returned from school in time to settle into the new family home. With unabashed joy, she realized the house had running water, indoor plumbing, and two rooms upstairs that were hers and hers alone.

CHAPTER 10

With his lively, busy, and inquisitive ways, little Thomas Roy seemed born to keep his parents guessing. By the time he was three, he thought nothing of striking out on his own. He explored the pastures and caves and rocky cliffs, bringing home lizards, horned toads, and robin's nests. Roy became the talk of the family and town: "He's a live wire, ain't he?" "Yep. T. H. might have met his match with that 'un . . . "

In the way that all children know, Roy knew he was adored. Not that extravagant praise came his way—far from it. Born in the post-Victorian era, children were to be seen and not heard. But he knew. Since he was the only son of the patriarch of the Cherryhomes clan, words of reassurance weren't needed. Roy was smart, even speaking in complete sentences before he was two. Charming, with a winning smile and sparkling brown eyes, his destiny seemed assured. But was it?

At the age of six, Roy was getting out of hand, and T. H. came down hard on his excitement-seeking son. The only thing for it, the only way to guide that boy, keep him out of harm's way, and maybe teach him some self-control, T. H. decided, was to put 'im to work—hard work—which proved a tall order even for T. H. Shouted commands fell on deaf ears. And when he wasn't hiding behind the chicken house, or scampering off, cane fishing pole waving in the west wind, fighting imaginary bad guys on the way to the fishing hole, Roy was stomping on red ant beds and yelling in pain from the stings. And Sallie, frowning at the notion of what he would get into next, sighed and ran cold water over his stinging legs and looked for T. H. to come take the boy off her hands.

And T. H. tried, but his stern barking at the child to do this or do that failed to do much good. By the time Roy was four, he showed a love and talent for music, resulting in what his Pa called wasted time and what the boy called fun. The screeching of fiddle strings eventually led to fast tempo tunes and almost anytime he wanted to shirk off chores, he could be found behind the barn, picking out new tunes on the fiddle or making up songs to sing to his ma at supper time. A born dreamer, sensitive to the extreme, Roy adored his sister, and when he had been especially bad-mannered or got caught throwing rocks at the ill-tempered strutting rooster who insisted on chasing him, Roy ran to Bertha and hid behind her skirts.

Bertha read to him and calmed him when hysterical crying took over his little body. Quick to anger, and even quicker to tears, Roy was a handful of mischief and surprises. Bertha knew better than to try to defend him to T. H. Instead she hurried him off out of Pa's quick anger, and for a long time that worked very well. But when he was eleven and still resisted taking care of his chores like the big boy he had grown to be, T. H. declared there was nothing for it but to send him to the Peach Orchard School House. Maybe the school marm would pound some sense into his thick head.

Avoiding hard work, pretending to know little about cattle or horses or chickens or hogs, he was, in fact, growing into a clever, handsome, charming young man. "If that kid would spend as much time workin' as he spends thinkin' of ways to get out of work, no tellin' what he could get done," T. H. muttered.

But sitting around the supper table when Roy began telling his hilarious stories of how the river, with its belly full of catfish, bass, perch, and water snakes, was a perfect spot to go lookin' for food and fun and "we should put out nets and catch some of those forty-pound catfish like Ma's cousin does," even T. H. smiled at the thought of catching bigger catfish than his wife's relatives.

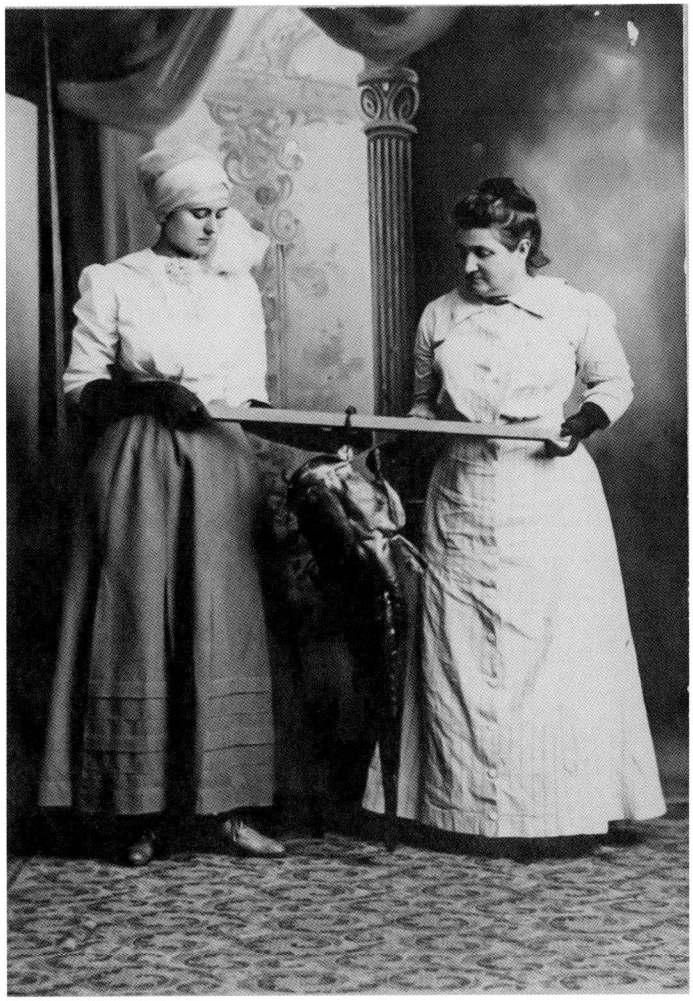

Bertha Cherryhomes, daughter of T. H. and Sallie, and friend with catfish caught in West Fork of Trinity River on Cherryhomes River Ranch. Family collection.

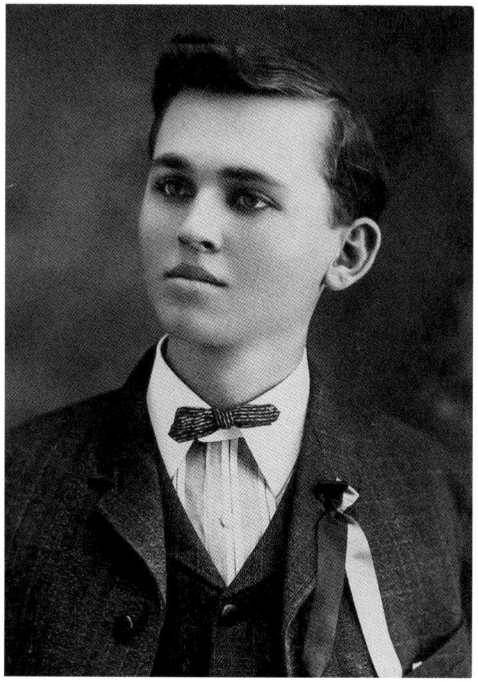

"Roy." Thomas Roy Cherryhomes, son of T. H. and Sallie. Family collection.

At sixteen, Roy was sent to Draughon School of Business in Fort Worth like his sister before him, staying with relatives. "Go get yourself some book learnin'," T. H. ordered. And while the classes were easy, so were the extracurricular activities. The notorious White Elephant Saloon welcomed him with swinging doors wide open and while the whisky poured, the poker games flourished. Sixteen-year-old Roy took to the night life like a duck on a June bug. Young and eager to show off his skills at cards and crap shooting, Roy had an amazing tolerance for sleepless nights and pints of whiskey. And those drunk nights mixed with his gift of gab and exaggeration brought him new friends and new assurance. "Buy another round. Don't leave. Git over here . . . the cards are just gettin' hot."

And against all odds, he won just enough money to keep him at the table and, some way or other, he also won a certificate of graduation from the business school. With that, T. H. summoned him home, back to the ranch and his future.

But when T. H. saw Roy taking a swig from his pocket-sized flask, he swore. "'I god . . . won't have it. Won't have a drunk on this ranch." T. H.'s pride and joy, his hope for the future, had learned far more than T. H. had bargained for.

CHAPTER 11

It was 1890, and while T. H. was busy with the ins and outs of being a ranch owner, while he worked and barked at ranch hands and his four-year-old son, his future daughter-in-law was born in the Piney Woods of East Texas.

East Texas was more like the Deep South than it was like the Wild West. Raised on good manners and generosity of spirit, Virginia Tipton's world was made up of kindness and regard for the needs of others. In the best of Southern tradition, weddings, births, and funerals were accompanied by fresh fruit cobblers, buttermilk pies, fried chicken, smoke-cured hams, and heartfelt notes of joy or sympathy, depending on the occasion.

In her world, neighbors and churchgoers stuck together while strangers were held at a distance. Memories of the Civil War and displays of the Confederate flag were common. Hard feelings and sideways glances met those who argued otherwise.

Treated like a little princess in a Southern fairy tale, dressed in gingham and lace, protected from riffraff and dissension, the small-boned, delicate-looking girl with blonde curly hair was her family's delight. Four brothers adored her, and her father Neely Tipton, known as Big Daddy, doted on her every word. Serenity shone from her big blue eyes, happy giggles announced her presence, and on her account a new upright piano shone like the evening star in her mother's parlor.

Having a real knack for music, playing the piano by ear by the time she was ten, Virginia mastered polkas, ragtime, and her parents' favorite hymns. Although she was pampered and rarely scolded, Virginia never crossed the line into peevishness or spoiled behavior. After she moved to Jack County, along with her family and her precious piano, the memories of East Texas with its lush green grasses and flowers never left her. And for all of her life she and her green thumb would try to recreate those memories in the unforgiving soil of her new life.

Settling into life in the Cross Timbers landscape, learning the three Rs in a one-room schoolhouse, Virginia grew into young womanhood with eagerness for life and music and fun.

The year she was seventeen, fate and a square dance changed her life. Mixing with other dancers at a Saturday night shindig in Cundiff, Texas, she met Thomas Roy Cherryhomes, and before the summer was over, she fell in love with his with brown eyes, quick laughter, and nice manners. The fact that the young man could not get her off his mind, and even told his sister and Ma about Virginia, puzzled and confused him. Roy was twenty-one years old, and if the thought of marriage had ever crossed his busy mind, he couldn't remember it. Granted, T. H. had brought it up a time or two, but between playing the big shot with the ranch hands, taking off for Fort Worth on the weekends, gambling, and raising some hell in the Jacksboro saloons, Roy gave marriage no mind.

Of course, Virginia's Tipton family knew the Cherryhomes bunch. In those days everybody knew everybody, either by reputation or business or neighboring. The Tiptons, ranchers like the Cherryhomes, knew T. H. and his big presence. Did Virginia's father, Big Daddy Neely, consider a union between his daughter and T. H.'s son? Did he arrange for a meeting of the two youngsters? Or did T. H. remind his twenty-one-year-old son that it was time to find a wife, go courting, meet a nice girl, and get married? It's not known for certain, but he must have believed, hoped, even threw up a prayer, that a good wife might help Roy settle down. And the Tipton family were

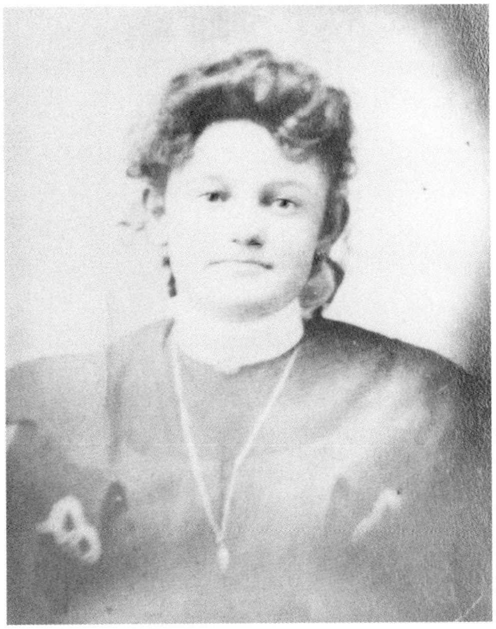

Virginia Tipton, age seventeen, engaged to Roy. Family collection.

good folks, well thought of. He knew them well . . . worked alongside some of the boys. And that seventeen-year-old, curly-haired blonde daughter of theirs, well, a real beauty.

As it happened, Roy, for once, agreed with his Pa. He proposed to Virginia. She said yes, and a date was set. But the wedding ring had to be special, so Roy sent word to a Fort Worth jeweler. When he ordered a size 3 ½ ring, the jeweler tried to argue that no grown woman had a ring finger that small.

Wedding plans proceeded while Roy dreamed of his fiancée's eighteen-inch waist, tiny size-four feet, and her delicate hands that raced over piano keys while he and his fiddle tried to keep up with the pace she set.

Big Daddy and T. H. were pleased, in their low-key sort of way. Sallie, cautious by nature, did not like the thought of another woman coming between her and the only son she would ever have . . . Sallie was not so sure.

Little Mama (Angelica Tipton), Virginia's mother and confidant, sat her daughter down for a woman-to-woman talk, whispering words of caution and advice: "Always obey your husband, even if your heart is breaking, and it might, because men rule the world. Despite the fact that they sometimes smell bad, drink too much, and break promises. That boy loves you. Comes from good stock. Someday he'll own a big ranch, and he's not bad to look at."

Tiny though she was, Virginia's spirit was strong. But she was emotional when Roy showed stoicism. She sometimes cried over broken hen eggs and dead kittens, and the sound of the hand-pumped pipe organ at the local Presbyterian church reduced her to stifled sobs and floods of tears. But the strength of pioneers ran through her veins. And a diet of farm vegetables, unpasteurized milk, fresh churned butter, home-cured ham, beef, and fried chicken nourished her tiny body. Taught early on the trick of snapping a pullet's neck with a flick of her tiny wrist, the skill of shelling fresh black-eyed peas and snapping green beans, Virginia helped her mother bake fruit cobblers and put three hot meals on the table seven days a week.

She was as prepared for marriage as any seventeen-year-old girl of the day.

A small black-and-white photo shows Virginia and Roy seated in a two-person black surrey, pulled by a black horse, and yes, it had a fringe on top. She dressed in ruffles and frills topped by a tiny hat nestled into piles of curls, a white parasol carefully placed over her left shoulder. He dressed in black suit and string tie topped by a dapper Stetson hat. When they moved into their new house on the Cherryhomes ranch—a house referred to as Greathouse, named for its previous owners—where five babies would be born and two of them would die, the young couple looked to the future with clear-eyed, but naïve, courage.

Even though T. H., with his big personality, could be intimidating, and Virginia's new mother-in-law was stingy with praise and had a habit of shooting critical glances in her direction, the young bride persevered.

It was often said by cattlemen that a small-boned Jersey cow almost always had an easy time calving. And perhaps T. H. compared his small-

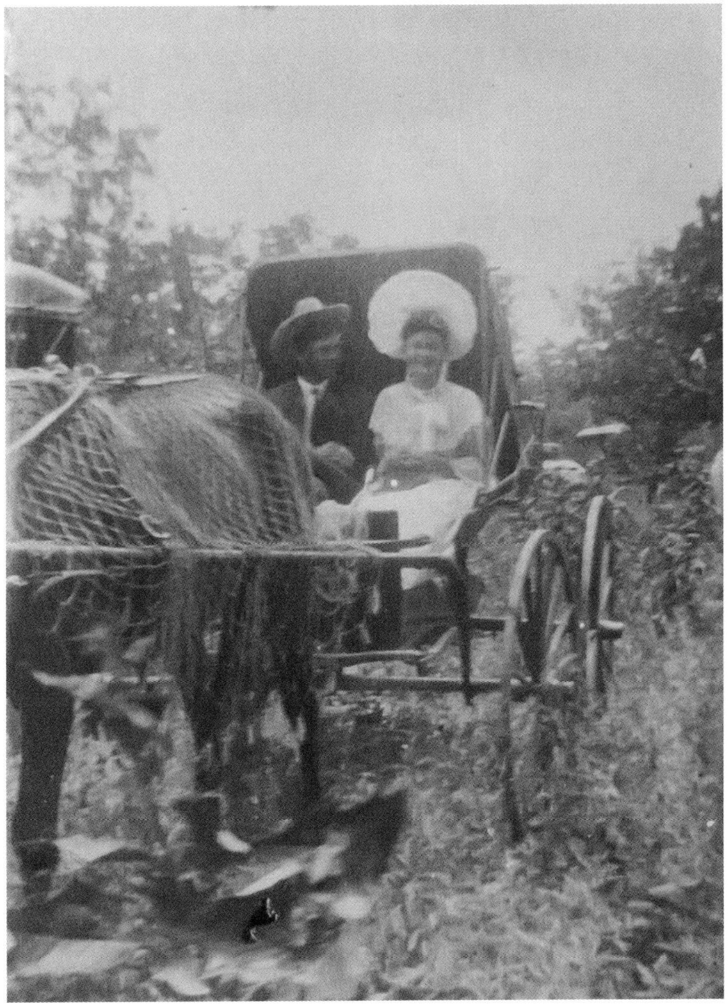

Virginia and "Roy," wedding day.
Family collection.

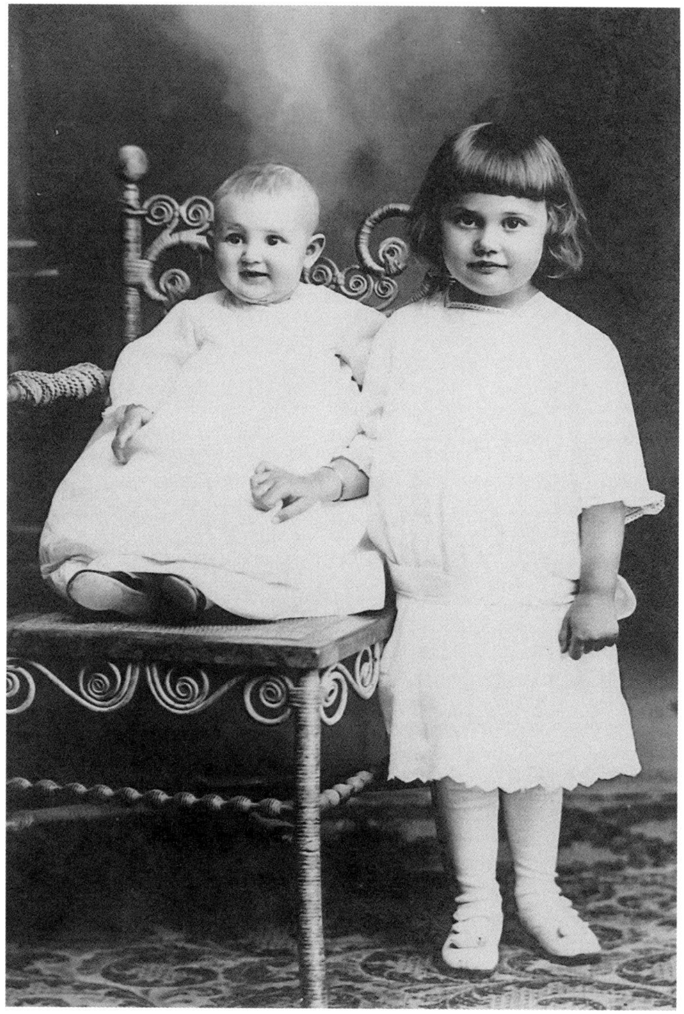

Mildred and Thomas Tipton, children of Virginia and Roy Cherryhomes.
Family collection.

boned daughter-in-law to such an animal. And the fact is, Virginia gave birth five times in quick succession and rarely seemed the worse for wear. Filling Greathouse with love, laughter, music, and babies, spending late afternoons rocking her babies on the big front porch, watching the big Texas sky blaze with color while it marked the end of the day, Virginia sipped iced tea and listened to the twilight sounds of song birds as they calmed with their music, and she knew the honesty and power of real love.

Yet to come were the long days of grief and the lonely nights when she would doubt that she could live through the sorrow of great loss.

But my tiny little grandmother was destined to survive and more. She would move off the ranch into a house in Jacksboro, transplant her laying hens and her much-loved rose bushes to her new yard, own a car, fly to the East Coast where she would see Broadway theater, climb to the top of the Empire State Building, and shake the hand of John Fitzgerald Kennedy. And to the end of her days, she would declare her loyalty to the Democratic Party and the Methodist Church.

Virginia Tipton Cherryhomes, a wife at seventeen, a widow at forty-three, never remarried and would die at the age of eighty knowing that, yes, she had done the right thing. Made the right choices. With quiet dignity she appeased T. H. and Sallie, lived on the Cherryhomes ranch as a widow, and saw her children inherit the ranch and benefit from its land, its cattle, and the sale of oil and gas under its surface. Steady and determined, Virginia had played the role—no—she had lived the life of devoted wife, mother, grandmother, and friend. And she had done it in service to the life and times of her family.

CHAPTER 12

With Roy's marriage, T. H. hoped his son would calm down, put his nose to the grindstone, and be more involved in the business end of things. And for a while, Roy did just that. Dreams of the future, persistent dreams, demanded T. H.'s attention. Like an eager cow pony, he took the bit and ran with it, and he did not shy from putting his money where his dreams were. Putting every cent of profit into new efforts, more cattle, and more land, he chased his dreams and never looked back.

Buying the Greathouse land was a stroke of good luck for the ranch. The new railroad ran through the middle of it. In fact, there was a mail stop not far from the house where Roy and Virginia lived. And that mail stop called Stewarton included a loading chute built to load cattle into the cattle cars and deposit them at the Fort Worth Stockyards. No more trailing cattle to market. No more days and nights of herding and guarding and hoping for good weather along the way to "town." And that suited T. H. just fine. He would be among the first to admit that life on the trail was a hard life, and even a two-day's drive was filled with danger and tension. And he damned sure would not miss even a short drive pushing cattle along the rough trails to the city.

After buying the Greathouse land, T. H. knew of some more land, prairie land, north of the River Ranch. While the River Ranch would always be his home, the White's Prairie land to the north, just a stone's throw across the dirt county road leading to Cundiff, was ripe with native grass—the kind of land every cattleman envied and wanted to own. T. H. wanted it. He wanted it bad.

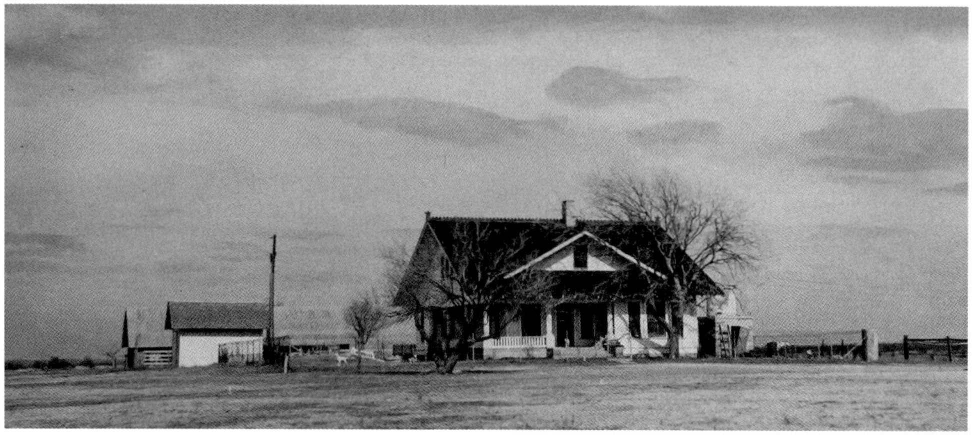

Greathouse. Home of Virginia and Roy. Family collection.

Always planning and looking ahead, T. H., without much fuss and without a hint of braggadocio, met with local bankers. He needed capital to outright buy the seven thousand acres of prime cattle grazing land. He was known and respected by the bank. In fact, there is an old family story that in his heyday, T. H. cranked up his Model A, drove to the bank, and honked his horn, loud and long. Hearing the sound, the bank's president stepped out the front door, gave a wave to T. H., who remained seated behind the steering wheel, car windows wide open so he could shout out to the businessman, "Goin' to town. Lookin' to buy some steers. Can you cover me?" With a curt nod, the banker gave his approval, and my great-grandfather drove off in a cloud of dust and gravel.

But that loan was for cattle. Buying the land required much more capital. After a daylong meeting with bankers, both in Jacksboro and in Fort Worth, a deal was made. The terms of the loan aren't known, but the fact remains that T. H. bought the seven thousand acres and paid off the loan long before he died.

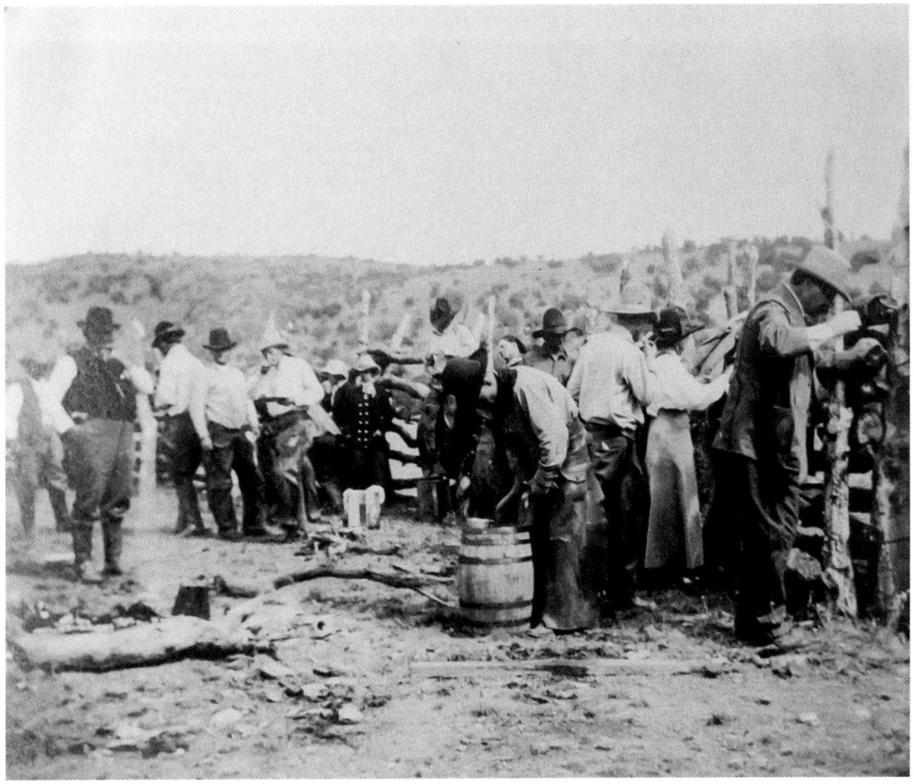

Onlookers: Cherryhomes cattle ready to be loaded onto train headed for Fort Worth Stockyards, circa 1930. Family collection.

Were there sleepless nights while he worried about being in debt? Nights of worry when the summer brought no rain and the grass was turning brown? Days of hearing Sallie try to ease his mind with, "It'll rain someday . . . always does"? Common sense makes it clear that of course he worried. But the facts tell us that those were the kinds of problems he relished and handled with firm hand. He wouldn't trade his place with the wranglers on the trails or return to a life on a few acres of dry dirt farm. No sir, his new life was much much finer than his life had ever been, and he was certain he could make it work out like he planned.

Managing the hired hands, keeping them reasonably happy and hard at work, required a finesse his family had never seen. Several families worked for him. The Frie family in particular played a big role in the early history of the ranch. As luck would have it, in 2014, I was fortunate to meet a man who had been born on the River Ranch and who had clear memories of T. H.

The youngest of five brothers, as a child Tom Frie lived in an old abandoned railroad car parked on a bluff overlooking the Trinity River. When he was old enough to work—five or six—my great-grandfather paid him thirty-five cents a day. "And I shore was glad to git it," he said. As we drove over the land where he was born, ninety years before, the land where some of his relatives are buried in the Rozelle family cemetery, Tom reminisced and told stories of the land and the man who owned it. Clear as a dinner bell in his recollections, the old gentleman recalled that he and his brothers and the other children living on the ranch called T. H. "Grandpa."

Remembering his childhood, with a clear and steady voice, the ninety-year-old chuckled as he said, "It seemed like ever time I got on a horse, I fell off, so Pa made a mule skinner outa me. But I got most places on foot." With sights and smells and cow trails etched in his mind, he talked of seeing wild hogs, deer and turkey, and the occasional panther. "Yep. Grandpa trapped hogs, fattened them, and sold them at local markets. Never forget that enormous black boar with long tusks and him smellin' of meanness . . . That devil musta weighed six hundred pounds or more." Pointing out landmarks, inclining his head one direction and then the other as he recognized certain hills and trails, he said, "Over yonder was a double log cabin. Dog run in the middle, ya know." And he was right. The remains of that cabin are barely visible today. Nodding toward a spot in the distance where the road disappeared over the edge of a bluff, "That must be Panther Holler down yonder. Yep, saw my grandmother walk up that rocky hill draggin' a dead panther. Killed it herself. Big one. She aimed to skin it, tan the hide, and use it . . . yes, ma'am, that's where it was all right."

Tom talked all afternoon that day, but one of his best stories went like this:

His older brother, the one who could ride a horse better than the others, was helping the other hands move a bunch of cows and calves from one area to another. The land was rough and rocky but thick with brushy scrub oak and tall grass. In grass as tall as a horse's flank, it was easy to lose sight of a cow and her calf. His brother spotted a cow and calf wandering away from the herd and, kicking his horse into a lope, went after her. But something spooked the cow and she took off runnin' like the devil *hisself* was on her tail.

Cowboy and horse broke into a hard run. In the excitement of the chase, his line of sight got blocked by the brush and mesquite trees, and the young man could not see that the cow was headed straight for the edge of a steep rocky bluff. She dropped out of sight, the horse and rider hot on her trail. What happened next is a story for the ages. Sliding on the rocky ground, tall grass blocking the rider's view, the horse jumped over a boulder that seemed to pop up out of nowhere. Landing with a stumble, head down, working to get his balance, the horse ran off the edge of the bluff. Losing control, but aware of the fall, the rider jumped off and fell sideways, avoiding an oncoming tree. The hapless horse, with too much momentum to stop, landed, but not in a good way. The boy, wedged between a "rock and a hard place" when he came to a full stop, heard the heavy breathing horse behind him, and when he looked back up the steep hill full of trees, rocks, and boulders, he was stunned to see his horse high above him, gasping for breath, legs splayed in four directions while he hung in the fork of a wobbly mesquite tree. What

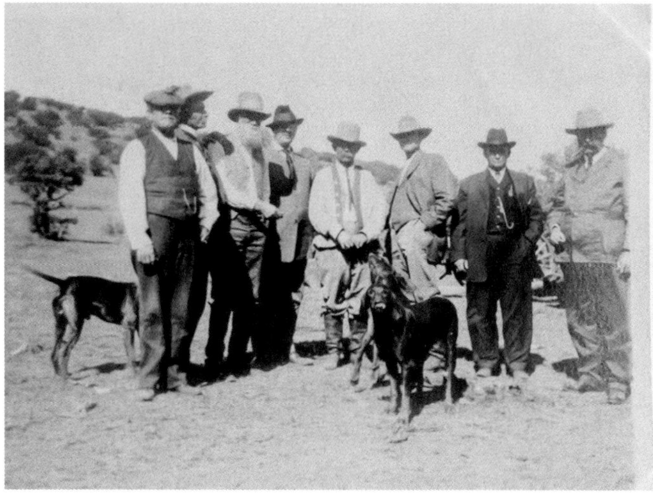

T. H. Cherryhomes, sixth from left. Serious talk with hunting buddies about hunting dogs, circa 1929. Family collection.

in God's name was he gonna do now? Mister Cherryhomes was goin' to be mad as a hive full of hornets. His good horse stuck in a tree.

But youth and bravery were on his side, and the youngster scrambled up the hill, reached the top, and yelled for his brothers, waving his arms and running. Seen by one of the older cowboys, both the stunned boy and the scared horse were eventually rescued and lived to chase other runaways on other days but were left with bruises and exaggerated claims and a whopper of a story to tell.

Tom Frie ended the day saying. "T. H. Cherryhomes was a fair and honest man. Nice to work for and tolerant of me, my brothers, and the other children living on the ranch. Never heard him say a cross word to any of the ranch hands."

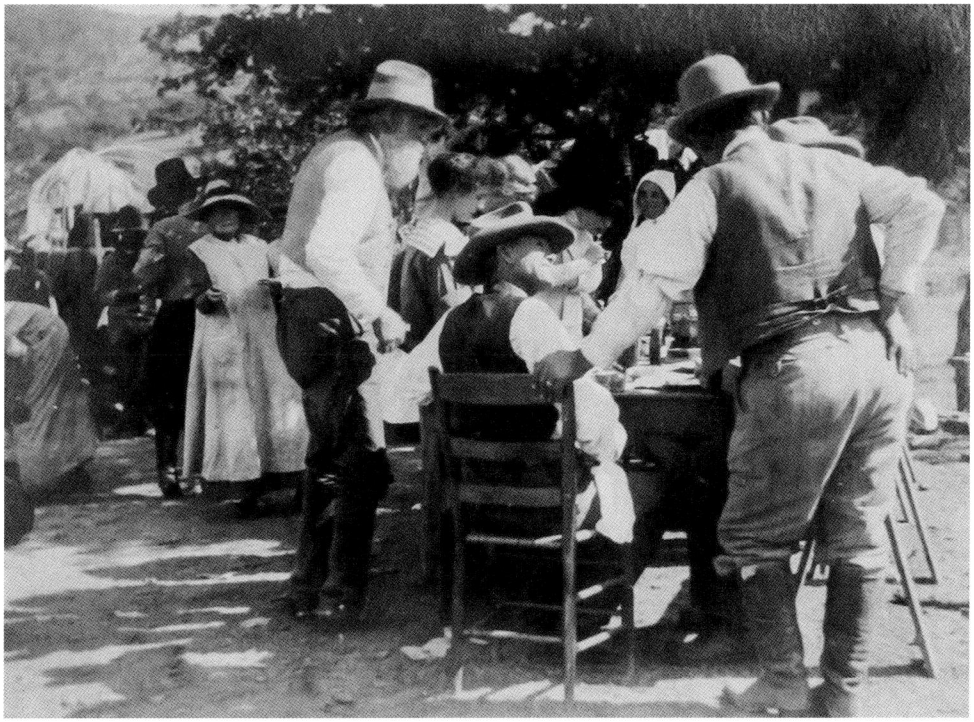

Fourth of July picnic on the T. H. Cherryhomes ranch with ranch hands and their families. T. H. is seated with his back to the camera and head turned to the side. Family collection.

CHAPTER 13

By 1870, T. H. had gained respect from his peers and extended family and was on his way to becoming the man he knew he was meant to be. And though he never spoke aloud of it, following the old adage of the day, "Do not walk too tall or act too proud," his pride in his family and his land was boundless.

His two children grew and thrived. Bertha and Roy were healthy, young, smart and inquisitive, learned their letters, read books, worked hard, and played the piano and fiddle. T. H. was comfortable in the knowledge that they would inherit his life's work, with the right grooming and guidance, and that they would have full and productive lives and be admired by all. At least that was his unspoken prayer.

Bertha never disappointed, and T. H. and Sallie made plans for her higher education. At sixteen, she was enrolled in business school, where she would learn mathematics and bookkeeping. The ranch business was growing. Overseeing the hired hands, the cattle, and the farming was a full-time job, and T. H. needed a bookkeeper. A trusted family member. And he was not much interested in acquiring a son-in-law.

Bertha was graceful, modest—with brunette hair pulled up in the fashion of the day—smart, and quiet, so perhaps she had suitors or offers of marriage, but none that she insisted on accepting. Well-respected, admired, and dependable, her love for family and friends was boundless. On the odd days

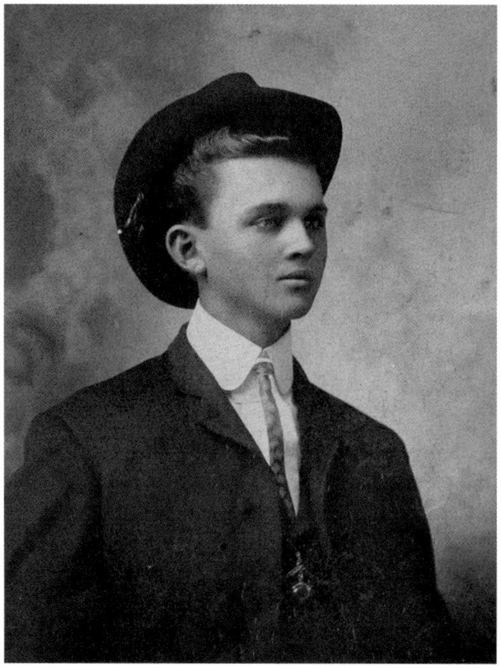

Thomas Roy Cherryhomes, age nineteen, son of T. H. and Sallie. Family collection.

when there was no bookkeeping to grab her attention, she could be seen visiting sick neighbors with her fresh baked bread and muffins and offering quiet words of comfort. The local chapter of the Red Cross enlisted her help, while the Methodist Church and membership in the local chapter of the Eastern Star kept her engaged with the community at large. Life was full and happy for the Cherryhomes's only daughter.

By contrast, Roy, who was three years younger than Bertha and growing tall and handsome, was filled with teenage angst, an ugly state of affairs. "What in the name of God was wrong with that boy?" T. H. wondered. One minute moping and surly, the next laughing and playing pranks on hired hands and cousins. T. H. wondered if he should whip him senseless like his own Pa would have done or just ignore Roy and his antics and walk away.

T. H. had run into the rock wall of another stubborn personality, and he was dumbfounded. That boy had responsibilities. Had he gone deaf? He sassed his betters and refused to finish his chores. Sending him to business school when he was sixteen might be the best answer. At least the boy would be out of his sight for a few months and maybe do some growing up in the meantime.

Roy was more than ready to leave home where his Pa's demands hounded him day and night. More than ready to be his own man and determined to become bigger and better than T. H., Roy's arrogance grew while his false pride and self-importance urged him to make clear to all who would listen that his destiny called him to be a big ranch owner, not a lowly cowboy. A cowboy with the dirt and sweat and worries. No sir, he had no taste for it.

But he soon developed a taste for something else. During his time away from home, a time in the big city of Fort Worth, when teenage fearlessness gave him a leg up on his way to adulthood, Roy tasted another fruit from the tree of life: whiskey and carousing opened a new door, and he began to feel even more sure of himself than he ever felt. When he returned from business school, high on book learning and hard liquor, he assured his Pa that he was more than capable of running the ranch.

And T. H., eyeing the young man, his only son, so able and strong, wanted with every fiber of his being for it to be true.

CHAPTER 14

Family stories skip lightly over his name. Thomas Roy Cherryhomes was a paradox of good, bad, and feigned indifference. The truth of the man lay somewhere in the middle of words not spoken, sadness not shared, sorrowful eyes and charming laughter.

He was a man who had success written all over him. The son of a hard-driving father. The husband of a southern beauty. The father of beautiful bright children, born into what seemed to be the lap of luxury on the Texas frontier, he suffered a flaw and lived with a handicap that would prove to be his undoing.

As was often the case with ranchers across the state, T. H. sometimes bought cattle out of Mexico. After listening to his son and watching him work with men and cattle and horses, T. H. made a decision. He would send Roy and five other cowboys to the Texas-Mexico border to receive a large herd of cattle. The cattle herd would be brought across the border, and T. H. told Roy that he wanted him to ride to south Texas to receive them. Roy was elated. Adventure knocking at his door. A chance to prove his worth to his pa. An opportunity that would last for at least a week, maybe ten days. He would wear the hat of the boss man, the big shot, the head of the family ranching business. Without T. H. around to cramp his style with criticism and frowning glares. Roy couldn't wait.

With cash and promissory notes in hand, Roy and five cowboys struck out on the long horseback ride to the border. It's not clear just how many days they rode, but pushing horses and men to the limit, they arrived around midday one Thursday afternoon. Making contact with the sellers, arranging to receive the cattle after a night's rest for the men and horses, Roy and his hands found makeshift lodging and decent food. Meeting with the Mexican representative the next morning, Roy was told that the cattle had not yet arrived. *Sorry for the delay. But please come across the border and pass the day with a game of poker and a steak dinner.*

The invitation sounded reasonable and, always eager for excitement and a poker game, Roy agreed. *Why not? A way to pass the time.* The whiskey proving plentiful and the Mexicans friendly, he settled into a game of five card stud.

The foray into Mexico, a no man's land of foreign language, a bottomless whiskey glass, and better-than-average card players, turned into a two-day life-changing event. Waiting on the herd of cattle, which promised to show up at any time, led to long nights, little sleep, and fragile nerves. And, as will happen, Lady Luck turned fickle. After a long winning streak, she deserted the young rancher. The results were devastating. Watching in horror as his cards turned cold and his winnings dwindled into almost nothing, my grandfather made a desperate decision: he went all in on a final bet. Scribbling IOUs on torn pieces of paper, signing his name with a trembling hand, Roy Cherryhomes wagered 1,200 acres of the Cherryhomes ranch land.

He lost.

The writer Herman Hesse (1877-1962) wrote the following words, words that Roy Cherryhomes might have written himself, had he the clarity to do so:

> *"My story is not a pleasant one; it is neither sweet nor harmonious, as invented stories are; it has the taste of nonsense and chaos, of madness and dreams—like the lives of all who stop deceiving themselves."*

The perfect image of defeat and despair, Roy began the long awful trail ride home to north Texas. Never had the days seemed so long, the sun so hot, the hours so slow. His head filled with unanswered questions of why and how and what should he do now. T. H.'s son, once full of optimism and self-confidence, slumped under the weight of dread and despair and shame while he slowly rode to the barn behind his pa's house, unsaddled his horse, and leaned over the water trough to splash his face. Sallie, spotting his arrival, knew immediately something was wrong—bad wrong. Where were the hired hands? The cattle?

How and when and where he broke the terrible news to T. H. and Sallie is not known. What is certain is this fact: T. H. never recovered from the shock. And Roy began an unraveling that would pound him into defeat.

"That gawd-damned boy," T. H. said. "Betting MY land, MY hard-earned land. Like it was worth no more than a handful of hard candy. Paid no more mind to it than some stupid, spineless, good-for-nuthin' son-of-a-bitch." Under the uncaring sky, his gut churning with anger, T. H. paced, staggered, slapped at flies, and growled at the hound dogs. Kicking up rocks, dust, hurling cuss words at a life that would give him a good-for-nuthin' son, T. H. tried to think. Tried to take in the news.

Declaring it was not his fault, Roy worked to paint a picture of himself as a man who was wronged by card cheats and thugs who had forced him into poker game after poker game and he was lucky to escape with his life.

Sniffing the afternoon air, T. H. shook his head at a thought, a stubborn thought about his own pa. A barely heard echo of long-ago pain. A time and place he had worked to forget. A shudder of recognition flashed through his fury. It was not that Roy resembled his pa in looks. Not at all. But there was something, some familiar pain, regret mixed with a memory of his pa's whiskey-smelling breath and the noise of his lying words.

If he had sired a stable full of sons, T. H. might have disowned Roy then and there. But that was a choice he could not afford to make.

"Partnership be damned."

That son of his, behaving like a wild-eyed young stallion, needed breakin' and he would by gawd try. Digging in his spurs, tightening the reins, riding the boy from sunup to sundown. "Hard work. That's the only answer," T. H. declared.

Stomping the ground, squinting his eyes at the glaring sun, and turning his back to the only son he would ever have, T. H. swore he would never give up control of his family nor his land ever again. And by God, he would get back his gambled-away land if it was the last thing he ever did.

CHAPTER 15

Always forceful, T. H. became unrelenting with his demands and critiques and criticisms. Shamed by his own son, refusing to be humbled, spurred on by anger and unwillingness to compromise, he became a tyrant. And somewhere during those hard days, Roy gave up his last shred of self-confidence. Covering his nagging self-doubts with unreasonable anger, Roy barked out orders of his own.

Beautiful Virginia, smothered by the grief of losing two baby girls and overwhelmed with five pregnancies in a span of six years, dissolved into tears at the sight of dead rabbits or her only daughter's skinned knees. Added to her despair were the hateful words from her handsome husband and the father of her children. "Git these young 'uns off my coat tail, wife." "Feed the damned dogs or they won't be fit to hunt with." "I'll be in for supper when you see me comin' and not before." Harsh and unreasonable, Roy's sudden coldness threw Virginia into fits of tears which often led to a daylong crying jag while she mourned the deaths of her baby girls and the loss of respect from her husband.

Continuing to claim that the fiasco in Mexico was not his fault—he was a victim—Roy vowed to join the Texas Rangers, hunt down bandits, anything to make himself feel important and strong and proud. Because deep inside, he no longer felt handsome or strong or smart or brave. How was it was possible that at the virile age of twenty-six, he had become a servant to the drudgery

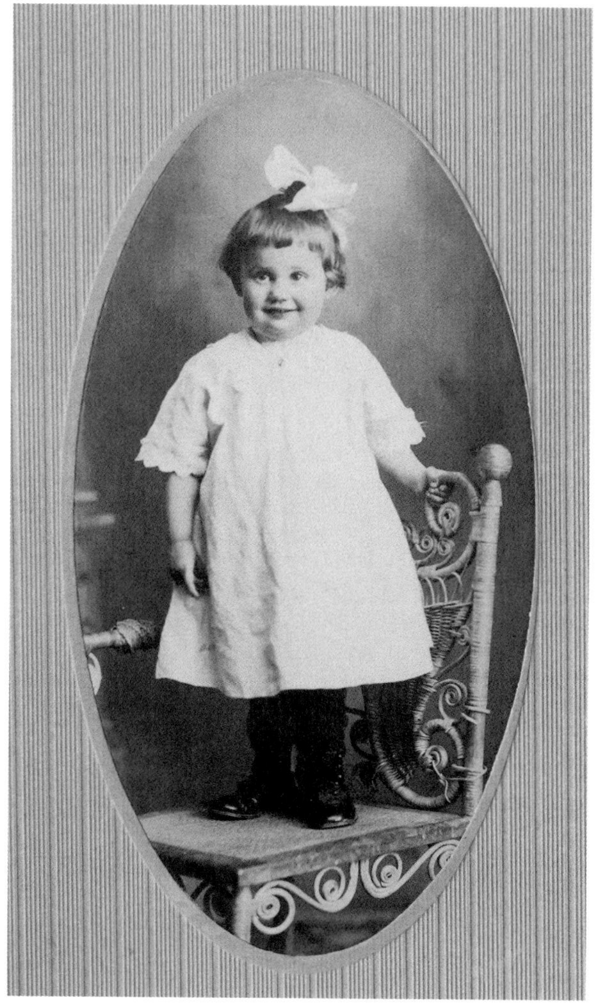

Mildred, daughter of Virginia and Roy. Family collection.

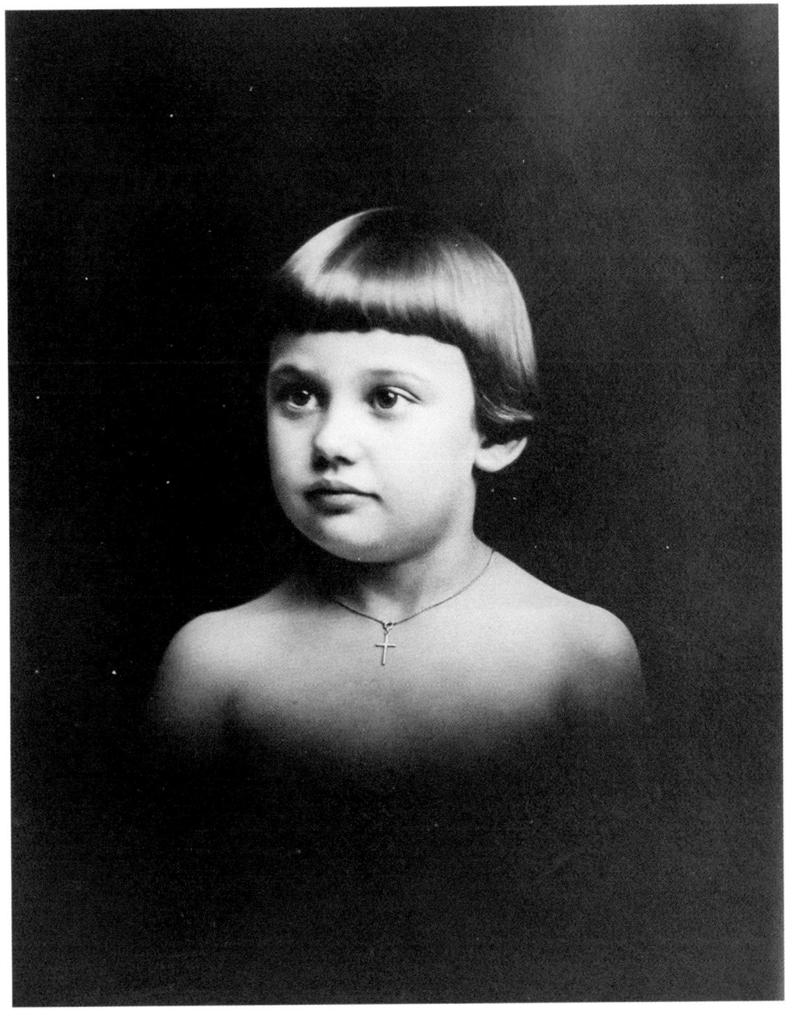

Mildred, age three. Family collection.

of everyday life? He who had been born to promise and prosperity had come to this: a man who had lost face and who, no matter how hard he tried, was the brunt of stern and angry rebukes from his father.

While his daughter, Mildred, and his sons, Thomas Tipton and Robert Roy, grew and rode horseback to the Peach Orchard School, and while his wife cooked three meals a day for her family, cooked biscuits and spoiled meat for the hound dogs, cleaned the laundry in a metal wash tub, gathered eggs and churned butter, and grieved over her lost youth, Roy spent weekends in Fort Worth under the guise of doing business at the Stockyards. In reality he hung his hat at the White Elephant Saloon, spent his nights at the Stockyards Hotel, and told made-up stories of how he once had an encounter with Bonnie and Clyde. His fall from a pedestal built of hope, promises, and high expectations had jarred every bone in his body, and the only medicine of hope, the only ease of pain was to be found in more and more gambling, hard liquor, and pretense. Looking for help in a bottle, he mused, he drank, and he cried.

CHAPTER 16

Sallie and Bertha loved their house in town. Running water, indoor toilets, a big white-washed kitchen. Life away from the ranch suited them just fine. Yes, they were aware of Roy's drinking, and yes, they were embarrassed by his gambling, but in their eyes he was still the good-looking charming, adorable son/brother he always was. Little did they know of the struggles between him and T. H., and that was just as well, because the worst of it was yet to come.

T. H., focused on ways and means of buying back his property, was preoccupied with meetings with bankers and attorneys, trading for cattle and more horses, and wolf hunts with neighbors. The ladies of the house seldom saw him during the day. Muttering while poring over his accounts, asking Bertha the whys and wherefores of the ongoing ranch expenses, always in the back of his mind was the thought: if anyone, anything, or any man thought they could take away what was rightfully his, they were sadly mistaken.

It was 1917, and rumors of oil well drilling were spreading. It was said that in some parts of the state, a man couldn't drill for water without hitting the nasty black liquid. "A damned shame," said the cattlemen. Shaking his head at the very idea of it all, T. H. vowed to never let speculators near his land.

In fact when the electric companies, new to the western part of the state, contacted him about routing a new electric line through the River Ranch, he said, not only "no" but "Hell no." But the company, persistent and aggravating as it was, kept coming at him with offers of money, promises of no harm being done to his land, and talk of benefits to his ranch houses and barns and all manner of things. "Hogwash," T. H. told them. "Won't have a bunch of by-gawd strangers roaming around on my land doing who knows what. Won't have it, I tell ya. Can't trust 'em, no sir. Think they can steal me blind, do they? Well they got another thing comin'." Outlining for him the proposed route for the line didn't help their cause a bit. In fact, it made T. H. mad as a hornet, and when word reached him that the company had a right to condemn his land and put up their damned line anyway, he began telling the hired hands to keep a sharp eye out for strangers in the daytime, chase 'em off the land. He grabbed a kitchen chair, took it to a spot where the line was expected to cross his open field, plopped it down, and sat in it night after night with his double-gauge shotgun loaded and ready. Afternoons found him riding his paint horse up and down the location, eyes and mind on alert, a loaded double-barrel 10 gauge shotgun balanced across his lap, "Not havin' it. Let the sons-a-bitches just try."

But even T. H., with his threats, finger wagging, and nighttime watch, could not prevent the inevitable. Within the month, he received a condemnation notice, and the electric company began digging holes for their tall poles and stringing a high wire slap dab across the middle of his River Ranch land. Electricity would prove to be a blessing to hired hands and family living on the land, but an ugly sight and source of aggravation to T. H., who kept a steady eye on every inch of the power line progress. Electricity was coming to Jack County farms, ranches, and homes. Years later, despite himself, T. H. would grudgingly admit its usefulness. "But gawd damn, those poles and high lines are ugly as nine kinds of sin."

Just as he was adjusting to the look of the tall electric eyesore, strangers working for oil drilling companies began knocking on the front door of his Jacksboro house. T. H., shouting to Bertha, "Don't be lettin' any strangers in this house!" finally gave in to their persistence and met with some of the lease hounds after all. Men who offered him money and who made big promises of wealth and security for his family.

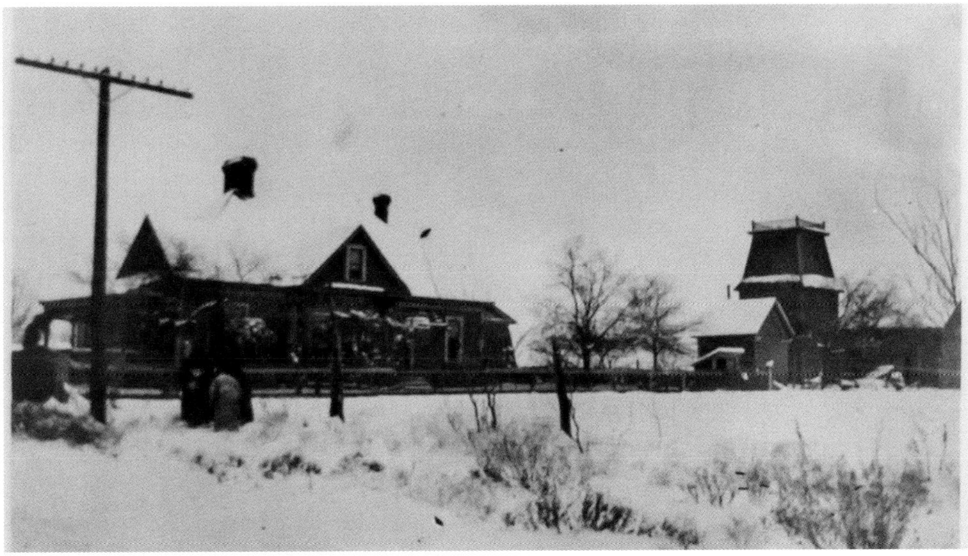

T. H. and Sallie's house on Live Oak Street, Jacksboro, TX. Family collection.

Worry absorbed him. Damned intruders always wantin' something from him. And all the while, hanging on the outer edges of his thoughts was the worry, fear, and uncertainty about his son. Aware that Roy was not just fractious and bad-tempered, T. H. had been told by his grandsons that their pa whipped them "for no reason at all." Feeling a need to do something to make his family situation better, he made a decision. Mildred, his only granddaughter, should live in town with him and Sallie and Bertha. Riding five miles on horseback through bad weather to get to the one-room schoolhouse was too much for the little girl. And she didn't need to always be around her pa with his loud talk and hard drinking. Living in Jacksboro, at least during the week, she would be close to the school, her friends, her beloved Aunt Bertha, and her stern but adoring Grandma Sallie. The thought of asking approval from his daughter-in-law, Mildred's mother, or Roy, her pa, never occurred to him. He knew what was best and said so. He knew that Mildred would not be away from her brothers and parents forever, just some of the time. And it's true that Mildred liked the idea, while her mother was not so sure, and her pa had little to say. Shrugging his shoulders with feigned indifference, he silently gave his approval. When Mildred saw her new upstairs bedroom only steps away from Bertha's bedroom, and when she looked out her new bedroom window at tree-top level and heard the winter songs of sparrows and the springtime cries of the cardinals and bluebirds, she felt warm and safe and happy.

If her brothers complained about her move, she paid no attention. She was, after all, their big sister, and with big sister words she announced her plans to go to the "big school on the hill" and learn to read and write and memorize her "times table." Little brothers had no defense against the wisdom of the older sister they adored, trusted, and believed in.

How did Virginia feel about her seven-year-old-daughter living away from her warm side? Never one to complain, or outwardly protest decisions made by her father-in-law, she remained quiet. With a mother's knowing, she understood that her little daughter would be better off with her grandparents and the opportunities of a larger school. Reality poked its ugly finger at her every morning when her once-happy whistling-with-joy husband stomped out of the house grumbling while he made his way to the barn, saddled his horse, and rode off to check on the cattle and hired hands. In her heart she knew that her daughter was better off with her grandparents and auntie. But, oh, how she missed the joy she and Roy once shared. She missed his fiddle playing and his once soft voice urging her to sit at the piano and join in the music making. She missed the sparkle in his brown eyes, his quick laughter, his sense of humor, and most of all, she missed their shared laughter and easy ways of talking. Fighting back tears at the sad thoughts, she went about her days with the hopes of a happier time to come, knowing that, as her own mother said, "this too shall pass."

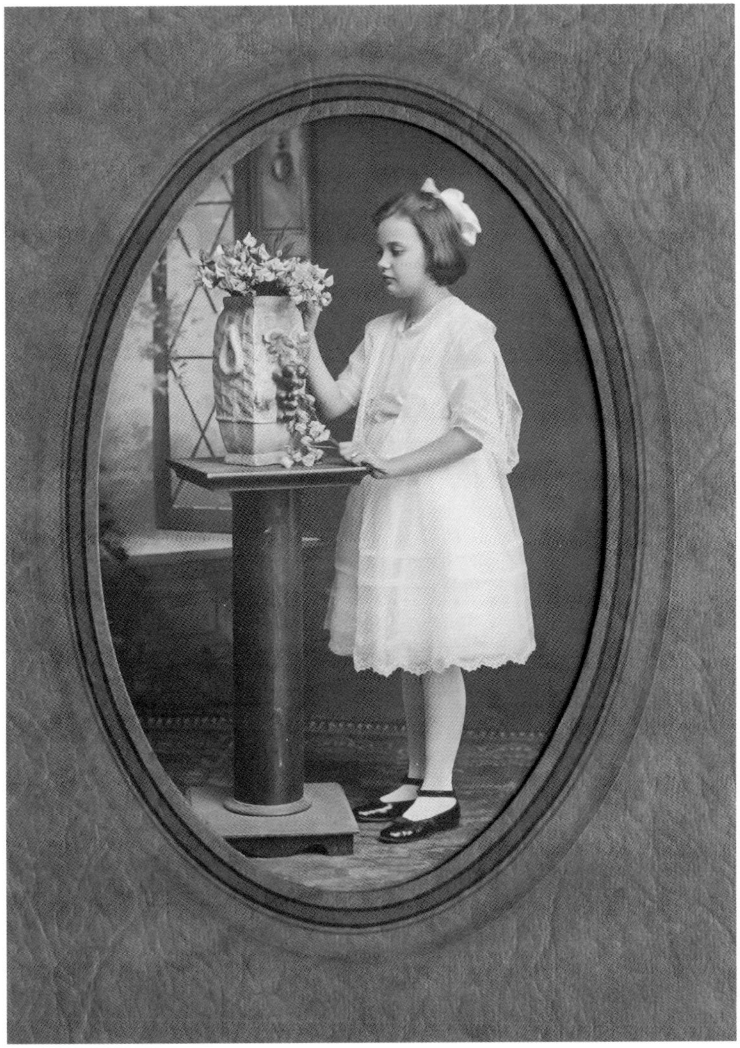

Mildred, age ten.
Family collection.

CHAPTER 17

Even though lease hounds continued their howling at his front door, the drilling for oil would have to wait. T. H., opposed to strangers poking around on his land, had other worries. News of the war in Europe hung in the air, and a new chapter of the Red Cross organized the women in town to make bandages and help as best they could with what was called "the war effort." *'I god*, T. H. thought. *The war could take care of itself. What the hell did it have to do with him and his people?*

But a catastrophe so big and overwhelming that even in his nightmares T. H. could not have imagined it was on its way, and nothing was going to stop it. Not armed soldiers. Not even prayers to God almighty. The winter of 1918 brought not only war news, but also rumors of a plague bigger and meaner and more deadly than any before.

Of course, Bertha, true to her nature, wanted to help the local war efforts in any way possible. Gathering steam as the war in Europe continued its awful carnage, the new Red Cross organization grew, and Bertha worked alongside neighbors and friends making bandages and gathering supplies to send to the American boys overseas.

T. H., while somewhat sympathetic to the war efforts, constantly warned Bertha against spending too much time helping others. He needed her bright mind and understanding of the ranch business. He wanted her to be in her office at home, where she should be. Hoping to keep her pa happy, while obeying her natural urge to help anyone in need, Bertha spent late nights poring over book work and losing sleep. Tired, but determined to be all things to all people, the stabilizer of the Cherryhomes family literally worked night and day.

What she did not know—what no one in her family or even the Methodist preacher who seemed to know a lot about a lot of things could know—was that a train of devastation was headed their way.

When a few cases of flu began popping up in the community, Bertha was quick to offer help. Nurturing sick friends and neighbors, simmering soup, baking bread to give away, her daily chores kept her even busier than before.

Of course, the family had heard horror stories about the war in Europe, but some of the most alarming news had to do with the spread of the Spanish flu. Yes, the awful disease was spreading like wildfire and heading their way.

T. H. vowed to protect his family, swearing to take care of them and his land, and raged at the thought of the runaway train called the Spanish flu intruding into his life and his family. "'I god, not in my family." Swearing he would not have it, he shouted orders to the help, his wife, and his daughter. "Bertha, you work too damned hard. You stay home away from those sick folks. . . . Sallie, make up some of that mustard plaster. And where are the Asphidity bags? Make some fresh ones. Hate the damned stink, but better safe than sorry. . . . Where's the horse liniment? I'll get the boys to bring some to town. Better stock up on it. Even if it blisters your skin, seems to take the mind off of aches and pains."

But, heading their way, the runaway train of illness was one that even T. H. could not stop.

Despite the fresh supply of Asphidity bags hung around everyone's neck, despite good hot chicken soup and fresh baked biscuits, everyone was tired and anxious and worried.

Bertha, with no children of her own, had filled a void in the life of her ten-year-old niece. Mildred turned to her for help with schoolwork and begged her auntie to read to her. Aesop's fables. The Brothers Grimm. Stories by Kipling. A devout Christian, Bertha fed Mildred's curious mind with Bible

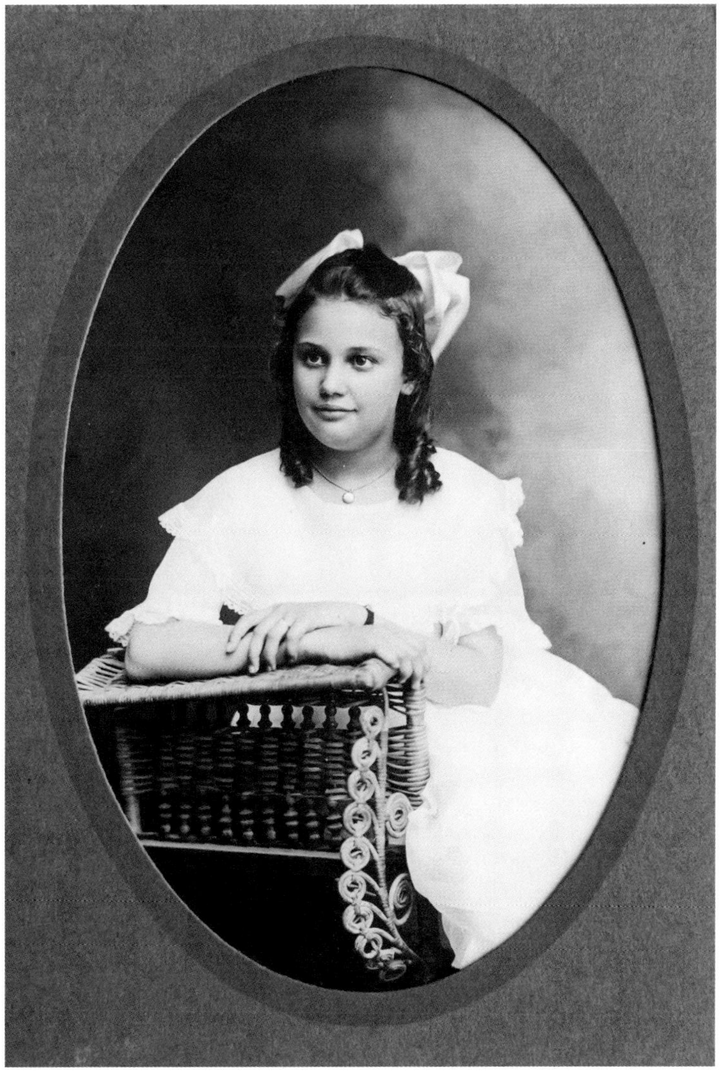

Mildred, age thirteen, daughter of Roy and Virginia. Family collection.

stories and taught her the art of memorizing poetry. Her maternal nature soothed everything from skinned knees to quarrels with third grade classmates. The little girl and her beautiful auntie shared an unbreakable bond. And for three short years, Mildred basked in the constant dose of unconditional love pouring from her auntie. She had thrived in a way not possible on the ranch.

But one awful day, Bertha, against all norms, stayed in her bed long past breakfast time and long past lunch time. When Sallie asked, her daughter replied that she was just tired and wanted to nap. By nightfall, wracked with bone-breaking pain, raging fever, delirium, and sweats, Bertha, too weak to leave her bed, lapsed into a feverish sleep.

Just the week before, Mildred had been sick with fever and aches, but Bertha stayed near her and bathed her little face with cold wet rags, assuring the little girl she would be fine and the fever would pass like it always did. Despite four days in bed, the little girl began to feel better and was soon up and about.

But Bertha's illness seemed different. She moaned with pain, refusing food or drink. The color began to leave her beautiful face, and the family feared the worst: Bertha might not recover.

How could it be possible? It was too much to bear. She was the bedrock of the Cherryhomes family, a benchmark of calm and serenity. How could life continue without her? Surely a miracle would happen, and she would rally and be her old self. Why, in the future they would talk about the awful flu and look back on this time and be grateful that Bertha had been spared.

But recovery was not to be. What they would come to look on as the worst day of their lives, Sallie and T. H., with the local doctor at her side, watched their icon of goodness and strength as she sighed her last sigh and was gone.

Little Mildred, shaking with fear, tears pouring down her young face, hid in the shadows while friends and neighbors gathered, drew the drapes, pulled down the window shades, and stood with bowed heads while Sallie's frail

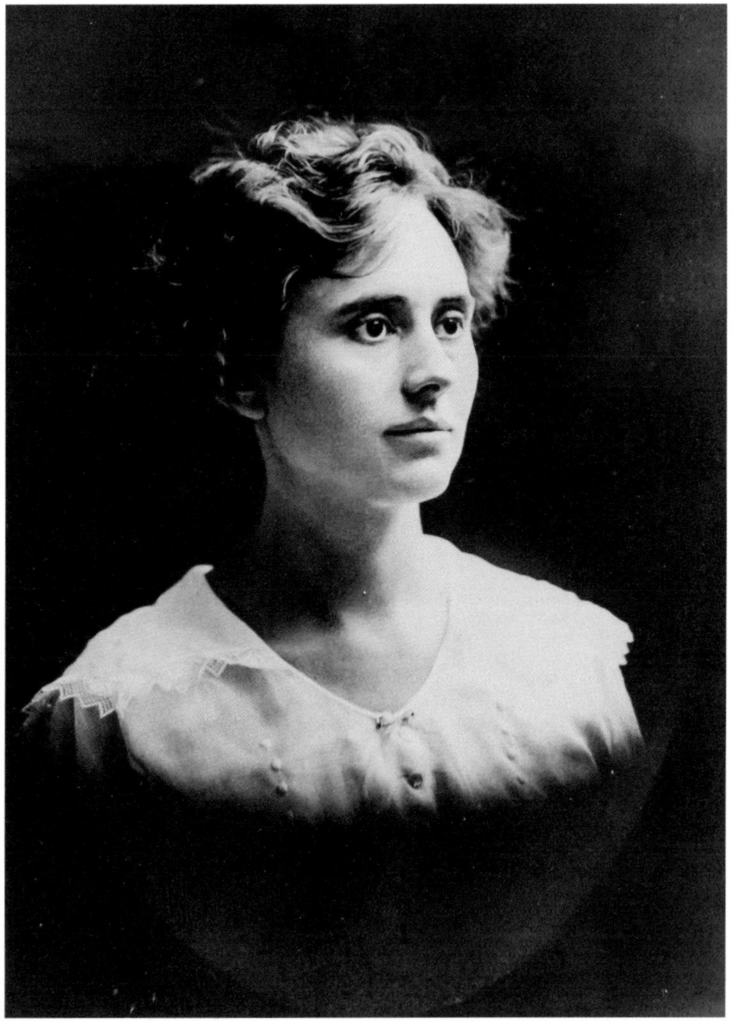

Bertha Cherryhomes, age twenty-five,
daughter of T. H. and Sallie. Bertha died in 1918.
Family collection.

body shook with moans of grief.

Why, just six months before, life had been normal, even when Roy, always on the lookout for action and daredevil behavior, chewed on the notion of joining the Texas Ranger force. He was too old at thirty-two to join the active military, and the Rangers was Texas's premier militia. Once an exciting idea popped into Roy's head, he was not equipped to think it through and consider consequences. By God, he would do it. Liking the idea of getting away from his pa's demands, loving the idea of becoming a hero, a high-ranking officer, he enrolled. Without pay, a loyalist to the core, he was welcomed and signed the enlistment papers in July 1918.

Nothing is known of how T. H. reacted to his son's impulsive decision. How could he object to such a patriotic action? And just maybe he was glad to have Roy out of the way, off the ranch. He was a flat-out worry to his pa. Maybe the break would do them all good.

But fame turned its back on Roy once again. Rigors of life in the saddle, infrequent meals, comrades with little or no education, none of the comforts of home. When Roy got word that he was needed at home because both his little daughter and his sister were sick, he reacted with bravado and quickness. It's doubtful he was reluctant to leave his new way of life. After all, he was needed at home. He would ride off to the ranch and take care of matters. Once again T. H.'s son returned home empty-handed and weary. Worst of all, the life he returned to could not be made right ever again.

Eerie shadows danced on the tall living room walls while candles flickered. And the dining room table, where family dinners and laughter were once common, had the unspeakable look of despair. Laid out on top of the table, nestled in a bed of white eiderdown pillows, dressed in her finest gown, the pallor of death settled on her once-beautiful face, Bertha looked for all the world like some imitation of her former self.

How could God be so cruel? Little Mildred, overwhelmed, frightened, and sad, falling into her own mother's gentle hugs, firmly believed that Auntie's death was her fault. If only she had been a better girl, if she hadn't come

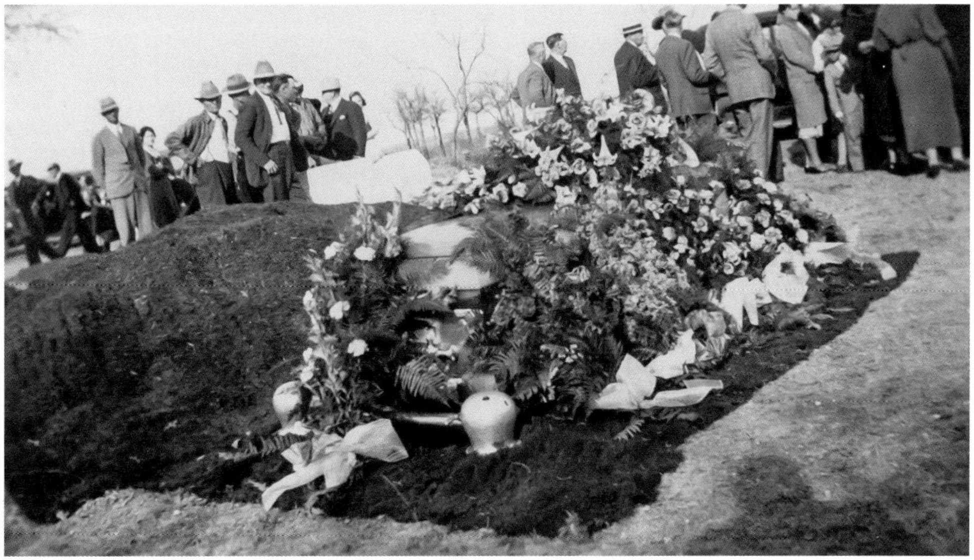

Bertha's grave site (funeral), 1918.
Family collection.

home from school sick and feverish, if she had not run to Bertha for comfort, if she had just not told anyone, Bertha would not have died. It was surely her fault. The curse of the utter despair and the youngster's exaggerated feeling of guilt would return at odd times to haunt Mildred throughout the rest of her life.

Roy, his wife Virginia, and the entire family was devastated. After three days of family and friends and neighbors coming and going in and out of the grief-filled house, the body of Bertha Cherryhomes was taken to Oakwood Cemetery on the outskirts of Jacksboro, where under impossibly blue clear skies, the seated family watched as she was lowered into her grave.

On the ride back to the big, now empty-feeling house, after the photographer took one last family photograph, Roy turned to Virginia and remarked,

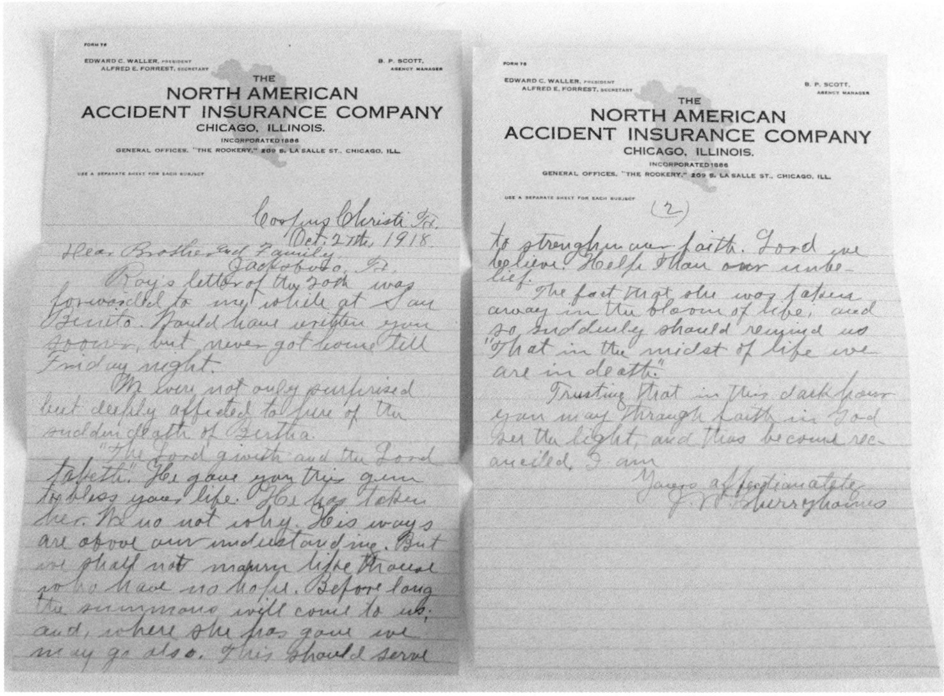

FORM 78

EDWARD C. WALLER, PRESIDENT
ALFRED E. FORREST, SECRETARY
B. P. SCOTT, AGENCY MANAGER

THE
NORTH AMERICAN
ACCIDENT INSURANCE COMPANY
CHICAGO, ILLINOIS.
INCORPORATED 1886
GENERAL OFFICES, "THE ROOKERY," 209 S. LA SALLE ST., CHICAGO, ILL.

USE A SEPARATE SHEET FOR EACH SUBJECT

Corpus Christi Tex.
Oct. 27th 1918

Dear Brother and Family,
Jacksboro, Tex.

Roy's letter of the 20th was forwarded to me while at San Benito. Would have written you sooner, but never got home till Friday night.

We were not only surprised but deeply affected to hear of the sudden death of Bertha.

"The Lord giveth and the Lord taketh." He gave you this gem to bless your life. He has taken her. We know not why. His ways are above our understanding. But we shall not mourn like those who have no hope. Before long the summons will come to us, and where she has gone we may go also. This should serve

(2)

to strengthen our faith. Lord we believe. Help thou our unbelief.

The fact that she was taken away in the bloom of life, and so suddenly should remind us "That in the midst of life we are in death."

Trusting that in this dark hour you may through faith in God see the light, and thus become reconciled, I am

Yours affectionately,
J. W. Cherryhomes

Letter of condolence from
T. H.'s brother, J. W. Cherryhomes.
Family collection.

as though it made perfect sense, "Better leave Mildred where she is livin' with T. H. and Sallie. Best thing for her." And almost like an offering, a sacrifice to some unknown god of death, the decision was made: take the little girl. It seemed the right thing to do.

No one would find the courage or the will to dispose of the hats and gowns and gloves belonging to the once vibrant Cherryhomes daughter. Sixty years later, a steamer trunk containing her finest clothes was opened and its contents donated to a museum in central Texas. Her best-loved books were saved and now are treasured by her grand-niece. The dead have their way of living forever.

CHAPTER 18

"He will not survive this," Virginia said to herself. "I just know it. Bertha was everything to this family and now she was gone and who knows what will happen to T. H., and then there's poor Sallie, never one to show emotion but now . . . . Oh my, now what will happen? And here I sit, the in-law, three children, a husband lost in his own grief. He will die from this. He surely will. Then what will become of us all?"

Virginia, lost in her emotions and miserable fear of the future without the steady influence of Bertha, watched with wide-eyed dread while her husband turned to the bottle, her boys acted out with anger and tantrums, and her daughter was taken over by her in-laws.

Years later, family stories of that time, 1918 to the early 1920s, skipped lightly over Thomas Roy Cherryhomes's name. Like a short story which ends too quickly, his story was told as a paradox, a vague cautionary tale mixing a little bit of good (handsome boy, kind and sweet and talented), a whole lot of tragedy, and feigned indifference. The truth of the man lay somewhere in the middle of words not spoken.

Virginia's fears of his death by grief would come true, but not for eighteen more years. Roy would hold his own for a while. Needed by T. H., the only son with his charming ways, still quick-witted and well-spoken, tried to pull himself up and to stand tall beside the father, who he hoped would turn to him for advice and strength. And he managed to pull off the charade.

For a while. After all, Roy knew he was adored by family and friends. If not exactly born with a silver spoon, he did enjoy privileges denied many: land, position in the community, respect from bankers and preachers and community leaders. By virtue of being T. H.'s son, he had it all. Or so it seemed.

Speculation in the little community ran high. "With Bertha gone, Roy will be T. H.'s right-hand man. He'll lay down the bottle. Smart as a whip, he is." "Those two will soldier through, and word has it that drillin' for oil will begin on the Cherryhomes land."

But Roy's outward look of confidence and charm had a dark side so powerful and insidious that deep in his soul he both feared and loved it. His inborn sweetness and genuine kindness were too often offset by a desperate need for excitement and drama. Showing an exuberant façade one minute, the next thrown off balance by a sensitivity to insult and bad weather. Irritability often won out over charm at the drop of a hat. A day filled with hard work and dusty cow lots and too much wind could tilt his world off track. A blue norther would turn him vicious.

In his element courting bankers and politicians, devoted to the Democratic Party, Roy was a natural at glad-handing. Yet his charm began to show chips around the edges. He often strained under the pretense of knowing much while in fact he understood very little. Sticking in his craw were the past bad choices which he tried to ignore even as his pa fretted and fumed and issued ultimatums.

Like a couple of territorial bulls, father and son fell into a powerful battle for control. T. H., forceful and unrelenting, became more tyrannical as time went on, issuing demands and critiques, barking orders to his son and hired hands and the gawd-damned dry weather. His rare moments of content had blown away. The land was his, by God, and the memory of his son's gambling it away would forever nag at him.

And during those dark days of working through grief and raw emotion, bad cattle markets, and his pa's ever-present criticism, Roy felt unsure in new

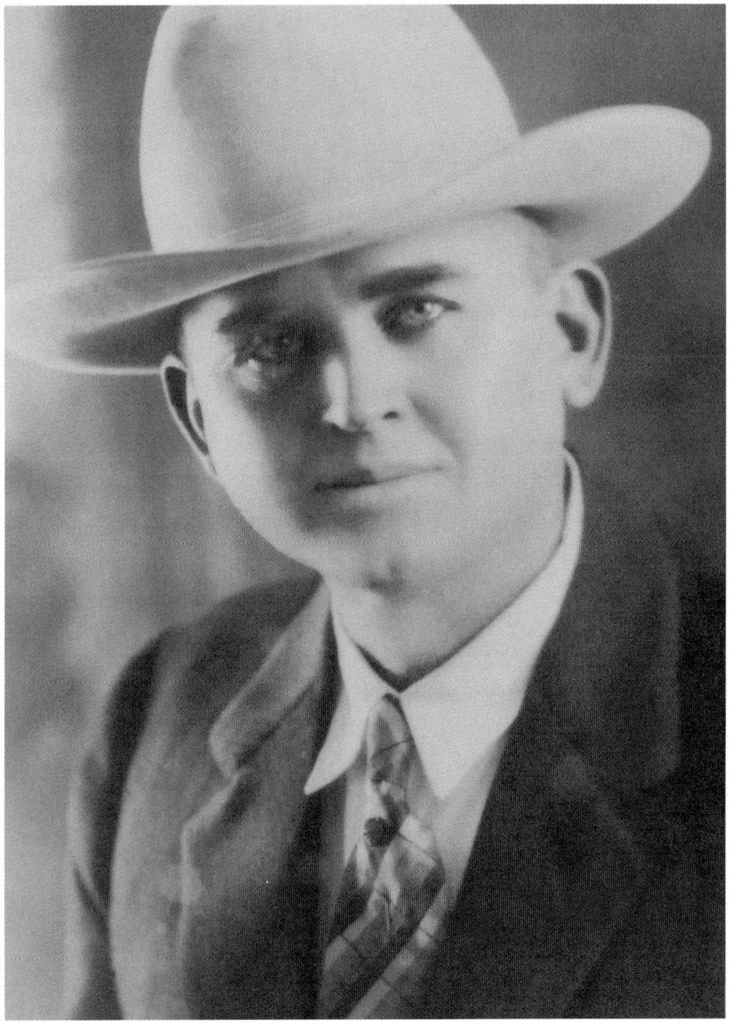

Thomas Roy Cherryhomes,
son of T. H. and Sallie, age thirty. Family collection.

and terrible ways.

Venting his anger and frustration, his confusion and guilt, he barked out orders of his own. Roy no longer felt handsome and strong. How was it possible that at the virile age of twenty-six, he had become a servant to the drudgery of everyday life?

Virginia, wincing at her handsome husband's harsh and unreasonable coldness, experienced her own doubts and fits of crying and loss while the memory of her two little girls dying before their time haunted her day and night. Where was the fun-loving man she had married? He who had been born to promise and prosperity had come to this: a man who had lost face. And watching from the shadows, feeling horror and helplessness, Virginia saw her husband look for help in a bottle while he drank and he raged and he cried. His terrible fall from a pedestal of hope, promises, and expectations began with the empty-handed return from Mexico, and only God knew where it would end.

CHAPTER 19

"He had to cry it out, and it took a long time," noted a cousin when asked about Roy and how he was coping with the loss of his sister. A light had gone out. Bertha was gone, and Roy, numb with grief, staggered under the reality. She had been there in all ways: three years older, quiet when he was rowdy, smiling with pride when he played his fiddle, taking joy in his children while she had none of her own. A raw and jagged emptiness filled his chest.

For friends and family, Roy had always been a puzzle to put together. Struggling to maintain a stoic demeanor, he might suddenly snap like a dry twig into hundreds of pieces. One minute calm and loving, the next a raging wildfire of emotion.

Plodding through the days following Bertha's funeral, Roy looked to his pa for reassurance that he would never hear spoken. On the good days, he pulled himself together and made jerky stabs at balancing the see-saw he rode with T. H.

But T. H.'s grey eyes hardened into a stern, unchanging glare. His voice deepened with a hoarse roughness, and his mind wandered into places unknown while Roy watched and shuddered with dread.

And his mother, Sallie. Roy hated the way she had lost all her softness. He noticed that her hair, once worn with almost careless ease, became overnight a tight controlled bun at the nape of her neck. Her once straight back seemed stooped, her always steady hands shook with anxiety at odd moments, and even her cooking tasted flat and indifferent.

And what had happened to his own sense of balance? Roy wondered. Everything in his world was off-kilter, and was it his imagination, or had the placid milk cow turned into a wild thing kicking over the milk bucket and shaking her head with a new fretful disposition?

It was obvious that the entire family was off balance without Bertha. Roy, many things but not stupid, realized with horror that he had become the scapegoat, the whipping boy, the-one-who-could-not-fill-his-sister's role in the world, and he went numb. When his daughter, Mildred, turned to him for love, he could not give it. When his wife and sons needed to feel safe and secure, he was at a loss.

And T. H., living daily with his own enforced numbness, increased his dispassionate need for control. Had he not sworn to see his family safe? His ranch land intact? His life on track toward security? What had gone wrong? Reasoning that his control had not been tight enough, his demands not rigid enough, he was propelled into a higher gear of determination. And he became the picture of a workaholic, a frustrated, powerful man working day and night to right the dangerous ship that had become his life.

* * *

Days and years crawled by slowly, and Roy came to believe that no matter how hard he tried, he could never satisfy the increasing demands of his father. Heavy with guilt and shame as T. H. steadily bought back the land that Roy had gambled away, pretending not to notice, Roy turned to other pursuits. Involving himself in politics, sending money and support to a Texas state representative, searching in vain to distract himself from the everyday pain of shirked responsibilities, while his bellyful of rumbling resentment and despair pushed him to his barely tolerated limit. His only relief came from the amber-colored liquid hidden in the oat bin of his big white barn.

Despite the ever-present family tension, his children, Mildred, Tom, and Roy Jr., survived and oftentimes even flourished. And although drunk at the time, Roy sat with his wife and parents and watched as his daughter Mildred graduated from Jacksboro High School in 1928.

Young Tom, fifteen and big as a strong ox, relished the physical skirmish of high school football. Watching the games excited Roy with their noisy energy and roaring small-town crowd. Nipping whiskey from a silver flask carefully tucked inside his khaki jacket, he raced up and down the sidelines shouting instructions to his son, the coaches, and the officials while exchanging insults with the crowd who sometimes tried to quiet him. Often out of control, picking public fights and yelling obscenities, he struggled when the local police were called and more than once was taken to the Jack County Jail and left overnight to sober up. Always remorseful afterwards, but unable to rein in his behavior, Roy Cherryhomes became a public spectacle and the talk of the town.

If his public behavior was outrageous, his behavior at home was worse. T. H. sent Mildred off to college in Fort Worth while her brothers stayed on the ranch and worked to please their grandpa. But there was no pleasing their own pa. Teenage Tom and ten-year-old Roy Jr. ducked and dodged the insults and cuss fights and turned to T. H. for direction. Their mother, Virginia, drank endless cups of tea and turned to her own mother for advice and comfort. The truth was terrible to face. Her husband, the father of her children, the son of a prominent upstanding family, was disintegrating into an uncontrollable mess, and no one knew just what to do to make it stop.

CHAPTER 20

T. H. was tired. Tired of worrying about everything under the sun. His son, his grandchildren, the cattle market, the price of land. Just tired. Crossing Main Street in Jacksboro, walking to the wooden bench on the Jack County Courthouse front lawn, bright fall sky overhead, cocking his head to hear the wild geese flying overhead, he took a seat, removed his Stetson hat, and rubbed his forehead. Feeling a headache coming on and giving in to a deep weary sigh, T. H. wished he could remember when the full moon was next due. A good time to hunt wolves, yessir. That's what he needed to do: saddle his old paint horse, call up the hound dogs, and spend a night thinking only of the sound of his dogs on the hunt.

T. H. was joined by a couple of other middle-aged men who had been hunting friends for years and whose friendly bragging about bird dogs and good horses took precedence over everyday worries. The talk easily turned to hunts past and present and future. "What about a bear hunt?" "I hear that the Davis Mountains are full of 'em and with a few good dogs, no tellin' how many a man could kill." "How's about it?" And before many more minutes passed, the notion became a near reality, and five Jack County men, imaginations on the run, made a decision: They would by gawd do it. They would make plans, contact guides, and set a date. And without much delay word got around, and they were as good as on the trail for black bears high up in the Davis Mountains.

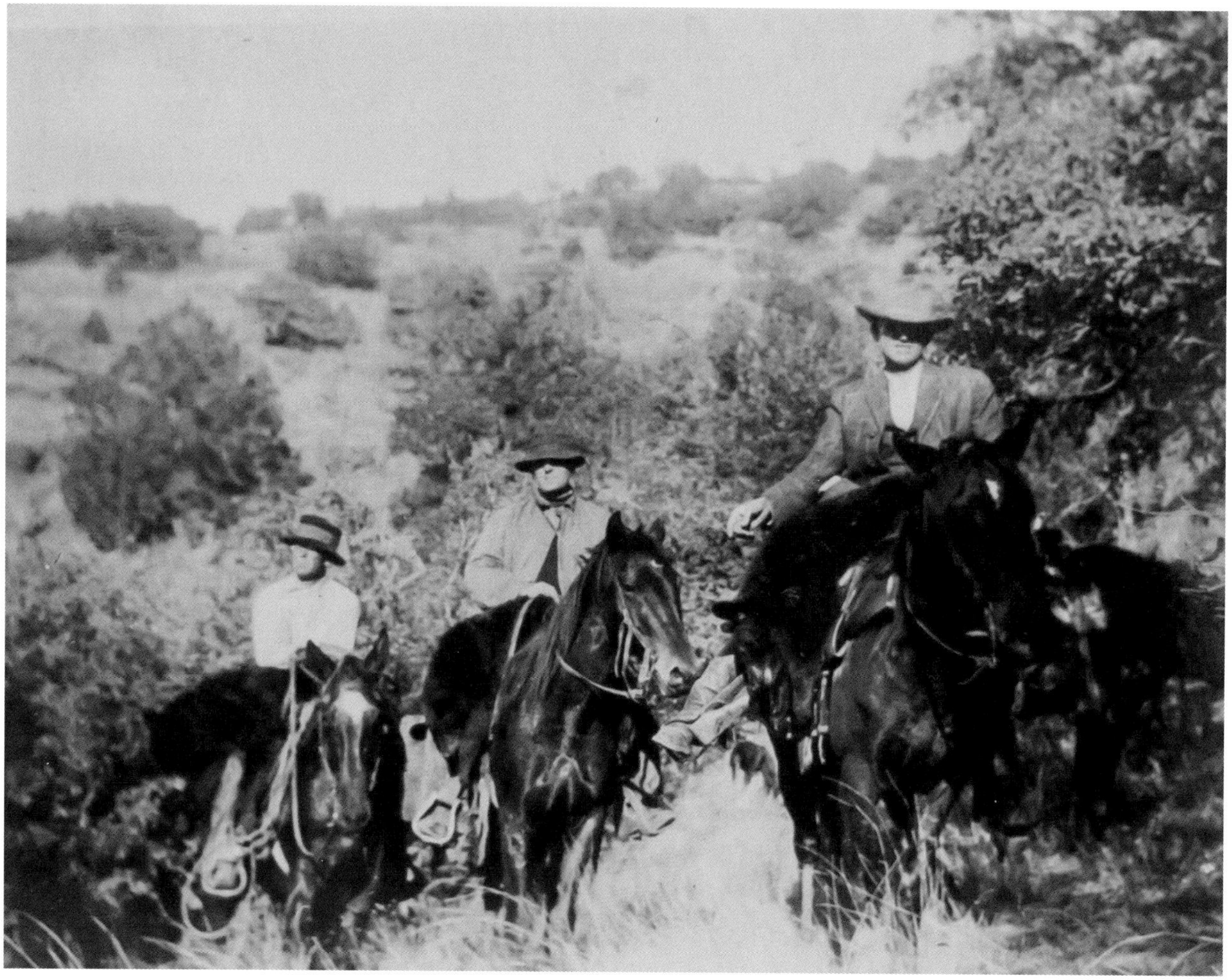

T. H. on the bear hunt in the Davis Mountains. He is on the lead horse. Note dead bears lying across horses of the riders. Photo appeared originally in Collier's *magazine, December 1913.* Family collection.

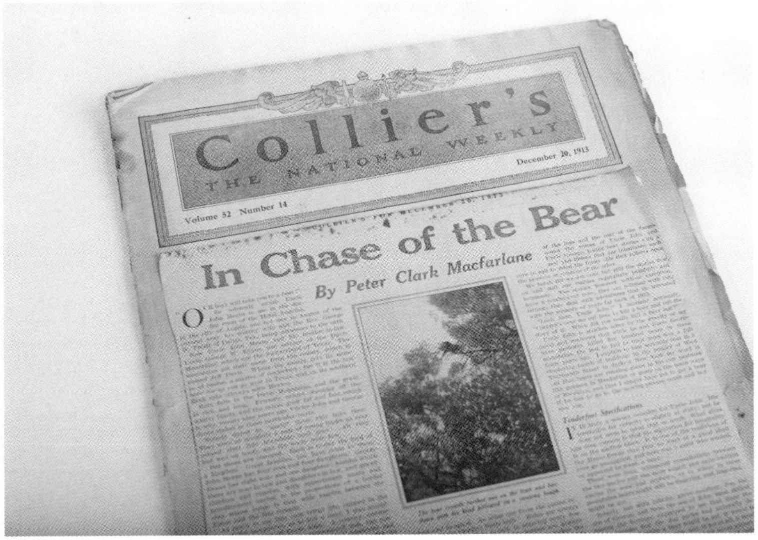

Collier's

THE NATIONAL WEEKLY

December 20, 1913

Volume 52 Number 14

In Chase of the Bear

By Peter Clark Macfarlane

PAGES 111-113
Pages from Collier's *magazine about bear hunt, 1913.* Family collection.

It's not known how *Collier's* magazine, a weekly national publication, got wind of the plans, but before the first 1913 snow on the West Texas mountains, these men were joined by a couple of strangers, including a *Collier's* journalist. They were on their way to a week or ten days of camping on the high desert that made up the land in far West Texas. The journalist, recording sights and sounds and photographing men, dogs, horses, and dead bears, reported the adventure, and in the 1913 December issue of *Collier's* magazine, a full three pages relayed a story of T. H. Cherryhomes and friends and how they camped and cooked and hunted and got away from their everyday work and tedium. And T. H. was sure glad of it, not so much glad about the magazine coverage, but for the relief given by two weeks without worry, without thinking about how to control his only son and heir, and without dreading what that boy might do next.

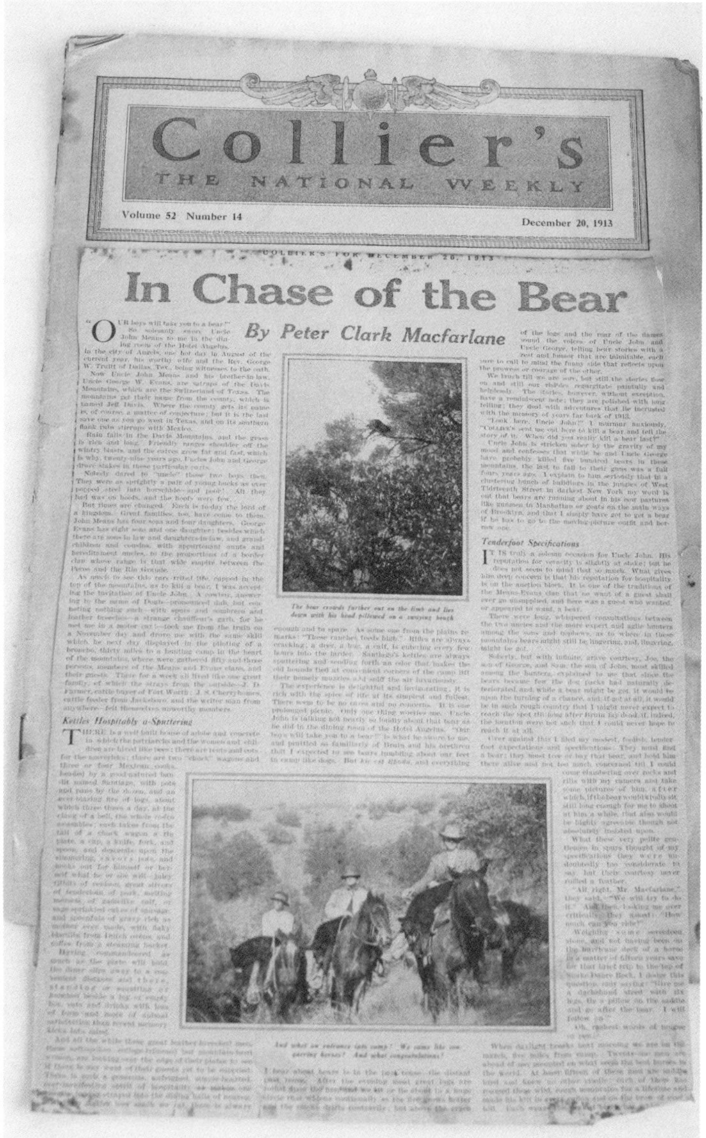

Collier's
THE NATIONAL WEEKLY

Volume 52 Number 14 — December 20, 1913

COLLIER'S FOR DECEMBER 20, 1913

In Chase of the Bear

By Peter Clark Macfarlane

"OUR boys will take you to a bear!" So solemnly swore Uncle John Means to me in the dining room of the Hotel Angelus, in the city of Angels, one hot day in August of the current year, his worthy wife and the Rev. George W. Truitt of Dallas, Tex., being witnesses to the oath.

The bear crawls farther out on the limb and lies down with his head pillowed on a swaying bough

Tenderfoot Specifications

Kettles Hospitably a-Sputtering

And what an entrance into camp! We came like conquering heroes! And what congratulations!

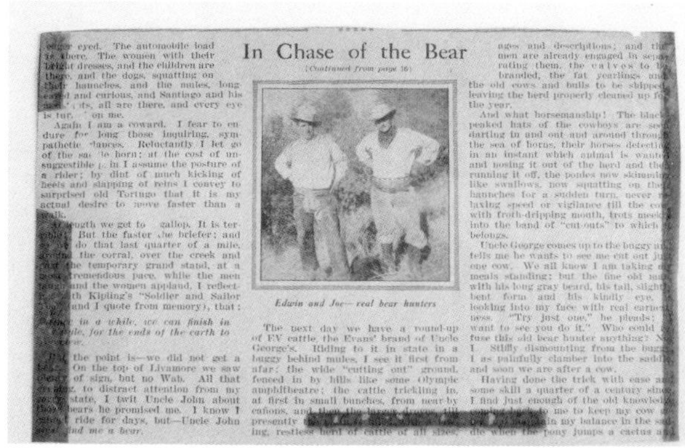

In Chase of the Bear

(Continued from page 16)

... eyed. The automobile load is there. The women with their bright dresses, and the children are there, and the dogs, squatting on their haunches, and the mules, long eared and curious, and Santiago and his ... all are there, and every eye is turned on me.

Again I am a coward. I fear to endure for long those inquiring, sympathetic glances. Reluctantly I let go of the saddle horn; at the cost of unsuggestible pain I assume the posture of a rider; by dint of much kicking of heels and slapping of reins I convey to surprised old Tortugo that it is my actual desire to move faster than a walk.

At length we get to a gallop. It is terrible. But the faster the briefer; and ... do that last quarter of a mile, ... the corral, over the creek and ... the temporary grand stand, at a ... tremendous pace, while the men ... and the women applaud. I reflect ... with Kipling's "Soldier and Sailor ... and I quote from memory), that:

... in a while, we can finish in ... for the ends of the earth to ...

But the point is—we did not get a bear. On the top of Livamore we saw plenty of sign, but no Wah. All that ... to distract attention from my ... state, I twit Uncle John about the bears he promised me. I know I ... ride for days, but—Uncle John ... find me a bear.

Edwin and Joe—real bear hunters

The next day we have a round-up of EV cattle, the Evans' brand of Uncle George's. Riding to it in state in a buggy behind mules, I see it first from afar: the wide "cutting out" ground, fenced in by hills like some Olympic amphitheatre; the cattle trickling in, at first in small bunches, from near-by cañons, and ... presently ... ing, restless herd of cattle of all sizes, ages and descriptions; and the men are already engaged in separating them, the calves to be branded, the fat yearlings and the old cows and bulls to be shipped, leaving the herd properly cleaned up for the year.

And what horsemanship! The black peaked hats of the cowboys are seen darting in and out and around through the sea of horns, their horses detecting in an instant which animal is wanted and nosing it out of the herd and then running it off, the ponies now skimming like swallows, now squatting on their haunches for a sudden turn, never relaxing speed or vigilance till the cow, with froth-dripping mouth, trots meekly into the band of "cut-outs" to which it belongs.

Uncle George comes up to the buggy and tells me he wants to see me cut out just one cow. We all know I am taking my meals standing; but the fine old man with his long gray beard, his tall, slightly bent form and his kindly eye, looking into my face with real earnestness. "Try just one," he pleads; "I want to see you do it." Who could refuse this old bear hunter anything? Not I. Stiffly dismounting from the buggy, I as painfully clamber into the saddle, and soon we are after a cow.

Having done the trick with ease and some skill a quarter of a century since, I find just enough of the old knowledge ... to me to keep my cow ... in my balance in the saddle when the pony jumps a cactus and ...

doubles up like a jackknife to go back on the trail of the wily, dodging beef. The pain is less than I supposed could be, and when warmed up I begin to like it so much that I stay in the saddle until the cutting and branding is done, when somebody proposes a deer hunt, and off I go trailing up hill and down with the hunters, ten hard, jolting miles, till nightfall brings us again into camp.

Next morning the sun shines beautifully, and the clouds drift lazily on the still tops of the mountains. Voices are subdued, no rifle shots ring out, there is a hush of peace and quiet in the camp. It is the day of the Lord in the mountains.

There is a service in the open air with the audience on the piazza, some sitting, some lying prone, some sprawling on rolls of camp equipage, but all listening intently to the preacher who stands beneath a great pine tree in the dooryard. At the end of the service they take up an offering to send the Gospel to the heathen in the valleys down below, and the sum is $262.

Dinner follows at the chuck wagon. And then: . . .

"Looky here," declared Uncle George, solemnly, falling completely into that vernacular in which his tongue is most at home; "We got to git this man a ba'r!"

"We shore have," assented Uncle John, whose own tongue loves that vernacular well, expectorating emphatically into the ashes, while he whittled long thoughtful shavings from the stick in his hand. There was whispered consultation with Joe and Sam and Will. Joe went off somewhere to telephone round the country for another pack of dogs. At three o'clock the plans were mature.

"These young bucks sleep on Livamore tonight," announced Uncle George.

Ugh! It will be cold to-night on Livamore. There are no hotels up there. Soon the party is off; Doub and El, Bug and Cole, Paul and Chunky, Lee and Hulie, Rube and Jess, and with them two of the older men, Brother Lally and Mr. Cowdon, who for the sake of adventure will dare the chill and discomfort of an impossible climb and a night on the highest spot in Texas.

But party number two—ourselves—is ready to depart; the cattle buyer and the correspondent, in a buggy behind a reckless span of mules, while the Feeder, long of limb and keen of eye, spurs a horse by the side of the real leaders of the hunt, Joe, Sam, and Will, two of whom are leading mounts for us, against that excruciating moment when we must exchange buggy cushions for saddles.

A COLLEGE MAN'S RANCH

WE drive fifteen miles, helter-skelter, over roads that for a buggy are worse than the sides of Livamore for a cowpony, all the while going higher till we find ourselves skimming over a broad, undulating plateau upon which scrub oak grows at orchardlike intervals. The boys call back to us that this is the highest ranch in Texas. It looks it. Far to the North is a frowning crack in the range.

"The Nation Cañon," calls Joe. "We hunt there to-morrow." And Sam adds: "I got five bears the last time I was in there."

This cheers us mightily.

Before us, in a pocket of the hills, a long, log house appears, chinked up with plaster, as rough and primal looking as the rocks that shelter it on three sides. To our surprise a woman greets us—it had looked a place for men only—a young and sprightly woman whose eyes and cheeks are bright, and whose white laughing teeth second warmly her cordial words of welcome. This lady is the mistress of the log house which we presently find more pretentions than it seemed. Another lady also appears, and we are presented—a daughter of the late General Kirby Smith, who greets us in the mellowing accents of middle Tennessee, from which we learn the lady is but two weeks distant in either direction.

Inside the house another surprise [illegible] awaits us. One side the long living room is lined with bookshelves and heaps on heaps of magazines. We scan the volumes quickly, searchingly, and every latest title seems to be there. One end of the same room is hung with large photographs of college groups, glee clubs, mandolin clubs, military organizations, baseball and football teams—mostly football—and there is one face that appears in all of them. That one is the face of Edwin Follkes, half a dozen years ago star center on a college eleven, now owner of the highest ranch in Texas.

The ranchman enters, but wearing no peg-top trousers or tiger stripes now. He is the typical cowboy in appearance, and the blood of a fresh-killed deer makes a dark stain upon his chaparajos. When his hand takes hold of yours you know that you are feeling the grip of a man. Three happy children complete the family circle.

How long have you been here? Seven years. Who reads all the books? Both of us? How old are the children? Six, four, and two. So goes the conversation.

And then comes a wonderful supper in a kitchen as long as the living room, with much good switch of talk, recounting of tales and matching of experiences. While Mr. Follkes and I are wiping the dishes, I corner him with my ravenlike question: "What about the chances for a bear?" He tells me that year before last he killed eleven bears; last year five bears; this year, none, so far. I do a sum in mental arithmetic and conclude that if the line of shrinkage holds there is exactly one bear to fall this year to the gun of Edwin Follkes—and that one will do for me.

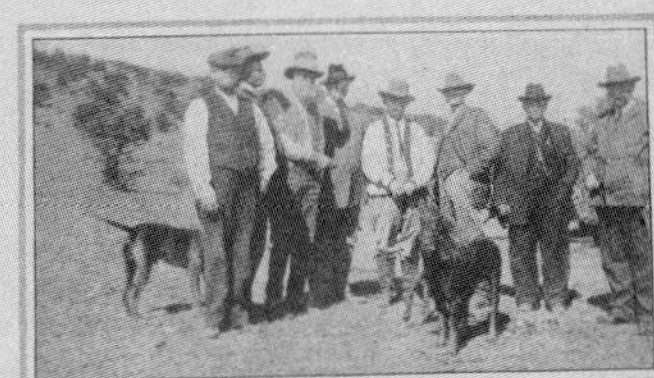

Not all bear hunters, but all bear fans — and all but one are Texans

So I go to bed in hope.

We are up and away while darkness still hides the very shape of the mountains. In five minutes the party divides. Joe and Edwin have decided to drop down into the cañon with the dogs.

"Every bear I ever started in the cañon always made for this high ground," explains Joe. "You fellows hit the high points as we are passing under and if we start a bear you'll be sure to get him."

This strategy sounds good. In a moment Joe and Edwin and the dogs have plunged out of sight in the river of mist that marks the flow of the cañon. With Sam and Will leading, the Feeder, the Buyer, and the correspondent are away on a six-mile jaunt to the first point at which we should come in contact with the trailers and the dogs.

TRACKS

THE sky to the eastward turns to orange, and then to flaming brass, with the curling edges of dun clouds jagging the sides of the picture. The world has been made new for us and we are glad to be alive. The horses feel it, and strike an extra shower of sparks from the rocks as they gallop.

Here and there the trail lies in soft earth which the boys scan intently until they make out the tracks of bear.

"As big as a nigger's foot," drawls Will; "look at 'em, will you?"

We outlanders gaze at the faint signs curiously, amazed at what they are telling the hunters, who read them as we would read our morning papers.

"See where they broke the bushes getting manzanita berries," exclaims Sam. "Right fresh, too!" He has swung from his horse and is crawling into the shrubbery to examine it more closely.

But we have no dogs. They are be- [illegible] for me, somehow, in that yawning chasm of the cañon. We can only prowl and wait and watch. A half hour passes. Our eyes strain at the blue-green back of Livamore, fifteen miles away in an air line. We wonder what is happening there. Perhaps this is the best place to tell what did happen.

SIGHTED

FOR the older men, after the hard climb up the sides, there had been sleep on beds made of slickers and saddle blankets; but the younger men scorned such ease. All night they sat about a roaring fire, toasting and smoking first on one side and then upon the other, laughing, joking, telling stories, and singing snatches of song from hour to hour, except that, as dawn approached, all voices were hushed, that no sound might give warning to the bear that there was one spot on the top of [illegible] more to be avoided like a plague.

When the firs[illegible] light began t[illegible] pear above th[illegible] the dogs were [illegible] out, and withi[illegible] an hour they [illegible] hit a trail the[illegible] arm. Cañon [illegible] ridge and cre[illegible] vocal with [illegible] music of their [illegible], which ranged [illegible] the way from [illegible] heavy-mouthed [illegible] of the old hou[illegible] to the falsetto [illegible] of the youngest [illegible].

Just at dawn [illegible] bundle shot [illegible] the top of the r[illegible] and rolled like [illegible] down the broad flank of the mountain [illegible] half dozen rifles cracked, but the f[illegible] thing rolled on and [illegible] appeared in the tim[illegible] with the dogs in full [illegible] after it. Half an [illegible] later the black bu[illegible] rolled over the top of [illegible] ridge again, and the r[illegible] cracked once more. [illegible] the pace of the galloping shadow never slackened.

"A two-year-old!" muttered one of the boys in disgust.

Now, a two-year-old bear is the special aversion of hunters. Strong of limb and not yet cumbered with the weight of years, he refuses to take to a tree or hole in the rocks or any other sort of trap, but puts his faith in legs, and in sheer delight and self-satisfaction humps himself and runs, hour after hour, galloping the hounds completely off their feet and retiring to the next range to laugh about it when he is tired of the game.

That was exactly what the bear on Livamore did. When he got done playing tag the game ended, and that was all there was to that.

But suddenly we forget the boys on Livamore. Shots are heard beneath us, and far back along the way we have come—very far back—shots—and silence—and shots again. We strain our ears, but no sound of baying dogs comes to us across the wrinkled, swimming depths of air.

At ten o'clock Sam decides to go back and look for the boys. After waiting for ages upon ages we hear from far, far back, three rifle shots in quic[illegible] cession, and then three more. T[illegible] the signal to return, that the ki[illegible] been made. Relieved that the [illegible] done and the agony of this deter[illegible] hunt is ended, yet depressed by th[illegible] fall of the hunter's providence, th[illegible] are not permitted to be in at the [illegible] we mount our horses and pick ou[illegible] out of the brush and over the hi[illegible] the home of the keeper of the hi[illegible] ranch in Texas.

It is a long, long ten miles befo[illegible] swing round the shoulder of the [illegible] tain and find the log house in [illegible] and the cattle buyer and I are [illegible] ing mostly of food to eat and of [illegible] cushions to sit upon.

But the yard seems all a-flutter, [illegible] citement. We see first Joe's buck[illegible] pony with the saddle empty, and then we make out Joe rushing the mules into the buggy. Mrs. Follkes spies us from the cabin door, and comes running, breathless, a hundred yards down the trail to tell me the news.

"The boys started a bear and two big cubs," she screams. "They killed the old one and one cub, and Edwin has the other cub treed, and is waiting for you to come and kill it."

Od's bodikins! Here were my specifications carried out to the letter. A [illegible] lump of joy [illegible] in my throat. [illegible] after all.

CHAPTER 21

Perhaps it was a psychotic break. Perhaps some inborn genetic malfunction. Perhaps it was nature's way of ending an alcoholic battering and breaking down of body and mind. The end result was clear: Thomas Roy Cherryhomes was out of control. He was a danger to himself, his family, and society. No matter how hard his family tried to talk some reason into him, he was beyond reasoning and completely out of control. It was the hot summer day of July 8. In the hope that confinement would calm him down, Roy had been arrested one week before and put into the Jack County Jail. But contrary to hope, prayers, and common sense, he continued to rage and rant and refused to eat. If there are degrees of insanity, he had reached his limit.

Mildred, his daughter, called home from East Texas where she taught school, joined her mother and her brothers, and together they met with T. H. and made a decision. Roy must be put away. The Wichita Falls State Hospital was the nearest place to house the insane in Texas and to clothe, feed, and treat victims of incurable alcoholism.

There was no other choice. And no easy way around it. Private hospitals where he might receive help did not exist in Texas. And under law, a man could not be committed to the state hospital without a public hearing before a judge and a court-selected panel of men.

So it was that a summons was issued to seven men. Of those seven, four men were chosen to appear before the county judge on July 11, 1932. And before that panel of Roy's peers stood his mother, his father, his wife, his daughter, and his oldest son, who each testified that Roy Cherryhomes had been uncontrollable and dangerous for ninety days. The legal document of complaint was signed by wife, Virginia; daughter, Mildred, age twenty-two; and seventeen-year-old son, Thomas.

To the Sheriff of Jack County:

You are hereby commanded to arrest the body of Roy Cherryhomes and bring him before us at 9:00 A.M. on the 11 day of July, 1932, for trial and examination, wherein he is charged with being of unsound mind, and further to inquire if it is necessary for welfare of the said Roy Cherryhomes and others, that he be placed under restraint.

But seven days in the Jack County Jail did little to change his behavior.

At the end of a week, the county sheriff issued a command, told to summon seven men to appear in court to testify on Roy's behalf. An equal number were summoned to hear and weigh the written complaints and consider the pros and cons of the matter.

In less than two hours, judge and jury heard the information and the decision was made:

"Roy Cherryhomes was adjudged to be a Lunatic and ordered to be conveyed to the Lunatic Asylum at Wichita Falls, Texas, without delay, for restraint and treatment . . . "

The county judge ordered two persons to guard Roy, handcuffed and shackled, as the sheriff transported him from Jacksboro to Wichita Falls. And in the late afternoon of July 11, 1932, Thomas Roy Cherryhomes was committed to the State Lunatic Asylum.

How had it come to that? A young man in the prime of his life, born to promise and prosperity, a gracious wife, three outstanding children, and a loving family. How, indeed.

Roy would live another seven months. On March 11, 1933, his death certificate listed the principal cause of death as branch pneumonia, pulmonary abscess, and chronic alcoholism.

Thomas Roy was buried in the Jacksboro Oakwood Cemetery beside the body of his sister Bertha and his two young daughters, Helen and Bertha.

Succeeding generations would observe that, unlike his sister's belongings, there were no clothes, books, bedroom furniture, trunks, nor storage rooms filled with Roy's belongings. Other than a shotgun and a few photographs, no personal items were saved.

*ADDENDUM:

It might be of interest to note that my mother, Mildred Cherryhomes, mentioned very little to me about her father's death. When she spoke of it at all to me, she mentioned only that he had died in the State Hospital, possibly as a result of a fight with a hospital attendant.

Late in her life, she offered this: "You must have felt left out when we didn't talk about family crises or my father's death. I was only trying to protect you."

I learned other information regarding my grandfather's life and death from old letters, legal documents, and family lore.

And the following letter:

Wichita Falls State Hospital
Wichita Falls, Texas
March 11, 1933
Roy Cherryhomes

Dear Uncle Tom:

I am writing this letter to extend to you my personal sympathy in this hour of your great sorrow in the loss of your only living child, Roy Cherryhomes. Although a number of things were afflicting this boy, he died from a chronic pulmonary abscess, which when it broke, released such extensive toxins into the body that he developed severe convulsions from which he died. The entire medical staff examined this boy concerning his condition, and I want to guarantee you that everything was done for him that could possibly be done for a man in his weakened and exhausted condition.

He leaves some fine looking children from what I have seen of them, and they are going on to have the life and accomplishments of their grandfather as an inspiration and an example of making fine and outstanding citizens and leaders.

Many members of the personnel and the entire medical staff join with me in extending our profound sympathy at this time.

Yours very truly,
Charles W. Castner, MD
Superintendent
Wichita Falls State Hospital

CHAPTER 22

A tsunami of grief roared beneath the surface of their creased and withered faces while the Cherryhomes family struggled to regain their lives. Vast. Monstrous. On the days when the pressure was too much to bear, which, at first, was most every day, T. H. fled to the ranch. Sallie's quiet tears slowly spilled down her pale face on their way toward the soapy dish water where her hands were never still. Scrubbing dishes, counter tops, baseboards, and floors, scrubbing them hard. Working in vain to scrub away the sadness.

The mailman brought letters of condolence from friends and faraway family. But few were saved. The Methodist church women brought food and sympathy, but few were invited to sit down and visit. T. H., encountering the menfolk at the feed store or the bank, tipped his hat, nodded, and avoided eye contact. Small talk, if any talk, was the best he could manage. "Might rain. Dry as powder." "It'll rain someday. Always does."

And as far as the community of friends knew, the Cherryhomes family bore up and never mentioned their tightly wrapped pain, shame, and remorse.

It was the land that offered comfort and relief. A place to come to. A place where T. H. had control. Ranch hands, cattle, horses, and hound dogs. Things he understood. Things that made sense. There was a rhythm to life on his land. An understanding between him and nature's ways. Always remembering that Mother Nature could trick him, he paid attention to dark banks of clouds when they gathered in the North or the smell of rain riding on the East wind.

And yes, he took pride in knowing that his gambled-away land had been recovered while he swore that as long as he lived, no one would ever take it away again.

Throw in the towel. Call it quits. Surrender to the unjust and unfair fate that left him childless? Not on a bet. T. H. was a practical man. A no-nonsense, straight-talking, clean-living kind of patriarch. And perhaps, just perhaps, deep down in his being, he felt an unspoken sense of relief when Roy died. At least there were no more worries about how his son acted in public or yelled at his wife or the million other things that cause parents sleepless nights and private hand wringing. As most men who knew him would agree, "T. H. is as tough as a run-over boot, and as bad as it is to lose a son, that man will never quit."

In private, where no one could see or hear his groans, the always-in-charge rancher, businessman, and trader sometimes felt sick to his stomach and too tired to hawk a good spit. But he would go on and on until at the end of his days, when squint-eyed, stooped, and deaf, he would simply lie down and die.

Nothing came easy. There were steers to load onto railroad cattle cars and ship to the Fort Worth Stockyards. Bank notes came due and had to be paid. There were ranch hands to keep in line, and on clear, cold nights there were wolves racing ahead of his baying hound dogs, and with luck and good aim they would be shot, skinned, and their hides sold for a good price.

The land was as much a part of him as his own heartbeat and his gray eyes. Even on the rare occasions when he was not standing or riding horseback on his land, when he drove to the bank or welcomed his granddaughter home for the weekend, the land never left his soul. Solid and firm, it responded to him in ways that humans never could. It lived. It breathed. It gave him hope as it went about the business of life and death and rebirth.

T. H. and Sallie had hope for their grandchildren. Mildred, who was educated and now teaching school, was strong and determined. She was a benchmark of support for her brothers.

Tom, with his square-jawed profile, had ambitions and strengths that mimicked his grandpa's.

Roy Jr. was thirteen and feisty and creative. There was hope for him, too. Together T. H. and Sallie could get his head out of the clouds and turn his strong will into a positive future.

* * *

Many years later, T. H's grown grandchildren gathered in the cozy living room of Tom's new house in Jacksboro. Tom, quietly sipping bourbon from a crystal glass, his blue eyes brimming with tears, reflected on a memory.

A memory so awful, so clear, and so intense it would not leave him alone. Mildred and Roy Jr. watched and listened while with trembling voice Tom whispered, "It was a terrible sight. His body covered with cuts and bruises." And no one in the room needed to be reminded who and what he referred to.

Roy Jr. spoke up next. Thirteen when his father died, Roy admitted he had felt confused and left out. Wanting and trying hard to be all grown up, but none of the adults who gathered around the family thought to explain much of anything to him.

At home, after the funeral, he remembered walking in and out of rooms filled with men who stopped talking when he appeared, and women who covered the silence with smiles and chattered nonsense. "Honey, where did you get that smile?" "So cute and bright-eyed." "Want some more cake, hon?"

Then to each other as though Roy was not even in the room, "Aww. Junior is the baby. Look at those big brown eyes. Just like his daddy's, God rest his soul."

How Roy hated being dismissed like that. To his siblings he blurted out, "The sight of T. H. stomping around the barns and cow lots after Daddy died, cussin' and spittin' out orders, it just flat scared me to death."

Then each of the siblings, having moved on with their individual lives, admitted that for a long time none of them felt safe anywhere.

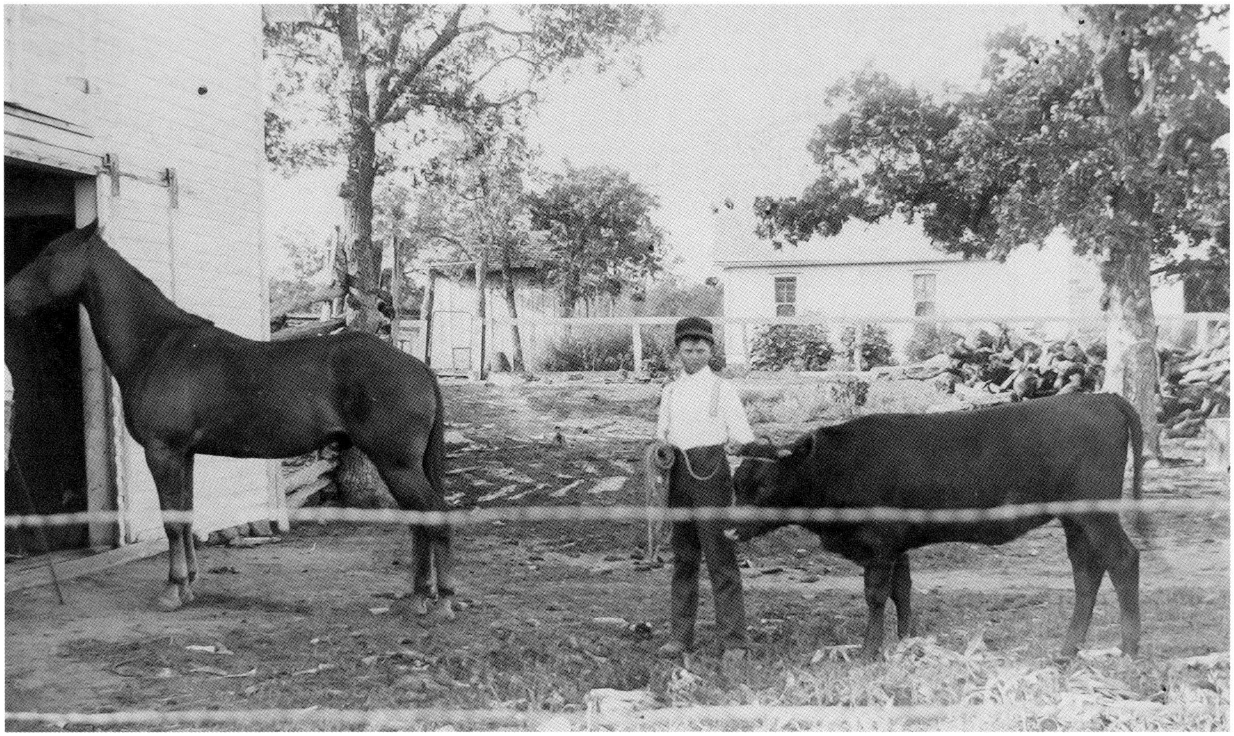

Roy Jr., age twelve, son of
Roy and Virginia Cherryhomes.
Family collection.

CHAPTER 23

Early one morning in September 1933, one month after Thomas Roy's death, T. H. arrived at Greathouse where Virginia, Roy's widow, lived with her two sons. Pushing his tall frame inside the kitchen door, he found his daughter-in-law sitting alone at her white kitchen table, a cup of steaming black coffee in front of her, a few dirty dishes stacked in the cast iron sink. A cool breeze disturbed the sheer white curtains covering the only window in the room. Virginia, lost in thought, had been debating with herself about drinking from the white cup or saucering the bitter black concoction. Startled at the intrusion, she looked up as T. H. stomped his boots at her back door and walked in.

He had not bothered to knock. Greathouse was his house. Only lent to his son and daughter-in-law, no need to knock. Without a word, T. H. looked at her and touched the brim of his gray Stetson in a silent acknowledgement. Virginia nodded.

Hands on hips, feet firmly planted on the wooden floor, T. H. took a deep breath. Virginia, scarcely daring to breathe, cocked her auburn curls to one side, trembled with the effort to smile, and said not a word.

"Well, he's gone. A damned shame. But that's the way it is. I want you and the boys to stay here at the ranch. Don't even think about moving out.

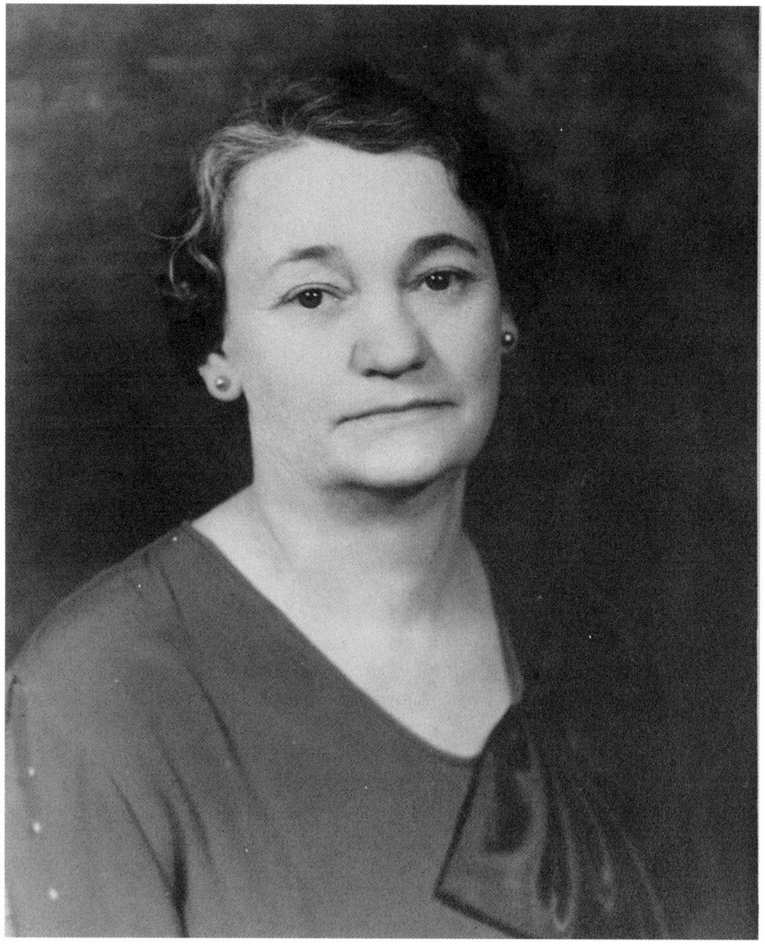

Virginia Cherryhomes, age fifty,
widow of Thomas Roy. Family collection.

The boys will work for me. Mildred is off on her own." And then lifting his eyes to meet hers, he straightened his back, cleared his throat, and continued. "There is something else that needs sayin'. If you ever marry again, I swear to God that you and your children will not inherit one red cent from me."

With that, the most forceful man Virginia had ever known rubbed his right hand over his chapped dry lips, turned away from her, and walked out of the back door.

Virginia, never able to hold back her tears, or her laughter, dropped her head to her hands, struggled to avoid a loud scream while she heard the contrary screen door creak and stick on the threshold. Tears flooded her blue eyes and spilled down her flushed face, pain stabbed at her young chest, and echoes of hurtful words bounced off the walls while a few determined flies buzzed in greed around the kitchen sink. Pushing back her chair, walking to the open window, and staring out at the midday sun, she wondered at the bleakness of her future.

Virginia would not see her father-in-law again for many weeks.

Lament
By Edna St. Vincent Millay

Listen, children.
Your father is dead.
From his old coats
I'll make you little jackets;
I'll make you little trousers
From his old pants.
There'll be in his pockets
Things he used to put there,
Keys and pennies
Covered with tobacco;
Dan shall have the pennies
To save in his bank;
Anne shall have the keys
To make a pretty noise with.
Life must go on,
And the dead be forgotten;
Life must go on,
Though good men die;
Anne, eat your breakfast;
Dan, take your medicine;
Life must go on;
I forget just why.

CHAPTER 24

"Man's Pilgrimage"
composed by T. H. Cherryhomes when he was less than fourteen years old

Man has a weary Pilgrimage
As through this world he wends
On every stage from youth to age
Still discontent attends.

From Infancy to school the little exile goes,
Torn from his mother's arms.
What's there to sooth his earliest woes
When the novelty of school has lost its charms?

Condemned to suffer through the days
With strict restraint which no reward repays. . . .
Time lengthens as she counts
The hours before his wished return.

On and on 'til matured manhood arrive
And other thoughts come on
But with the baseless hopes of youth
His generous warmth is gone.

It's to this end that all men see their fate
And can but say
That old experience is learned too late.
Too late . . . Too late . . .

* * *

Many years after T. H.'s death, I found this poem in a tattered leather-bound scrapbook. The scrapbook, filled with old letters, various documents, and memorabilia, the remnants of his long and rather brutal life, begged to be opened and investigated.

Reading the poem for the first time, I was doubtful that a fourteen-year-old boy could have written it. But, considering the fact that childhood in the 1800s was short, considering what I had learned about my great-grandfather's early years, I now believe that he did write the poem. T. H. grew up fast and determined and shouldered big burdens. To know that along with the hard work he had an introspective and intelligent mind makes perfect sense. I believe he lived with a wisdom born of hard times and curiosity which was enhanced by a mother who taught him to read and write and question life.

When faced with a life empty without his only two children, perhaps as the poem says, there were times when "His generous warmth was gone." But with friends and acquaintances, he remained cordial and thoughtful. Perhaps it was his two grandsons who caught the brunt of his determined strength and need to control. And there is no doubt that there were times when he questioned the need to go on living.

Following Roy's death, unmistakable signs of aging set in. And T. H. did not take it well. Too hard. Too immediate. Too disabling. When his hearing began to fail, he was irritated beyond measure. "Gawd Dammit. Open up your mouth and talk." Years later his grandchildren chuckled over the memory of Grandpa shouting and fuming. Eventually he owned a Trumpet

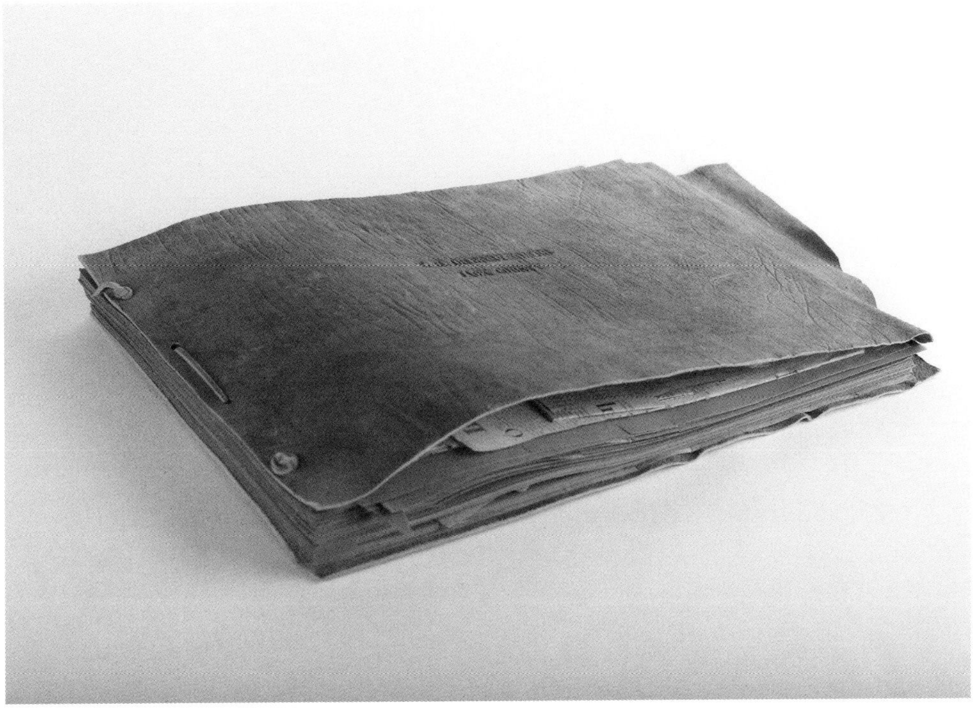

T. H. Cherryhomes's leather-bound scrapbook.
Family collection.

Horn—a large morning glory-shaped device designed to help the hard of hearing, but not the best of aids.

Yet, determined to persevere, T. H. hired a local black man, Cecil Williams, who was a shoeshine man at the local barbershop. Cecil became his driver, his nighttime hunting buddy, and for a long time, Cecil was the only one who knew the sound of the hunting dogs well enough to report to T. H., "Yessir. That's old Blue Dog on the trail for sure. YES. He got that

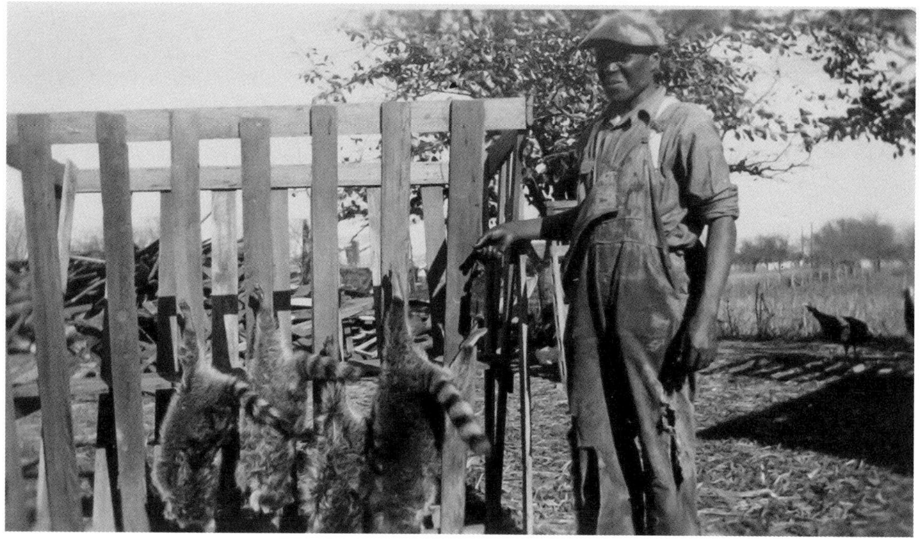

Cecil Williams, T.H.'s hunting sidekick.
Family collection.

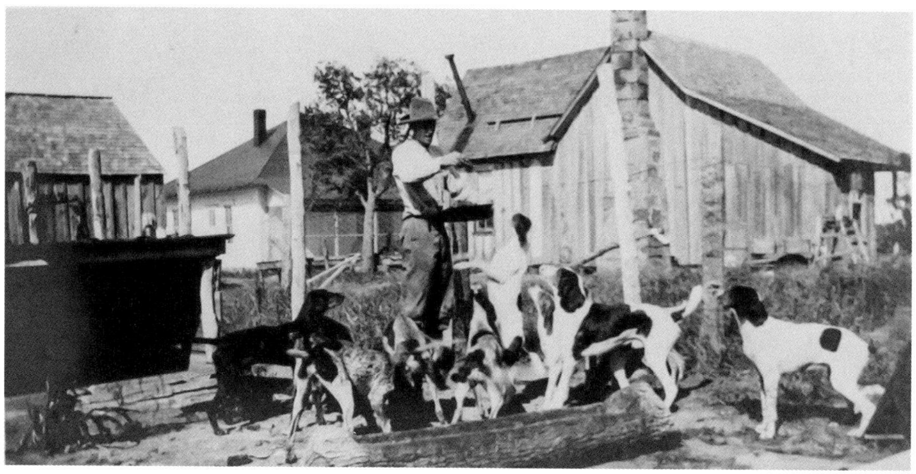

Prize hunting dogs. Family collection.

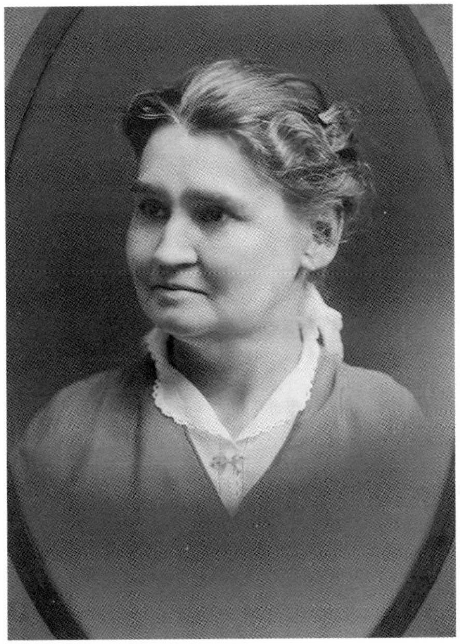

Sallie (wife of T. H.), middle age.
Family collection.

coon now, he surely do." And somehow with the aid of Cecil and others, when the full moon gave them light, T. H. made a recording of his dogs while they tracked, located, and trailed the raccoons, wolves, and coyotes. Years later, when Cecil himself was in the last years of his life, he listened over and over to "Mister Tom's" hound dogs and chuckled and remembered.

T. H. would have ten more years to get his affairs in order, and he, by gawd, would get it done. As bad as he hated the ugly sight of the black wooden box hanging like an eyesore on his living room wall, he shouted to Sallie while she cleaned up the kitchen, "Come in here wife. You need to call the lawyer. It's time for me to make a new will." And call him she did. And drive from Eastland to Jacksboro he would . . . the next day. Business details made Sallie nervous, and she knew without a doubt that "Mister Cherryhomes," as she referred to him in front of visitors, would know best what to do about the ranch land. And "let it be soon. That man is worrying me to death with his complaining and barking and fretting."

Beneath his grief, even with his eyesight dimmed by sadness, his focused mind was sharp and his determination clear. His land was as much a part of his family as any other living person; he was not going to risk losing it to strangers. He never got over learning about "right of eminent domain" and how the electric company just came on his property and ranch and put up that damned ugly line held up by wooden posts and cutting right through his River Ranch. Damnation. He had tried to stop them, but no. The court or some other fool thing condemned that part of the land and slipped in to his ranch without so much as a fare-the-well and set those posts in the middle of the night. "Nervy bastards. Bustin' in and ignorin' me and my horse and my shotgun."

No, sir. He would do everything he could to keep strangers from nosing around and trying to take over his land. He would not by gawd have it.

With his battered soul hidden from public eyes, T. H. sat down with his attorney and dictated the new will.

Here's how it went: Total acreage equaled thirty thousand-plus acres. He had three grandchildren. The math was simple. At his death, an average of ten thousand acres would go to each grandchild. Mildred would inherit the River Ranch—the heartbeat of the property. The original acreage he had paid for. The land where the West Fork of the Trinity ran through on its way to the southeast. The river with its belly full of catfish, crappie, mud cats and snapping turtles, and yes, water snakes. Each year on the banks of that river he hosted Fourth of July picnics for the hired hands and their families. As a young man, he had waded and pitched nets in that river to trap the big fish. This is the river where his jon boat delivered him from one fishing spot to another, where the crappie laid their eggs in the springtime, and where the big ugly gar fish still swam. Yep. That would be Mildred's. She knew that land, knew it like the back of her little hand.

The land to the North, the White's Prairie land would go to Roy, Jr. Open prairie for the most part. A man could make a good livin' with cattle on that grass land. Good prairie land. Yep, Junior could make that work out just fine.

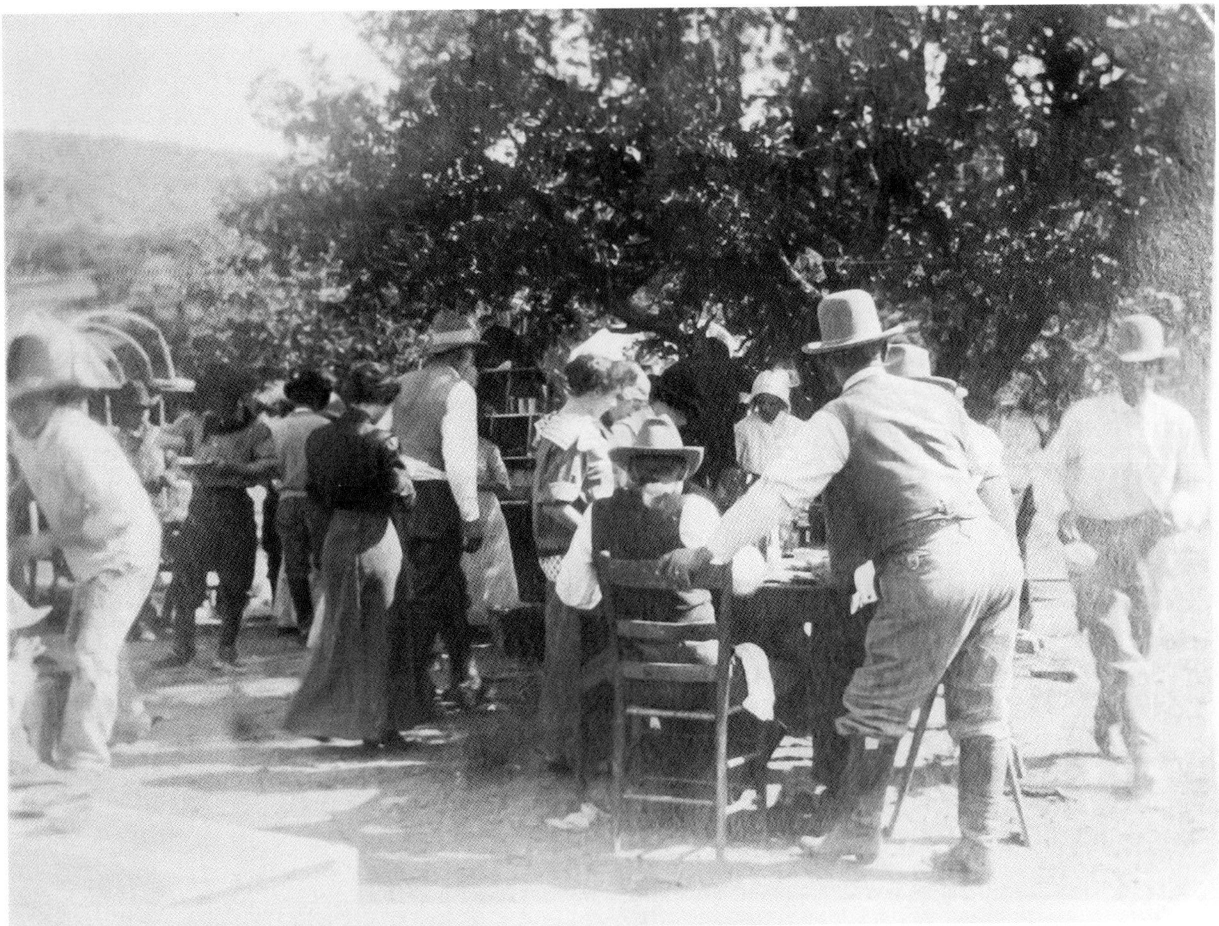

Fourth of July picnic on the T. H. Cherryhomes ranch.
Ranch hands and their families. T. H. is seated with back to camera.
Family collection.

And Tom, the oldest, the young grandson with his new wife and already living in that old house where Mildred and her brothers were born: Greathouse, a good house where Roy and Virginia had lived and been happy. Yep. That house and land would be Tom's. Tom knew all of the land. Knew where the best grazing was, knew the water holes and the tree-shaded draws, and knew how to make use of that railroad with its cattle cars and its sparks a-flyin'.

The plan made perfect sense to T. H. Sallie agreed, though she knew it didn't much matter; the mister was going to do what he made up his mind to do. She just had one request: let Mildred inherit the house on Live Oak Street. She would like that.

The will was written, witnessed, signed, and sealed. And all the while, Sallie prayed: "Dear Lord, help us all draw an easy breath now."

OPPOSITE
T. H. Cherryhomes, circa 1900.
Family collection.

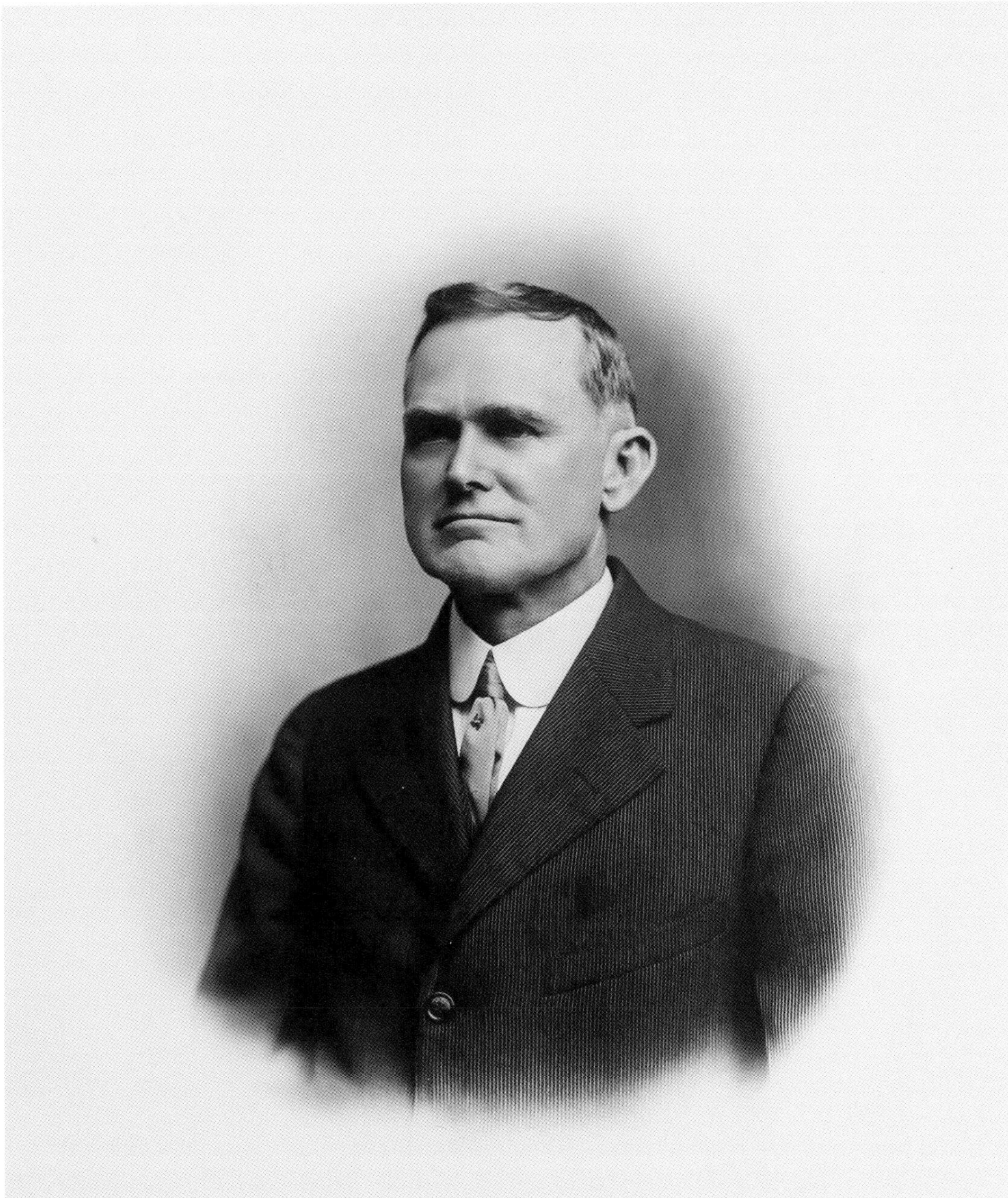

CHAPTER 25

My mother, Mildred Cherryhomes, became the first of T. H.'s flock to live away from home. Of course, her father and auntie had lived away while they went to business school, but that was for only a few months. But in 1925, when Mildred graduated from Jacksboro High School, she enrolled in Texas Woman's College (later merged with Wesleyan College) in Fort Worth, lived on campus for three years, and received a teaching certificate. Roommates, parties, big lights, and big city—she thrived on it all. She was well-read for a sixteen-year-old girl of the time, so college classes and study were right down her alley. She joined the Thespian Club, starred in Shakespearean plays, went to dances, and had boyfriends.

With her teaching certificate tucked under her arm, she traveled to Carthage, Texas, and applied for a job. And she was hired as the only teacher in the one-room schoolhouse. The Great Depression was in high gear, and jobs were hard to come by. But in Carthage she could live with relatives and avoid most living expenses. And because she had never worked outside her home and ranch land, she didn't expect much of a salary. Her exuberance mixed with her love of adventure and newfound freedom gave her the push she needed for life in the lush green piney woods of East Texas. It was pleasant there, and safe. And, best of all, T. H. gave his approval.

Well educated, self-reliant, smart, and self-assured, she eagerly stepped into her new role as a schoolmarm.

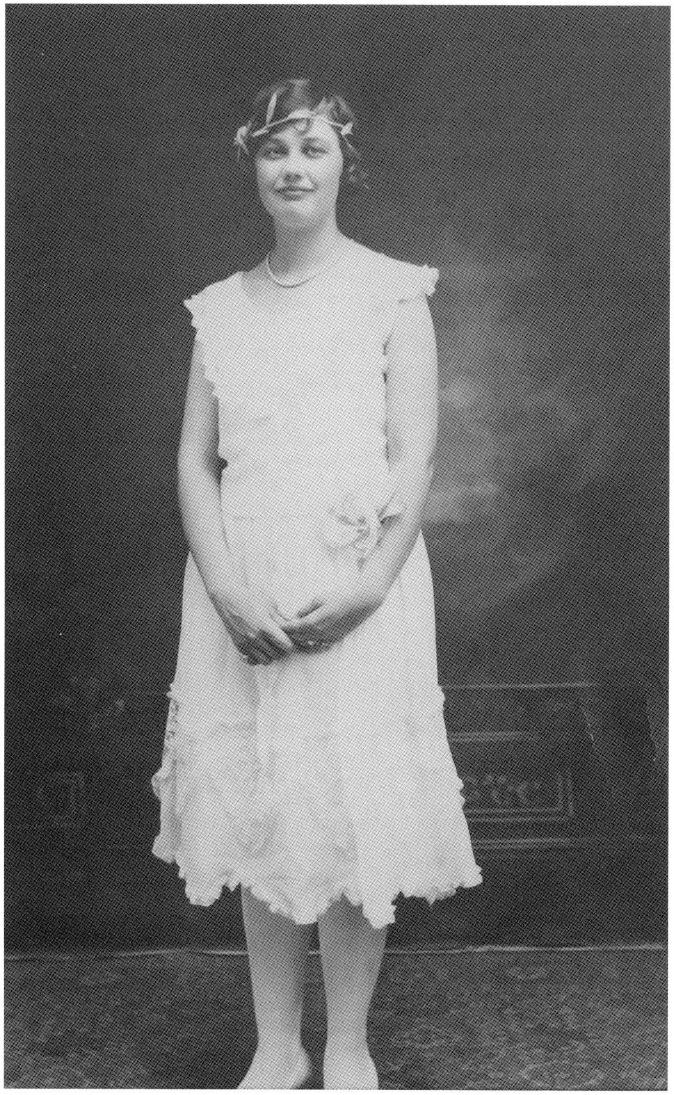

Mildred, age sixteen, Jacksboro High School Graduation, 1925.
Family collection.

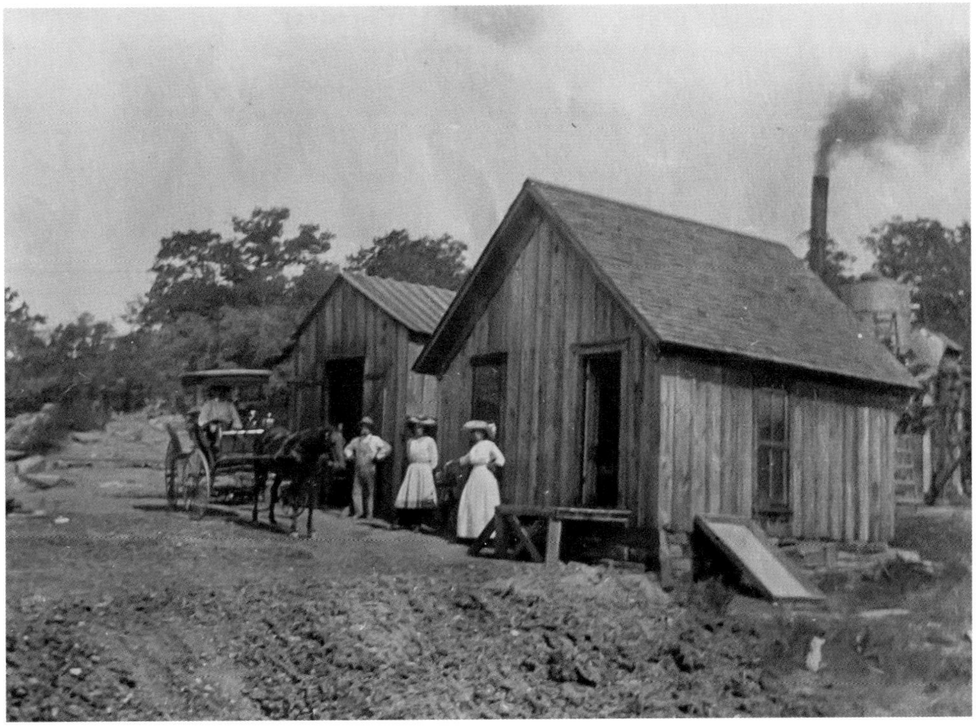

Glimpse of daily life: "Dressed to go to town."
Family collection.

Her stories of life as a schoolteacher were many and colorful. Theater experience had taught my mother just the right amount of stage presence: forceful but not too much so, witty but not silly, great eye contact with her audience, naturally beautiful features and self-assurance, intelligence tempered with patience. The young children in the one-room schoolhouse adored her.

When paying jobs could be found, the older children in the area had been put to work. Dropping out of school by the age of eleven or twelve was common practice in the 1920s. When the boys in a family grew big and strong enough to lift feed sacks and walk behind a mule-pulled plow, they were expected to work.

Living with her grandparents, being doted on by her Aunt Bertha and the older cousins, Mildred had led a sheltered life, leaving her a bit naïve. As a result, Mildred was shocked to see that most of her pupils wore tattered overalls or dresses made of feed sacks, and worst of all, they came to school barefoot.

Adding to her surprise were the number of little girls who came to her asking, "Can I tell you a secret?" Whispering in her ear, they said, "Miss Cherry, someone stole my lunch." Mildred tried to hide her shock. The children brought their lunches wrapped in cloth and tucked under their desks. How could they be stolen?

"Miss Cherry. It was that boy over there," one of the little girls said, nodding toward a very small, scruffy-looking barefoot boy standing in the far corner of the room.

"Are you sure?" Mildred asked. The solemn nod and grave look told her what she needed to know. "This must be stopped. It's my job to help teach these children right from wrong." She stopped the little boy at the end of the school day. Waiting until all the others had gone, she stood, looked the boy in the eye, and asked, "Do you know that it's wrong to take lunch food from your friends? Unless they give it to you."

Ducking his head, blushing and embarrassed, a frown growing on his dirty little face, he said, "Didn't do nothin' wrong." Then turned and ran out the schoolroom door.

* * *

He did not return to school the following day or the day after.

By the end of the week, early on Friday morning, he reappeared, and he was not alone. Walking slowly behind his angry-looking parents, the boy quietly slunk into the schoolhouse while his parents stopped and glared at Miss Cherry, demanding to talk to her outside—alone. On the front stoop, with the sun just peeking over the tall pine trees and the fading moon still visible overhead, the boy's father growled, "Told 'im to take that food... He's hawngry." And with that, the barefoot man and the tired looking woman turned and walked away. Mildred, who had never gone hungry a day in her life, gasped. "Oh, I did not know that. If I had known . . . " and her voice trailed off behind the angry parents.

Following a couple of sleepless nights, Mildred made a decision.

Monday morning, Miss Cherry arrived at school early, carrying a wicker basket filled with apples, nuts, and cold biscuits. As the children took their seats, she rang a small brass bell, the signal for quiet, and in a clear voice she made an announcement. Noting that the shy perpetrator was sitting in the back row, head down and frowning, she spoke with a clear and calm voice. "Children. This basket on my desk has a surprise for each one of you. Today and every day from now on, that basket will have treats in it for you. When you stand to go outside for recess, stop by and take one or two things that you would like to eat. You may eat it outside."

With that, class began. And for the rest of the school year, no more lunches were stolen. And, to add to Mildred's delight, the quiet, shy little boy in the back row learned his ABCs, his "two-times," and read the first book of his life.

Mildred taught school in that one-room Carthage, Texas, schoolhouse until she went on a blind date with William Joseph Durham. That date that would change her life and take the young couple on the journey of a lifetime.

CHAPTER 26

With Mildred gone from her hometown, from the ranch, the hum of her grandparents' everyday life lost more of its happiness than they might have thought possible. Roy's death was a bitter pill; Mildred's absence made it worse. And conventional wisdom probably suggested that T. H. and Sallie demand that their granddaughter come home. Return to help them regain some footing, some sense of direction. But the grandparents were smarter than to insist on that. Mildred had her own strong will and determination, and when she did return for short visits they could see that she was happy and becoming very much her own person.

And they still had the grandsons. Tom, who was married to his high school sweetheart, Maxine Grable, and had thoughts of a baby soon on the way, was busy night and day. Never failing to report his daily activities to T. H., Tom was good-natured and toed the line his grandpa had set. And he excelled as a rancher. Tom scarcely had time to look up from his responsibilities: entering his Hereford white-faced cattle in competitions at the Fort Worth Stockyards, winning blue ribbons and trophies, riding herd on hired hands and livestock, prompting his brother, Roy Junior, to toe the same line and walk the same expected path, and making big efforts to keep his new wife happy and the front porch swept.

But he did miss his big sister. She had always been able to calm the waters when T. H. went on a tear or Roy Jr. acted out.

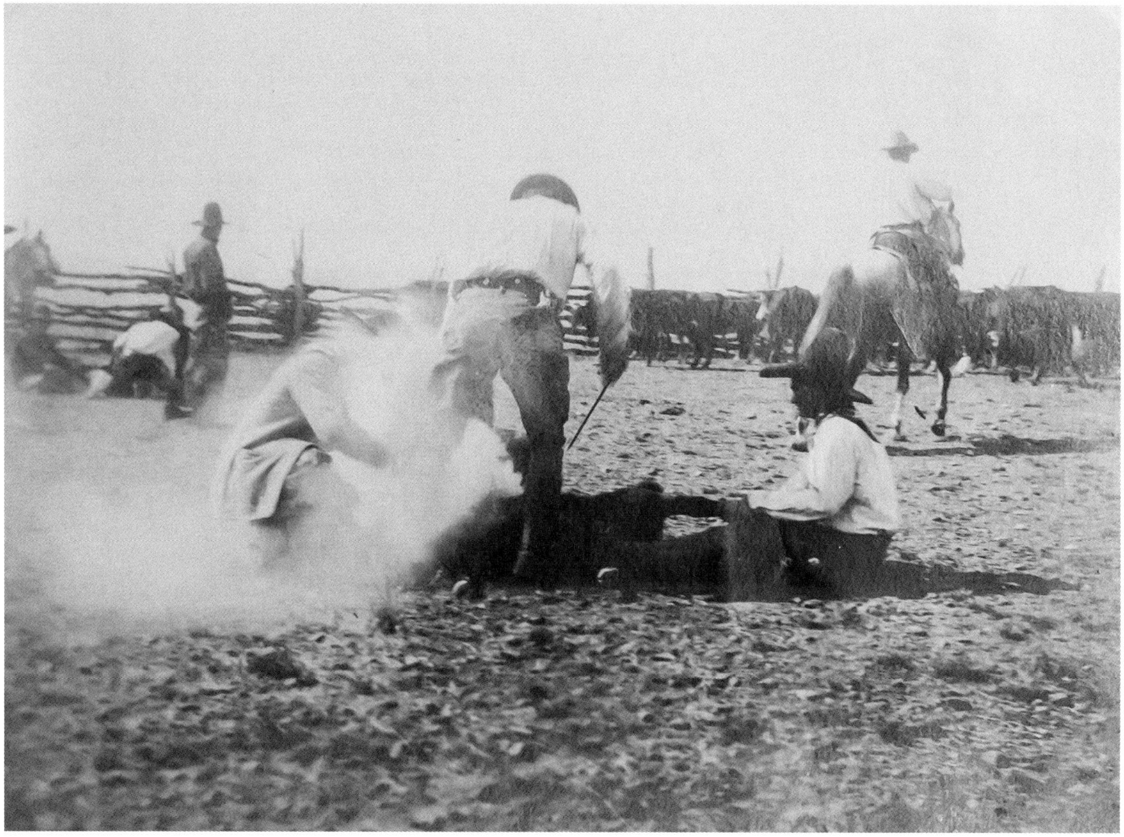

Branding calves. Daily life on Cherryhomes Ranch.
Family collection.

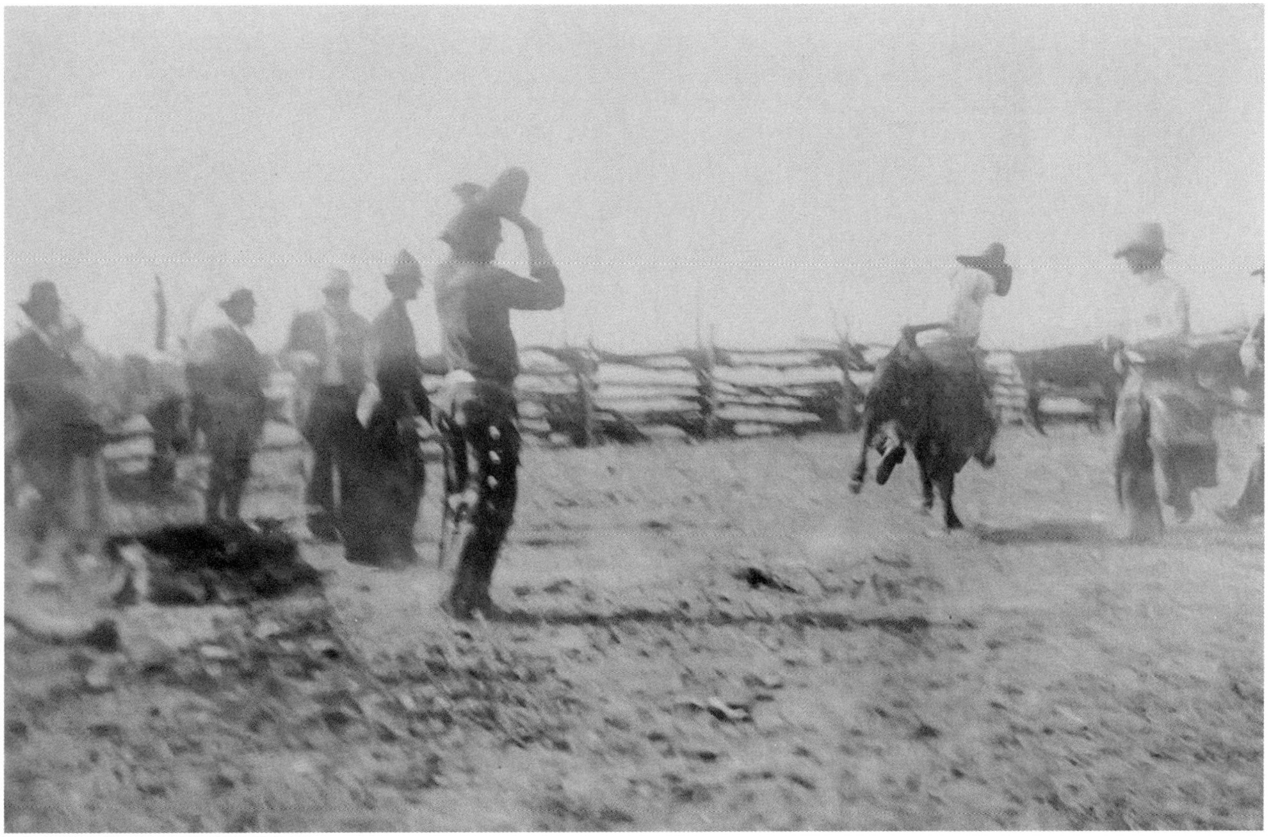

Cowboys having fun.
Family collection.

* * *

In 1934, the world was in turmoil. It was said that Europe was in the hands of a madman, and America was called to arms once again. The whole idea of it gave T. H. the heebie jeebies. He felt the disease of war deep in his bones. Witnessing the dregs of the Civil War, the economic impact of World War I, the disease and poverty of the depression, the personal losses from futile attempts to control the future, he was exhausted.

Like a senseless paradox, he and Sallie were living a life that was at once empty and full. The cattle market was good enough to give them a good living, and the drilling for oil on the ranch land was going better than expected, but it all felt empty and futile somehow.

Shaking off the blues, listening to the quiet of his living room with its faint ticking of the mantel clock, T. H.'s ruffled feathers were soothed by the chiming of the hour. And yet, life was moving along too fast. He had too much to do. And he was well aware that he had a short time to do it. At seventy-four, he looked at the possibility that he had no real control over much of anything. That didn't mean he would not keep trying, and trying hard, to control the life and ways of his family. But his fierce love for his family too often sounded like harsh criticism and anger to the grandsons. And the day that Roy Jr. broke the threshing machine, well, that just about put the icing on the cake.

It was a day in late August. The hay cutting had begun, and the threshing machine was doing its damndest to keep up with the hired hands. Roy Jr., at fifteen a big strong boy, just didn't have his heart in the whole enterprise. Working an hour or so, and then slipping off to sit in the shade of a big oak tree, taking longer than he should to drink water from the tin can, wash off his sweaty face, and cuss at the hotter'n hell noontime heat, he was not gaining any good will from the hired hands or Grandpa.

"Dad dammit, boy, you rested long enough. Git up and git with it," T. H. told him. Roy Jr. glared up at the boss man through the heat waves and dust, scratching under his sweaty arms at the prickly shards of hay sticking to everything, and ambled over to the waiting pitchfork and took hold.

The afternoon droned on as storm clouds began to gather in the West. Not looking good for the fresh cut hay. Not at all. When five o'clock rolled around, clouds growing bigger and wind picking up, there remained a field full of cut hay to gather and haul to the machine. "No stoppin', boys. No stoppin'," T.H. declared. "Git that hay picked up before she blows in."

Threshing machine chugging, men silent and sweating, the smell of rain in the air, Roy Jr., tired and mad, had enough. Jamming the sharp tines of the pitchfork into the dry ground, looking at the field around him, Roy found just what he was looking for: a big jagged rock about the size of a big prickly bale of hay. Strong and sure of himself, Junior stepped over a pile of smaller rocks, looked at the big red sandstone rock, and not caring how much it weighed, nudged it out of the ground. Taking a deep breath, leaning over, and bending his knees, he bullied the rock out of its resting place, picked it up, and slowly walked toward the hateful threshing machine. Standing close to the machinery, face red with heat and strain, raising the big rock over his head, he threw the boulder toward the machine and made a direct hit. The motor jammed. The blades stalled. The threshing machine groaned in its death throes and came to a grinding halt. Deaf as he was, Grandpa heard the commotion and looked at the startled faces of the hands. He watched his grandson, an heir to the land he loved, stomp his feet, put his hands on his hips, and shout, "I quit." Not pausing to take a breath or look at his audience of hardworking men, Roy marched toward the nearby ranch house, and he never looked back. As some of the hands said later, "The rain began then, and we all called it a day." T. H., red-faced and furious but not saying a word, turned to his own vehicle, revved up the engine, and in a cloud of dusty rain, drove back to town.

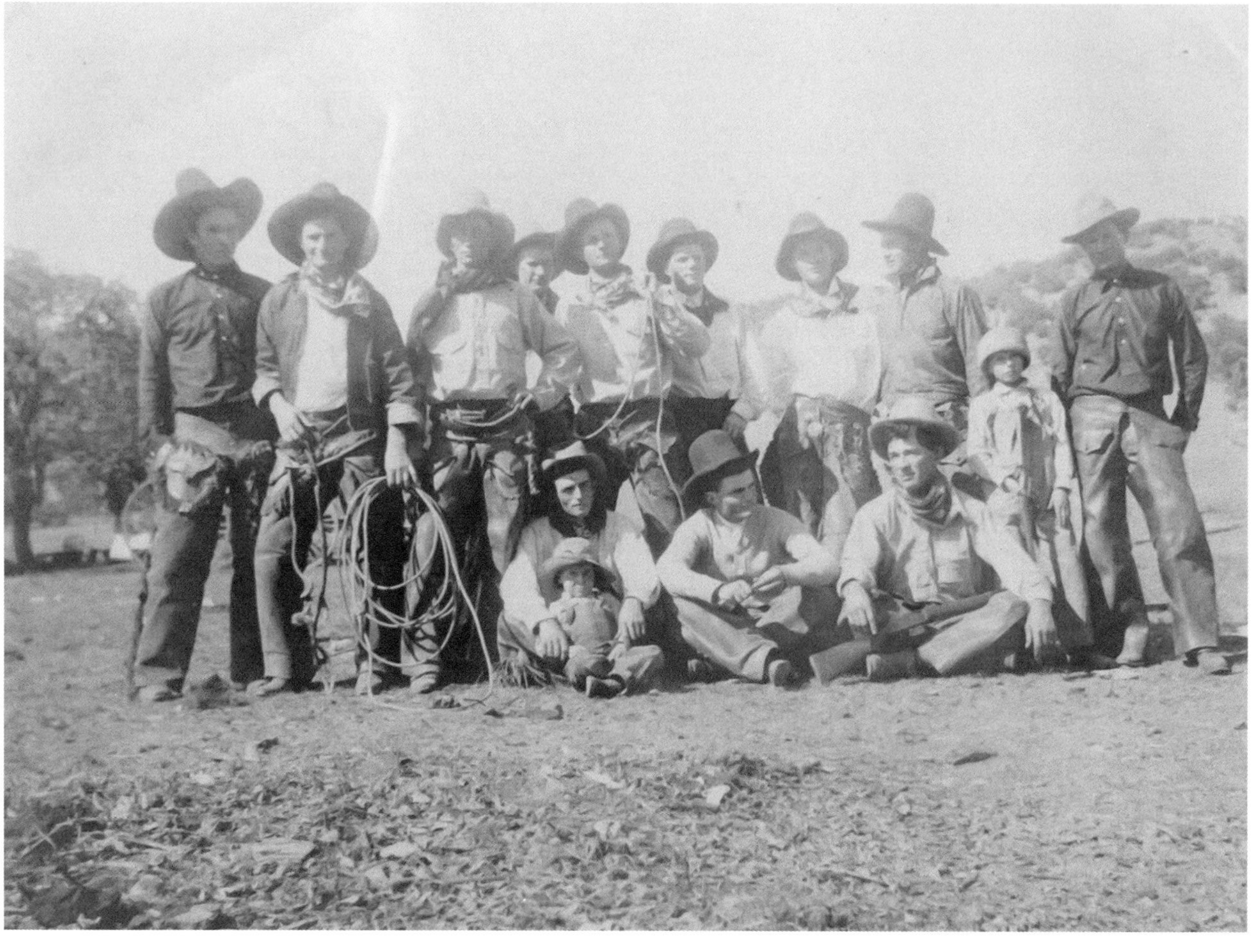

ABOVE AND OPPOSITE
Cowboys on Cherryhomes Ranch and some of their family.
Family collection.

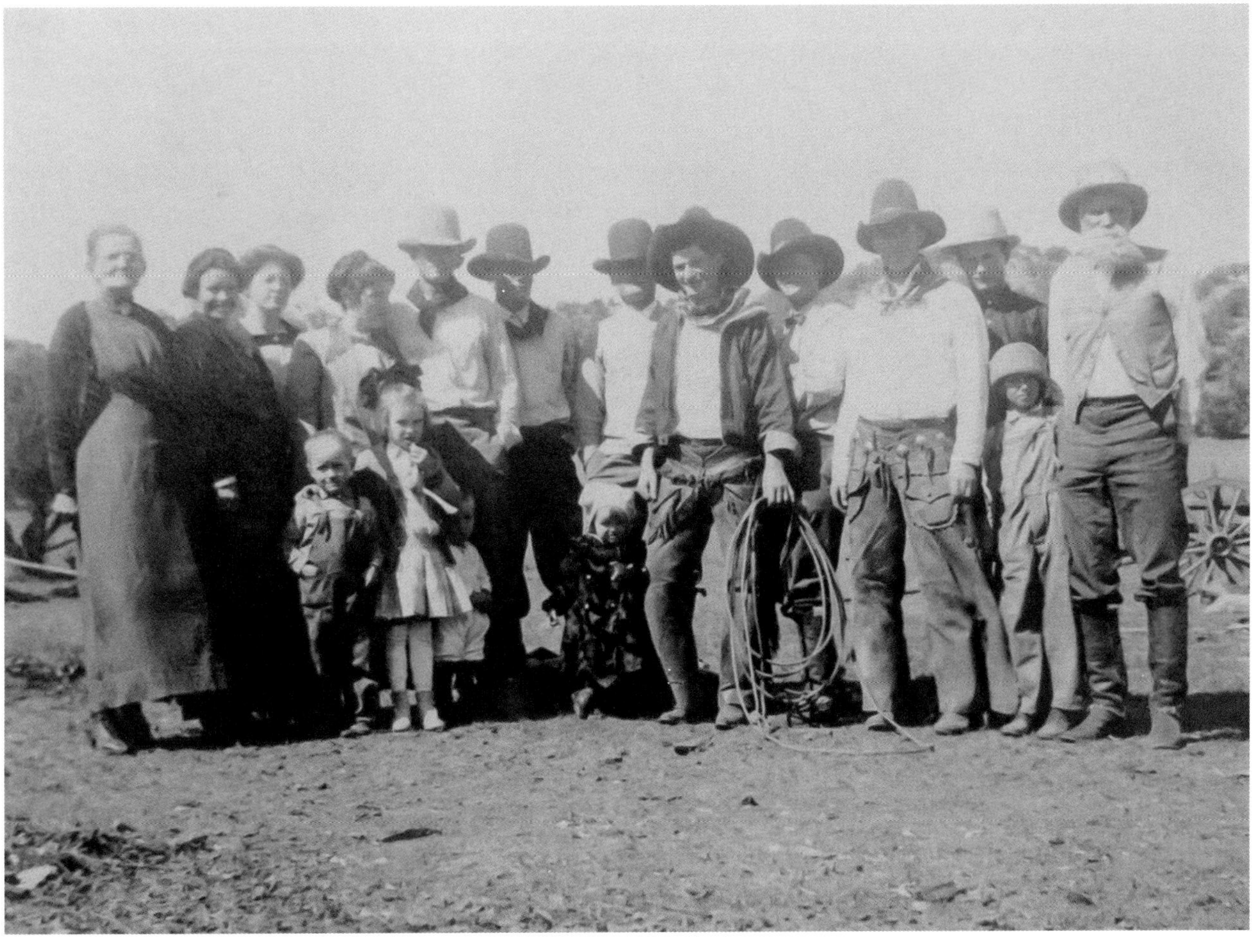

CHAPTER 27

If the town gossips continued talking about T. H. and how he sat for hours on his big paint horse patrolling the land, hoping to keep so-called progress at bay, well let 'em, T. H. thought. In fact, he was proud of it. Proud of his ownership of the big ranch. Proud of his ability to stand up for its rights. Yes, he had tried to prevent the big electric line from cutting though his River Ranch. And yes, electricity had come anyway. And yes, he hated the idea of outsiders drilling for oil on his land and making a mess of it, and strangers roaming who-knew-where, nosing around his houses and barns and his prize hound dogs. "Dad dammit," T. H. had said. "This land is private. I won't have strangers gawking around lookin' at the houses and the huntin' dogs and makin' ruts in my roads." But he supposed it was inevitable that some damned fool landman was going to throw enough money his way to cause him to relent and lease some of his acreage. And of course he did sign leases, but not without driving a hard bargain.

To his surprise, it was not so bad. An experienced trader himself, T. H. did not suffer fools. He could spot a shyster a mile away. And by giving no truck to glad-handers and bullshitters, as far as records show, he never got blindsided by a shaky business deal.

He told Sallie to call the attorney again. Because he owned the mineral rights on all the land, he wanted his will to state that proceeds from the minerals would be evenly divided between the three grandchildren, no matter

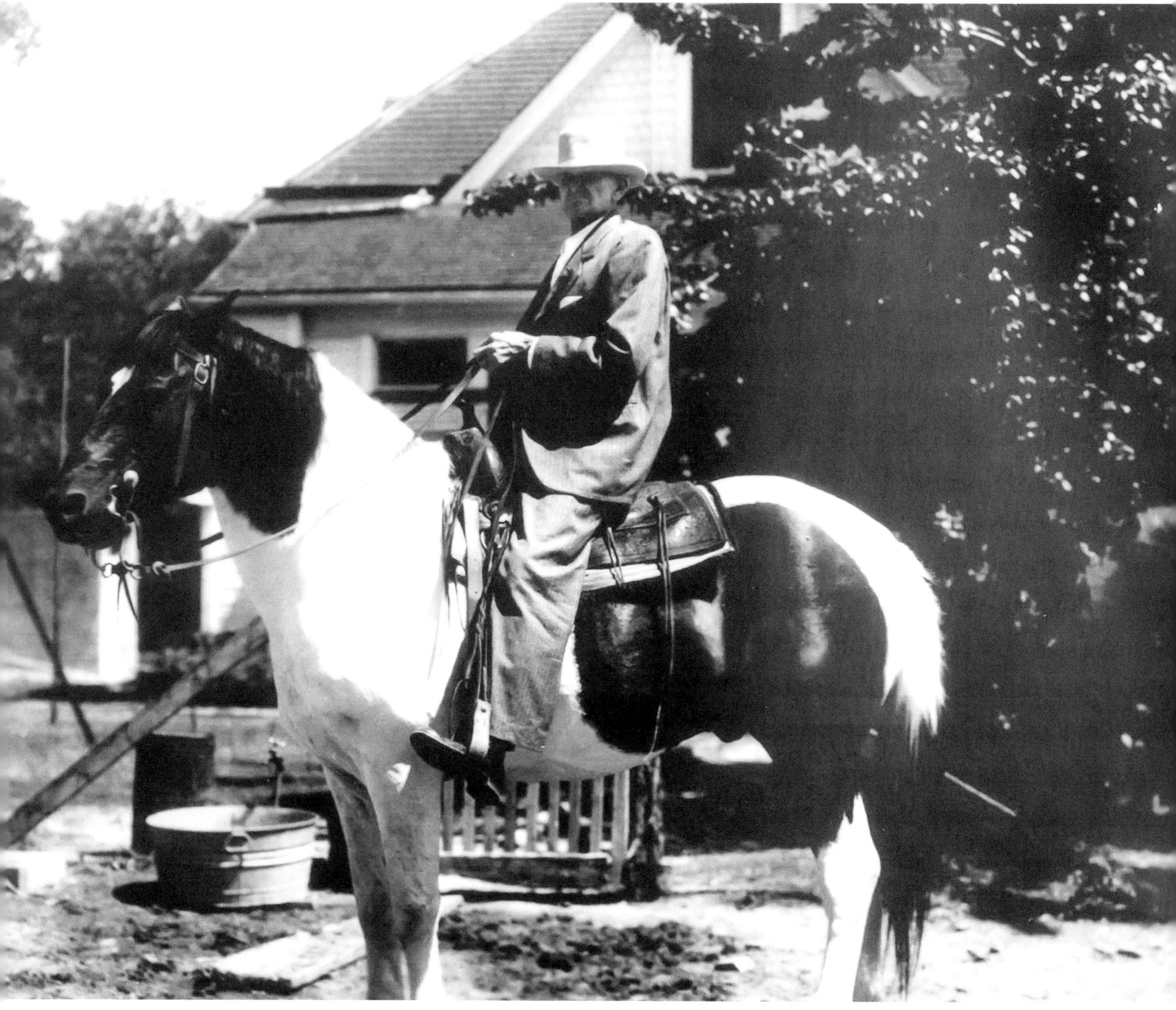

which part of the ranch the production happened to be on. He was farsighted enough to know how that decision would affect his land and his heirs. It was a gift. And by stipulating that proceeds be divided evenly between his heirs, bitter jealousies were avoided.

As it turned out, the sale of gas and oil on the Cherryhomes ranch land would produce income enough for his descendants to maintain ownership of the land and for cattle ranching to continue far into the future. When taxes rose, the royalty income kept pace, cushioning the blows from erratic cattle markets and drought.

Beginning with the drilling of the T. H. Cherryhomes #1 well in 1917, just as T. H. had predicted, everything on the ranch changed. And some of the change, disguised as progress, was inevitable and good, bringing electricity and increasing the family income. But like everything else, when one thing changes, so do others, and the days when the walls of slush pits broke, spilling sludge and killing large parts of grass land, or when the electricity came and went and he had to buy more kerosene to feed the lanterns, T. H. was heard having a few walleyed fits.

OPPOSITE
T. H. on one of his favorite forty paint horses.
Family collection.

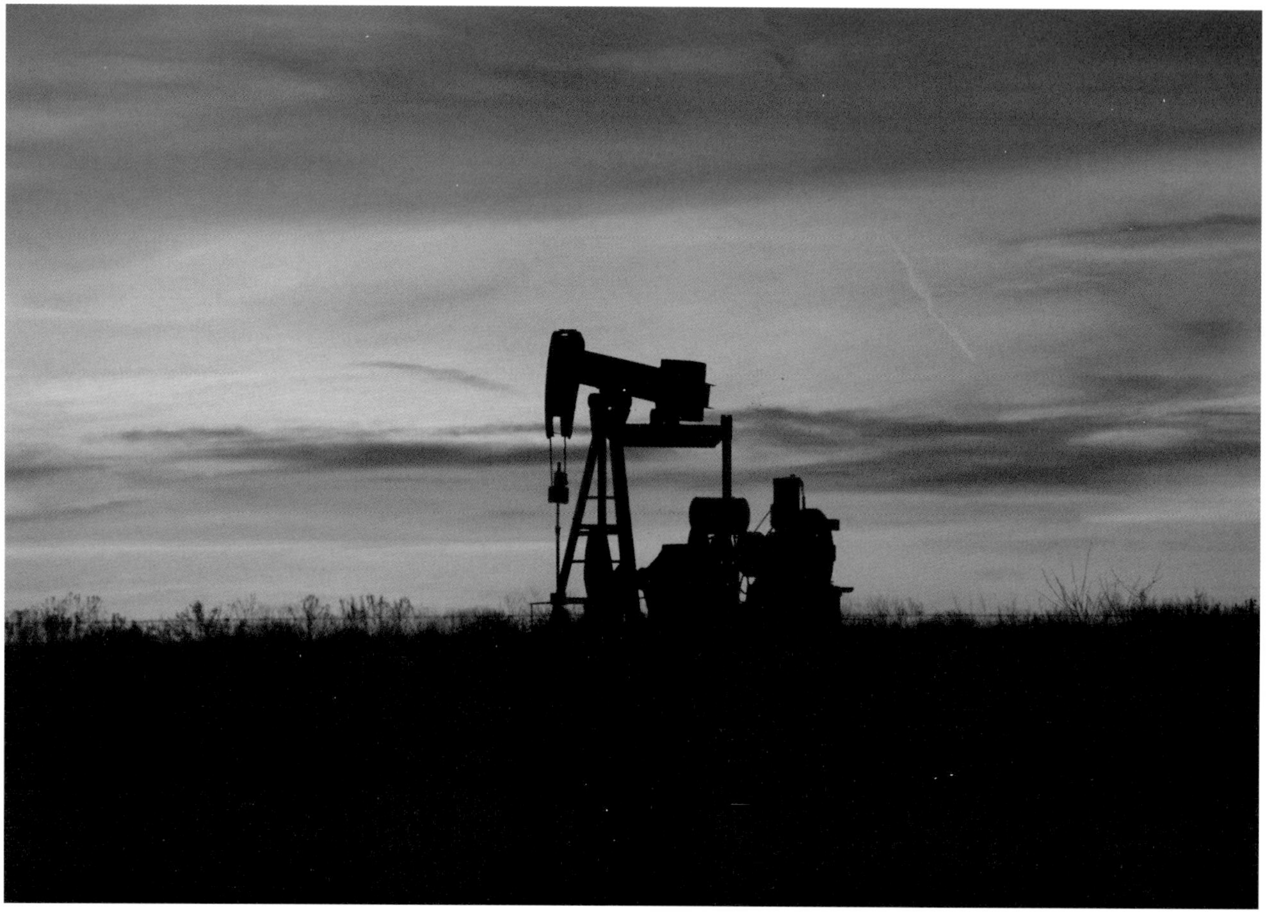

Pump Jack, H&D Ranch, 2020.
Photo by Donna Henderson Craft.

OPPOSITE
Invitation to Join Kennel Club.
Family collection.

President, Brown Harwood. Sec.-Treas., S. F. Collier.

FORT WORTH KENNEL CLUB
STOCKYARDS NATIONAL BANK
P. O. Box 697
FORT WORTH, TEXAS

February 7th, 1921.

Mr. Tom Cherryhomes,
Jacksboro, Texas.

Dear Mr. Cherryhomes:-

You have, no doubt, noticed in some of the Fort Worth papers where there has been a club organized under the name of the Fort Worth Kennel Club. I have the honor of being elected its first Secretary and am very proud to be associated with as fine a bunch as compose the members of the club. In talking the matter of membership over today with Mr. Frank L. Miller he asked me if I had ever written you and asked you to join us, said he felt sure you would be glad of the opportunity, I am, therefore, taking this occasion to write you and ask you to join us. While you will realize that from the standpoint of making financial returns it will not be what one would call an investment, it will be of great assistance in furthering the interest of the Dog in that it will teach men and women more about how to care for and attend to the needs of him who would not hesitate to do his bit.

We are now preparing for a Bench Show to be held during the Stock Show and have 37 very beautiful cups already paid for and are expecting to make it one of the best shows of its kind that has ever been held this side of K. C. I received a letter from a man in Chicago the other day who intends to send a string down and we are hearing from them all over the state saying they will show with us, surely would like for you to send a few down, whether you join the Club or not, and let the people see what a real dog looks like, and that reminds me, we have several members who are interested in Hounds and one of them, Mr. R. W. Plummer, of Joshua, Texas, who was talking about his dogs some time back and I begun telling him about your bunch, how fast they were and what all I had heard of them and he said that while he wasn't a gambling man he would put up a good hat that if you were to take three or four of your Hounds and he take an equal number of his and take all of them to new ground that after they made a strike his dogs would lead. I would love to see a chace like that.

Am enclosing a card, which if you will sign and enclose the required check, I shall take great pleasure in presenting it before the next meeting which will be next Tuesday night, February 15th. May I not hear from you?

Very respectfully,
Sam Collier

CHAPTER 28

Leaning back in his wheelchair, head turned toward the kitchen door, T. H., now old and infirm, barked, "Sallie. Come in here. Crank up that contraption on the wall. Call Mildred."

As if the aches and pains of old age weren't enough, Sallie's niece had been fluttering around him all morning, and he was irritable to the extreme. Old age had refused to soften his rough voice. But it gave him a focused wisdom, and he was damned certain that the big-boned, dark-eyed, flat-footed middle-aged woman was up to no good. Acting all nicey-nice, eyes darting like a damned old hen looking for something to peck and scratch at. He hated the sound of her high-pitched nasal voice and the awful way she clucked and whispered and never seemed to stop to catch her breath. And a foul-smelling breath it was. Damn it all. T. H. did not like it one little bit. "'I god, I'm not dyin' yet," he said.

Mildred would know how to keep her away, he ruminated. Damnation. "Ever body just tryin' to get into my pockets." Even the mailman brought bad news. Glaring at the stack of mail, missing Bertha in the worst way, T.H. muttered and frowned and hawked a spit with a direct hit into his spittoon. Talking in a gruff voice to no one in particular, he could be heard growling out words of complaint. "Bought this house in town. Now the gov'ment wants to charge me a tax on it. Pure-dee gall. That's what that is. Have a good mind to move back to the ranch. Show the sons-a-bitches who's boss." Chewing on his worries like an old hound dog worrying with a dead coon skin, T. H. had worked himself into a fine lather.

Pushing back from the cluttered desk, tired of shuffling papers around and missing Bertha, he barked, "Hell's bells, woman. Make that call. Find out how soon Mildred can get here. Living off in Midland with that husband of hers. She belongs here in Jack County with her people."

Hearing T. H. perfectly well the first time he barked, Sallie, two rooms away in her kitchen, sighed. Snatching a white dish towel from the countertop, wiping her hands, wet from morning chores and dishwater, she slowly walked into the living room.

"Yes, I heard you, T. H. What do you want with Mildred?"

"I want her to chase away your nosy relatives."

Sighing again, Sallie, with a reluctance reserved for suspicious objects, approached the ugly brown wood box hanging on the living room wall. She did not like the intrusive thing and at first had refused to have the thing in her house. What did anyone need with a telephone? Never had one. Never missed having one. Didn't want one.

But their grandson, Tom, talked them into getting it. Praising its wonders, telling how much they would enjoy it, how much they needed it, Tom even promised that if they did not like it after it was installed, he would take it away. "Give it a chance," he smiled. "Think of it. You can call the grocery store and order you some food. Why, you can even call Dr. Fillmore if you get sick. It's easy to use. Easy as falling off a log," he chuckled. "Imagine all the trouble it will save you."

"Save trouble, will it?" T. H. grumbled. "Ha. Cost me money is what it will do." But, as Tom knew he would, T. H. relented. Tom managed the details, and the ugly thing was hung on the living room wall in front of God and everybody. After Sallie reminded him that Tom was usually right about the newfangled world they found themselves living in, T. H. nodded his okay, but that didn't mean he had to like it.

He knew all along it would be a problem. The damned thing crackled and buzzed and he couldn't hear worth a tinker's damn even when the receiver was pushed tight against his ear.

But Sallie could hear well enough, and that was all that mattered. "Wife, have you called her yet? Tell her to bring that little girl of hers, while she's at it. How old is that child by now? Must be three or four. Haven't seen her since she was a mite of a thing."

"Yes, yes, I'm ringing up the operator right now. Hold your horses. It takes a minute." Hearing the static and waiting for Mable, the local operator, to answer, Sallie thought to herself that Mildred should come to visit. Wouldn't hurt a thing. Havin' another woman in the house besides Mamie the maid. Oh my, she did miss Bertha.

"Number please. Miz Cherryhomes. That you? What can I do for you?"

"Yes, Mable, it's me. Need to talk to Mildred out in Midland."

* * *

My memories of T. H. and Sallie, of seeing them in person, of being in their house, are few, but very real.

When my mother told me that she and I were going to take a car trip all the way from our house in Midland to Jacksboro, I was excited. We were going to visit my great-grandparents. Reminding me that I had met them when I was very little, I nodded. But I really did not remember the visit. After all, I was four going on five, and lots of things had happened since I had been little.

We had lived in Pecos, where Daddy's job seemed to make him grumpy. And then we moved to Midland, which was better because there was a Piggly Wiggly store and a picture show and new friends next door.

But hard as I tried, I did not remember ever seeing Grandpa and Grandma, as Mother called them when she told Daddy we were going for a visit.

After what seemed a very long time, at least three days, we loaded the car late one afternoon because we were leaving early the next morning, and

I went to bed too excited to sleep. So when Mother came into my room, turned on the light, and said, "Let's go," I jumped up and hurried to put on my blue dress and black patent leather shoes. Gulping down a glass of milk and begging to take a piece of toast with me to the car, I then settled next to Mother in the front seat of the blue 1940 Ford sedan, because Daddy wasn't going. And best of all, the car had a radio that sometimes worked, and when it did, we might hear music. I was so excited that it was hard for me to "settle down," like Mother said to do. The morning was still dark and with headlights on and the radio crackling, we left our four-room house in Midland and drove off into the adventure.

Mother chattered a bit about the big house where Grandma and Grandpa lived and told me that it was the house where she had grown up. And "guess what?" it had an upstairs with two extra bedrooms. There was plenty of room for us.

I tried really hard to hold my eyes open, but with the darkness and the music and Mother's soft voice, I must have taken a long nap because the next thing I knew, Mother's voice was louder, "Wake up sleepy head. We're here."

After five hours of travel, the sun was now shining, and I felt really hungry. The car turned into a big dirt driveway. Mother drove to the back side of a big, two-story white house and stopped. Looking at me with her "don't be a slow poke" face, she opened the car door, stepped out, stretched her arms up to the sky, yawned, and walked across the big backyard. Jumping out of the car, I caught my breath at the sight of the tall house with its tall steps leading up to a black screen door.

Who knew what kind of magical things lurked inside? I hurried to climb the steps and catch up with Mother as she opened the creaky screen door and stepped onto a big porch. Ahead of us was a white door with four little windowpanes, and before I knew it we walked thought that door into the biggest, whitest kitchen I had ever seen. An old woman, dressed in a muted print dress and white apron, her grey hair pulled into a tight bun, a hint of a smile dancing across her thin lips, put her hands on her hips, looked me over with big gray eyes, and in a soft voice said, "Well, it's about time you got here, Missy." Mother gave the old woman a gentle hug and said, "Carol, this is Grandma. Do you remember her?" I didn't, but before I could answer, Mother turned away again and whispered, "Where is he? Is he asleep?"

Grandma patted me on the head, nodded toward a doorway on the far side of the room, and said, "Go on in." A walk across the kitchen led into a dining room with a big round oak table and ten chairs. I followed Mother as she went past the table and turned to walk through another door, a tall, transomed doorway, and whispered, "Grandpa will be in there." I was not at all sure why we whispered, but whispering seemed to be the thing to do. Maybe he was asleep. I had been told to never ever wake Daddy when he was asleep. Should I tiptoe? Entering a large room encompassed by dark tea stained wallpaper, I squinted my eyes to see better in the dim room with no windows. And there, like a spotlight in a stage play, a single lighted floor lamp shown behind a high-backed, ornately carved wooden chair. Seated in that chair, his spidery thin hands dangling from the arm rests, was the oldest human I had ever seen. Face crisscrossed with track marks of eighty-two years, track marks so deep that the scattered whiskers, thin and sparse, could not cover them, thin lips searching for a smile, the old man, harrumphing to clear his throat, nodded at Mother, looked at me, and commanded, "Come here little Missy. Let me take a look at you."

Looking back at that time and place, I don't know why I wasn't afraid or intimidated. But as Mother silently urged me toward the ancient old man, I was simply curious. Was he really my grandpa? Why were his whiskers so long? Daddy shaved every day and never had those long scratchy-looking hairs on his face. And the eyes that met mine, shot through with sparks of interest, silently pulled me toward him.

Even though his clothes were modest, gray work shirt, khaki pants, hair disheveled and oily, his commanding presence took me over. I watched in amazement as he picked up a morning glory-shaped wooden horn and stuck the small end of it into his left ear. But if he had hoped to hear what I had to say, he was disappointed. I knew he was a man not interested in idle chatter, and as I stood there in awe, I had absolutely nothing to say.

With a brief nod and trembling hand, he removed the horn, set it on the table beside his chair, and leaned toward me. Motioning me to step closer, reaching his arms toward me, his face drawing near to mine, he gently lifted me up into his lap. This was the man I had heard about. Strong. In charge. I had no doubt that I was supposed to sit on his bony legs and be very still. We looked at each other, my little girl eyes staring at the hair growing out from his ears and his nose, and as he gave me a brief hug, I hoped that the next time I saw him his face wouldn't feel so scratchy. "My, my. Just look at you," he muttered. He might have commented on my dress or said that I looked like my mother, I do not remember. What I do remember is this: His presence was huge. But his manner kind and gentle. He was not a man for me to fear.

And soon, I was wiggling and squirming and needing to go to the bathroom. I slipped from his lap and looked at Mother as she pointed to another doorway and said with a smile, "The bathroom is through that door."

After washing my hands, I slipped past Mother and Grandpa and skipped toward the kitchen, where I hoped Grandma was up to something more interesting. And sure enough, she was doing mysterious things with eggs, sugar, and flour. I heard Mother talking to Grandpa and decided I needed to stay in the kitchen with Grandma. "What 'cha doin'?" I asked as I watched her crack open a dozen or more hen eggs. Separating the yoke from the whites, she said, "You'll see," which told me nothing except that I would have to wait. Since I was not very good at waiting, I looked around the big room and spotted a partly opened door, and since no one was looking, I slowly walked toward it, pushed it all the way open, and saw amazing things. White-washed wooden shelves stretched from the floor higher than a grown up could reach. And on those shelves sat sacks of sugar, flour, buckets of lard, and white china plates stacked neatly next to metal pots and pans. And the smell of spices made my mouth water. When I spotted a white china plate covered with a blue cup towel, I glanced over my shoulder to see if anyone was watching and lifted the corner of the cloth. "Hungry?" I jumped at the voice. Grandma stood in the doorway of the big pantry. "Go ahead and uncover the plate. Fried chicken left from lunch. Still good. Bring it to the table and take a seat. I'll get you a cold glass of sweet milk." I was soon to learn something else: In Jacksboro if you wanted a glass of milk, you needed to say "sweet milk." Or you might get a glass of buttermilk and be in for a big surprise.

Sitting at the wooden kitchen table, biting into a drumstick, I decided that I had never tasted fried chicken that good. And, though I could not know it at the time, while I was eating cold fried chicken, my life was about to change forever, and the unfamiliar house would become as well known to me as the back of my own hand. But for that moment in time, all I cared about was that delicious taste of happiness.

CHAPTER 29

Stars of the stage, women who were great beauties, writers or musicians sometimes made a name for themselves in the America of the nineteenth century. But the women who made up the stabilizing backbone of the frontier, the behind the scenes women; the strong, determined women who birthed babies, planted gardens, and fought off wolves; the unrecognized heroic women; the women without whom the West would not have been won, the country civilized, the churches attended, often remained anonymous. Through no fault of their own, their heroic deeds were left to family lore or lost in the dust of faded memories.

Peeking from the pages of the era are the well-known names: Sharpshooter Annie Oakley. Lillie Langtry, the beautiful mistress of King Edward VII. But while they made their well-known splash in history books, the Sarah Alice Berrys of the Texas frontier worked their own magic, helping tame the land, establish ranches, and work in tandem with their menfolk to raise and feed good Christian families.

As Carmen Goldthwaite writes in her book *Texas Dames*, “Anglo women would build a republic and a state stepping into the deep footholds notched by Indian and Spanish-speaking women they did not know . . . women who . . . made the wild country ready for later women and families. . . . They would enable church and churchmen, schools, villages and towns, and embrace the arts. . . .”

Sarah Alice Berry was one of those women. Born in 1864, she was the daughter of a pioneer mother who rode in a covered wagon from Tennessee to Texas with about $1,000 tucked in her skirts. She fought off Indians, thirst, and wild animals.

With the courage and strength of that pioneer mother running in her veins, Sarah Alice (Sallie) Berry was the epitome of the early ranching wife. Silent, strong, and determined, Sallie learned to read and write at the age of seven, and by eight, she learned to tend a garden and wring a chicken's neck. Chores occupied hardworking Sallie's life until she first laid eyes on T. H. Cherryhomes. The strapping young man rode a horse onto her family ranch, offering to buy land and cattle, his blue eyes snapping, and Sallie never looked back.

To say she was swept off her feet would be an understatement. To say that she flirted and giggled and batted her eyelashes at the handsome young cowboy would be an overstatement. Reserved, clear-minded, and smart, she set her cap for T. H. and that was that. Their union made sense to her family. He was a young man on his way to big things, and Sallie was just the girl to help him get there.

Native to Jack County, Sallie was taught the importance of weather and its whims. The survival of her hearty family and all settlers of the Cross Timbers lands depended on nature, and a child who never understood the importance of sniffing the breeze for information was doomed to an unhappy, brief existence.

Taught by observation that the wildlife had lessons to teach, she knew if the hunting dogs whined and paced for no apparent reason, or the songbirds went silent or she heard thunder in February, well . . . the weather was apt to change.

The menfolk in Sallie's young world were tough, straight talkin', and rough-mannered, and she learned to keep her feminine ways to herself.

She knew that a life with T. H. would be rough and tumble, but there was no way around it. She would marry him, even as he paid cash for a big chunk of her family land, amid some grumbles from a few of the Berry menfolk.

And marry they did and settled into a small wood-frame house with a wood-burning cook stove and two rooms. The stove worked just fine so long as T. H. remembered to cut the firewood short and often. When he forgot, well, Sallie knew how to use the axe when she had to, but never said she liked it.

Plans for their life together didn't require much conversation. Major decisions would be made by her husband, and unless they rammed into ideas Sallie was adamant about, she kept quiet. But no one ever doubted that T. H. had married a woman of strength. Carrying herself with an air of authority, she moved though her days and nights with confidence.

But when she was pregnant with their first child, Sallie laid down the law. She told T. H. in no uncertain terms that she would be a good, firm parent, and the bottom line was this: the child raising was her territory and if she needed advice, she knew how to ask.

Unspoken was her knowledge that life was fragile, children died too young, crops failed, cakes would refuse to rise, and she would never cry over spilt milk. Throwing in her lot and life with T. H. Cherryhomes, Sarah Alice Berry seldom looked back while with a straight spine and determined eyes she walked with him into an uncertain future.

And at the end of his long life, T. H. would hold up his head and comment to anyone who cared to listen, "Yep. Sallie was a good 'un."

CHAPTER 30

"Mercy. Cold as a well digger's behind this mornin'," Mother said as she came inside through the back door. "We better get a move on. Started the car so the heater can warm up." Peppering Grandma's backside with questions, I had not noticed the cold. Always busy doing something or other in the kitchen, Grandma didn't act like she heard my important questions, and I was determined to get some kind of answer. "Why does Grandpa snore so loud?" "Is Mamie coming today?" "Can I have another biscuit to take with me in the car?"

It was time for us to leave and go back to Midland and Daddy, and why did everyone have on such sad faces?

Mother's soft voice broke my stream of "whys" and "why nots": "You should say, 'May I have another,' Carol, not, 'Can I?'"

Ignoring Mother, I reached for the nearest biscuit and stuffed it in the pocket of my coat that all at once seemed too small. Where were my mittens? And no, Mother, I had not seen my wool cap. With a "Bye Grandma, see ya later," I turned to follow Mother down the back steps, shoes crunching on the gravel path. The blue Ford was chugging and bellowing white smoke in the cold frosty air as I hopped inside. Grabbing the radio on-off button, hoping the sound was strong and not full of static, I turned to the first music I could find. "*I'll be seeing you in all the old familiar places . . .*" I merrily sang along with the voice on the radio.

I rolled down the car window and waved goodbye to Grandma, who was dabbing at her eyes for some reason and seemed too busy to wave back at me.

Grandpa was standing in the back doorway, ramrod straight and frowning. And there was Mamie after all, waving a white dish towel at us. At least she was smiling.

Even Uncle Tom, who drove up just as Mother was about to back out of the drive, wore a worried face. Jumping out of his Model A, walking to the driver's side of our car, sticking his head inside the window, and giving Mother a little kiss on her cheek, he said, "I wish you weren't leaving so soon, Sis."

"Well, for goodness sake," I mumbled, like my Sunday school teacher said when she was exasperated. I couldn't see one thing to be gloomy about.

Pulling out onto Live Oak Street, Mama murmured, "Sallie does not look well. Not at all. Color is bad. Grandpa can't hear thunder. He's a handful. I hope Tom can get them both to the doctor. She doesn't look well at all." Curious about Grandma's color, she looked just the same to me, but knowing not to ask what Mother meant, I turned my attention to the radio.

* * *

One month later, in the windy cold of a February day, 1942, rain clouds gathering in the North and Grandma's bones aching, the seventy-eight-year-old woman decided that a warm soak in the big white claw-footed bath tub was just what she needed. A warm bath would do just the trick. Filling the tub with hot water, a luxury she never dreamed of in her youth, steam filling the small bathroom, Sallie peeled off her clothes, turned off the water, and gingerly stepped into the inviting pool. Remembering what Mamie had said just the day before, "Yessir, this be a mighty big house to keep up . . . hm . . . Miz Cherryhomes, you needs to have yourself a lie down. That's what." Sallie did just that. Stretching out in the warm water, inhaling the scent of bath salts, watching the bar of Ivory soap as it floated away, her eyelids feeling relaxed and heavy, head rested against the edge of the big white tub, feeling warm and safe and grateful, Sallie drifted off to sleep.

Mamie, hair tightly wrapped in her ever present "head rag," busied herself, waving her feather duster at cobwebs, both real and imagined, sweeping up the bread crumbs on the kitchen floor, humming to herself, and rearranging the blue plaid wool lap robe over Grandpa's knobby knees where he sat in his big high-backed chair, noticing, with approval, that he had dozed off. She suddenly stopped. Standing up straight and as tall as her 5'1" frame allowed, she looked around, cocked her head from one side to the other, and thought *Where is the Missus*? The big house was filled with silence, and it gave her a chill. Yes, it was nineteen degrees outside, but the chill she felt was not from the cold. "Too cold for that woman to be outside, that for sure. She do like takin' a hot bath from time to time. Whar can that woman be?" Looking from room to room, hurrying in the direction of the bathroom, she called, "Miz Sallie. Where you at?" Met with more silence than her curiosity could stand, listening at the closed bathroom door, she lightly tapped. "You in there?" No reply. Slowly opening the door, seeing the frail pale body stretched out in the soapy cold water, Mamie gasped.

With that, Sallie's eyes popped in surprise. Sitting straight up, giving a shiver, "Oh I must have dozed off."

"Lord God. You gwine take yo death of cold, Miz Sallie. Now you git on out a that water."

Trying to smile, Sallie asked, "Will you help me out of this thing?"

And with effort, strong arms, and a great deal of fussing, Mamie did just that. "Let me git you warm and dry and into the bed." Wrapping two big white towels around her trembling little body, briskly rubbing her back and arms and legs, Mamie gingerly led the woman she admired most in the world to her bed and helped her put on a long-sleeved white flannel gown. Guiding her thin body under the clean sheets, piling on quilts and blankets, Mamie barked, "I'm gwine fetch the hot water bottle fore you catch your death." Scurrying past Grandpa, the man she feared most in the world, she tapped him on his sleeping shoulder, "Mister Cherryhomes. You best wake up. Miss Sallie, she not lookin' too good."

But Sallie was too chilled, too tired, and too old. By nightfall she began to run a fever and developed a hard, dry cough. She assured T. H. that she only needed more quilts and a good night's sleep, and he agreed she was right. But he would have felt better about the situation if she would just agree to drink some broth or warm milk like he told her to do. He had never seen Sallie down for long, and rummaging through the pantry for leftover biscuits, he decided to sleep in the guest room. By morning all would be well.

But morning brought high fever and a cough that turned wheezy. Dr. Fillmore came and took Sallie's pulse, offered comforting words, and motioned for T. H. to follow him into the living room. With a sad look into T.H's squinting eyes, he sighed, frowned, and gave his head a worried shake. "I'm afraid it's pneumonia, T. H. Can you get her niece to come in and help? She needs to rest, drink liquids, and we'll see what tomorrow brings."

* * *

Slipping in and out of consciousness for five long days and nights, her will to live became more fragile by the hour. But ever the strong, determined woman, she clung to life long enough for the grandsons to rally around. Long enough for Tom to call Mildred and tell her to "Git home quick. Sallie's mighty sick." Long enough for Dr. Fillmore to make three house calls. And long enough for T. H. to sit up straight and bark out orders to anyone and everyone.

The doctor was called one last time, and while the three grandchildren, Mildred, Tom, and Roy Jr. gathered round her bedside and T. H. struggled to his feet and made his way into the bedroom, the little group looked at each other with anxious faces and turned away. Stethoscope dangling from around his neck, Dr. Fillmore felt for a pulse. Not finding one, as the cold winds whistled around the corners of the Cherryhomes house, Dr. Fillmore with a simple shake of his head and a quiet voice declared that Sarah Alice Berry was dead.

"Well, I swan," T.H. muttered, shaking his head in disbelief. Looking at the doctor, whose slow nod validated the family's fears, T. H. questioned in a voice thick with emotion, "You're sure, are you? She's gone?

"My, my," he said in a hoarse whisper spilling from his dry mouth, "never figured Sallie would die 'afore I did."

With that the old man turned away, and with a slow shuffle walked into the living room. Looking around as if to see something other than the gathered shadows from the late afternoon sun, his shoulders sagged while he heaved a sigh and transformed into a drooping heap of a man. With all the effort his body could muster, T. H. slumped into his favorite chair, put his face in his hands, and sobbed.

* * *

They were all there. The grown grandchildren, the niece, and Mamie all gathered and milled around as T. H. cleared his throat and pronounced, "She will rest in Oakwood with the others." Mildred nodding, understood. She would make the arrangements.

Days later, after the funeral, the grandchildren scattered. Mildred went back to Midland. Roy Jr. drove to the ranch. Tom and T. H. talked. "You're going to need someone to stay here with you," Tom advised. Mamie can make your breakfast, but . . . " Knowing his grandpa would never agree to such an idea, Tom nodded goodbye, mumbling he would be back later. There were decisions to be made. Were the weaned calves still in the big pasture? Had the ranch hands moved the bulls? Was there enough hay in the barns to make it through the winter?

And in the long run, T. H. would never recover. Sallie had been his anchor, his rock, his touchstone. Bent and deaf and with shaky hands, he made one more revision to his will and was tempted to call it a day, a lifetime . . . call it quits. And perhaps that was when his will to live began crumbling. But even in his darkest hours, the land pulled at him. Not one other living soul understood its whims, its needs, its promise. The land was as much a part of him as his once tall frame and his gray eyes and his faltering heartbeat. And to the bitter end, it called his name.

* * *

At the end, the family wondered if the patriarch found any peace of mind. One thing was certain: they would never hear the answer to that from T. H.'s own lips. Tom drove him to the ranch every day or so for a few months. He lived to see the spring calf crop and to remind the ranch hand of the coming three-year-old colts that needed breaking. He put the Pierce brothers in charge of planting the new hay crop, and Tom agreed to tend to the hunting dogs.

"You leave that old paint horse be," T. H. said. "He can die out in the pasture while he remembers those nights I rode him by the light of the moon and followed the howls of the hounds."

And T. H. saw to it that Virginia, his daughter-in-law, got moved into town. No longer any need for her to stay on the ranch, Mildred located a nice, white two-bedroom house with a big kitchen and a sleeping porch. Situated on Main Street across the street from the Presbyterian church, the house was purchased by Mildred and her brothers for their long suffering mother, Virginia. "Don't seem possible, but Virginia's no spring chicken either," the old man mused.

He lived long enough to hear that Tom and his new wife, Maxine, were expecting a baby. "Humpft," T. H. snorted at the news. "One more person trying to get into my pockets." But he gave Tom power of attorney of his life and property. Told his attorney to designate Tom as executor of his last will and testament. Business-minded to the end, he did the best he could to control his precious land, his life's work, from the grave.

And through words, actions, and legal documents he made it clear that the ranch land was Cherryhomes land, bought and paid for and debt free. And as far into the future as was possible, the land would remain under the ownership of his descendants.

CHAPTER 31

"A man of sterling character, there has ever been associated with Mr. Cherryhomes' name an integrity that is one of his proudest assets. He can borrow money at any time, without security. A typical old-timer, Mr. Cherryhomes is of a genial nature, fully endowed with . . . hospitality for which the west is noted. . . . he is ready at anytime to go out of his way to do a favor. He counts his friends by the hundreds, throughout the ranching area of North Texas and is one of the outstanding ranchers of the old regime."

—"**THOMAS HENRY CHERRYHOMES,"**
from *The New Encyclopedia of Texas*, 1939, p. 973

* * *

Ruminating, chewing his cud like an old bull put out to pasture, muttering to himself, and wishing Sallie's niece would get out of his face, T. H. grumbled, "Damned in-laws. Like a bunch of buzzards waiting for their next meal. Can't trust 'em."

Knees aching, back catching, stomach growling. the old man knew he had friends aplenty, but he was not of a mind to see any of 'em. "Here I sit. Good for nuthin'. Damnation. Where is Tom when I need to talk to him? Time to wean that mess of calves in the north pasture."

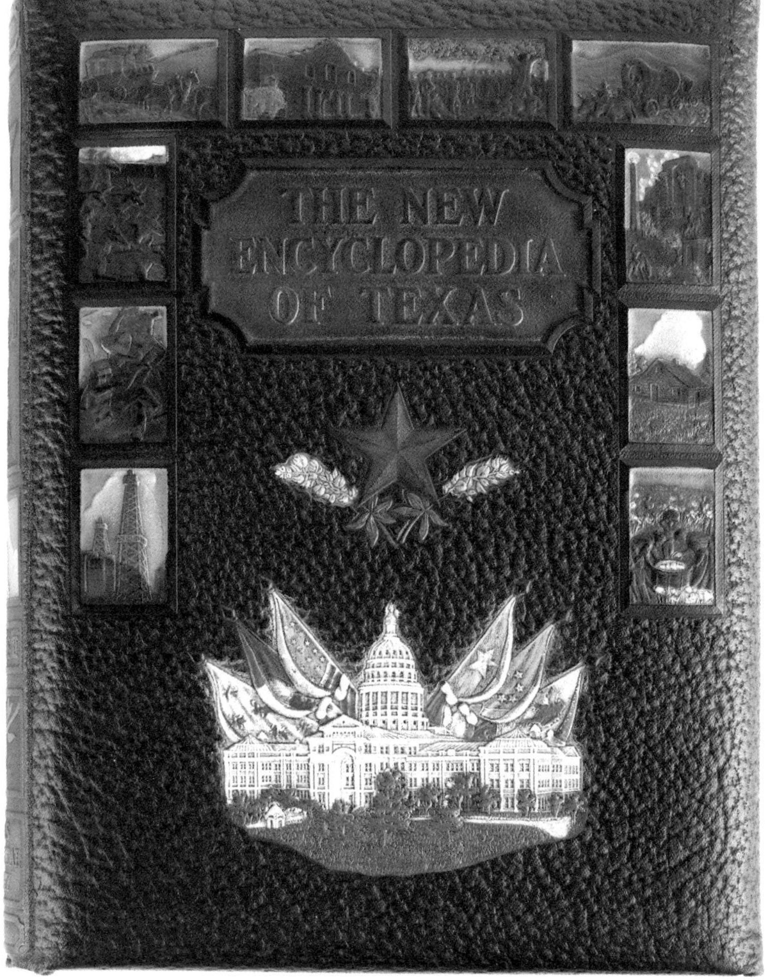

Encyclopedia of Texas with information on T. H. Cherryhomes. Family collection.

OPPOSITE
Wild turkey at H&D Ranch, 2020.
Photo by Donna Henderson Craft.

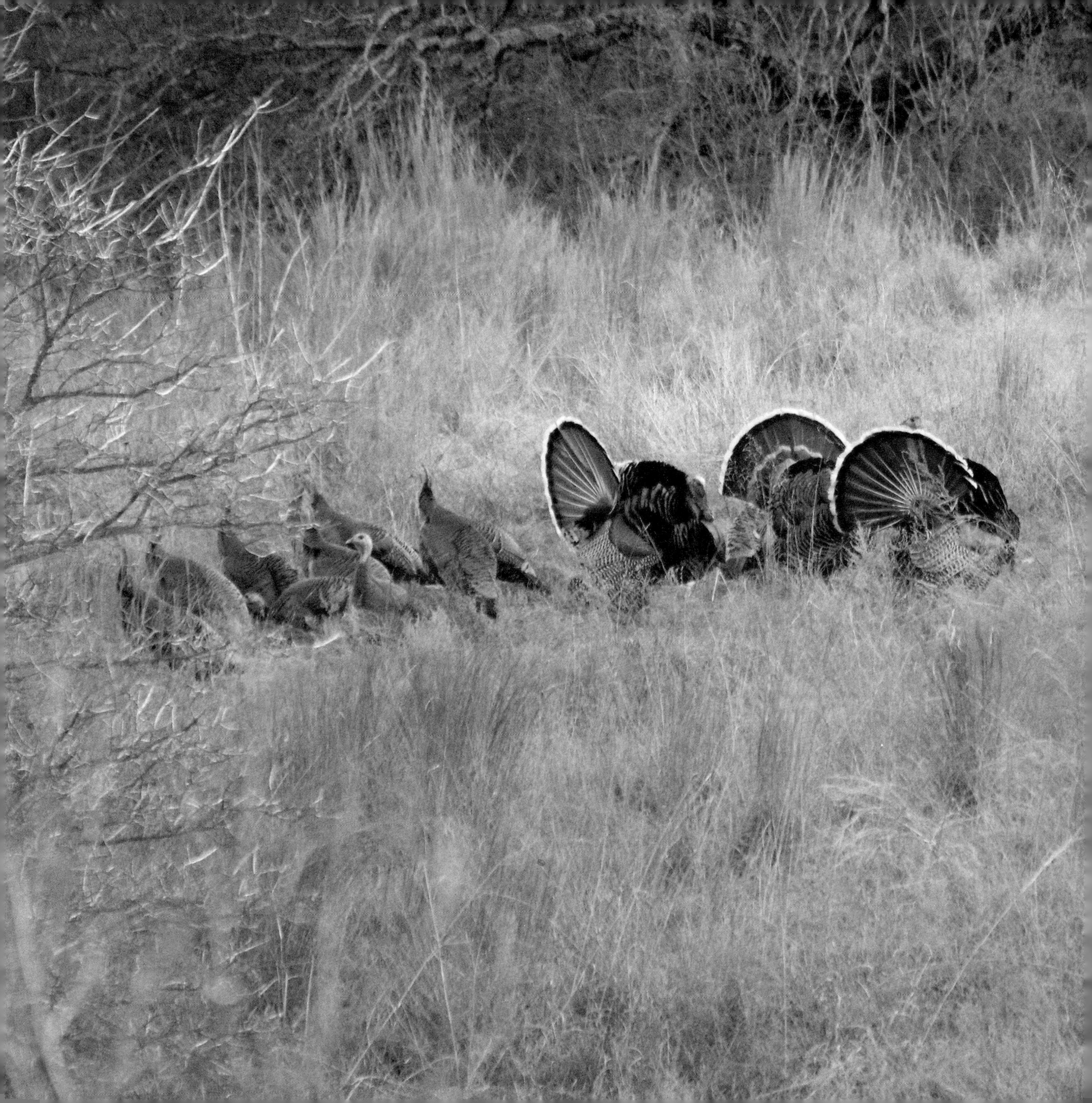

Lonely with the missing of Sallie, his mind lingered on a talk he and Sallie had not long before she died. He had been telling her how the world had changed, even while she reminded him about the way their own land had changed. Even though they could still see the ruts made by the Overland Stage on the far side of the river, the stage itself was long gone. . . . "I remember when that plowed field over there was covered with wildflowers every spring."

Yep, he had captured some land and coaxed it to make him a living. Not ashamed of it. Not one bit. But seeing the writing on the wall, feeling the shadow of death hovering in the corners of the dark living room, he wondered, *Was it all worth it?*

Life had been full, that was for sure. Battles on the home front, some won. Reminding himself that he had recovered the gambled-away land, but hating the way the world crowded him and his territory. Strangers wanderin' on his land, drilling oil wells, hookin' up electricity—had to admit, some of it brought him a kind of comfort he never dreamed of—but damned if he didn't like the old ways. By gawd, sometimes he missed the open spaces and the quiet early mornings when the gobbling turkeys and the gentle rain were all he could hear.

And here he was, weak-kneed and about to die and leave it all to youngsters. Those grandchildren would always look like youngsters to him—and did they have enough sense to take up the reins and keep the ranch going? Did they even begin to understand the land and how it was their mainstay?

With jumpy mind and shaky hands T. H. turned in his desk chair and reached for the phonograph. Turning the crank to get it going, pushing the start button, he leaned back and listened, with the help of the detested trumpet horn as best he could, to the music of his own hounds dogs baying at the hunt. By gawd. There it was. Old blue dog's howl. He would recognize that dog's sound anywhere.

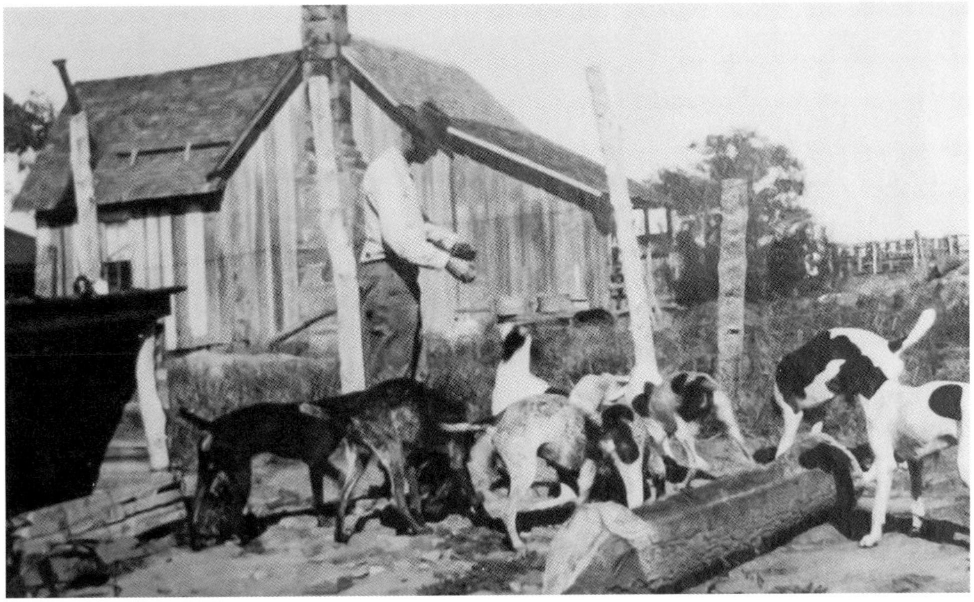

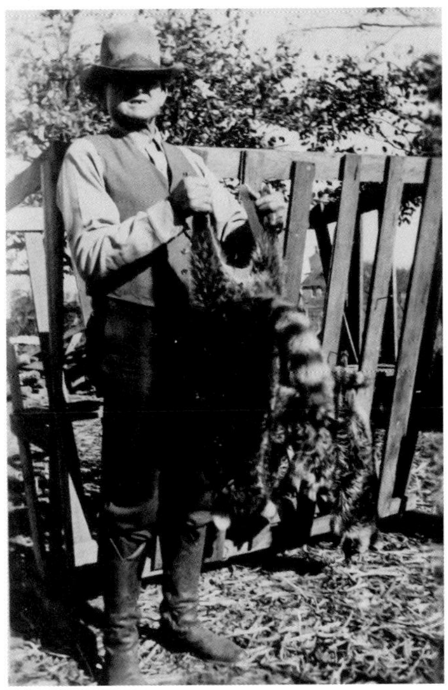

Prize hunting dogs.
Family collection.

T. H., after the hunt.
Family collection.

* * *

The summer of 1943 was hot and dry, and no matter how often the help said, "It'll rain someday . . . always does," it did not. The brass fan with its whirling wooden blades scarcely made life bearable in the high-ceilinged house on Live Oak Street.

T. H. was fading. He knew it. His family knew it. Fading fast. Grandchildren and in-laws hovered around but steered shy of stepping too close to the old man with his growling, grumbling, restless groans. He could not find an easy place to sit. The old high-backed chair, once his favorite, was too hard. The mattress on his bed, too lumpy. The kitchen smelled of yesterday's bacon grease, and the open windows refused to let in some breeze.

Tom put out the word. Roy Jr. came around but could not abide the stink of old age or the musty smell of the house where his grandpa had lived since Roy was a little boy.

Mildred drove in from Midland. Taking one look at his tired, pale face, she leaned over the old patriarch, patted his arm, and whispered a few words of love and thanks. And soon after she arrived, T. H. slipped into a deep, quiet sleep. A sleep the doctor would later call a coma. Relaxed at last, free of worries and glad of it, on July 3, 1943, one year and a few months after his wife's death, while the chickens clucked in the pen behind the house, while the blistering sun drove away any hint of a cloud, and while Mildred and Tom, wide-eyed and disbelieving, stood by his bedstead, the life quietly ebbed out of their grandfather.

In death, as in life, Thomas Henry Cherryhomes and his wife and his children rested on a family-owned plot of land. In the Jacksboro Oakwood Cemetery, marked by a granite monument, a lone juniper tree and individual foot stones noting dates of birth and death, T. H. and his family were once again together. Where they belonged.

FUNERAL ANNOUNCEMENT

The Funeral Services of
T. H. Cherryhomes
Age 82
Will be held at the Cherryhomes Residence at
3 O'clock Sunday afternoon, July 4, 1943

With Rev. Guy E. Perdue, Officiating
Interment In Oakwood Cemetery

*ADDENDUM:

T. H. Cherryhomes Dies in Jacksboro

Tom H. Cherryhomes, 82, who entered the cattle business at the age of 19 with a saddle horse and six steers, died early Saturday morning at his home.

At the time of his death, he owned the 35,000 acre Cherryhomes ranch in Jack County. In which approximately 3,600 of his cattle grazed.

Survivors include a sister-in-law, Mrs. M.T. Berry of Jacksboro, and three grandchildren, Thomas Cherryhomes, foreman of the ranch, Roy C. Cherryhomes* of Jacksboro, and Mrs. W. J. Durham of Midland.

Funeral services will be held at 3 o'clock Sunday afternoon from the residence. Rev. Guy Perdue, Methodist pastor, will officiate. Interment will be in Oakwood Cemetery here at the side of his wife, who died February 15, 1942.

Pallbearers will be Herbert Flowers, John Pitts, Mizell Stewart, Roy Reid, Guy Berry, and Wes Tipton.

Cherryhomes was widely known throughout the ranching fraternity of Texas. In addition to beef cattle, he raised fine horses.

*Roy C. Cherryhomes should read Robert Roy Cherryhomes or R. Roy Cherryhomes.

CHAPTER 32

Tied to the land and each other, the three Cherryhomes siblings would live and ranch in Jack County all the days of their lives. Lives lived in tandem. Lived in the same town, two of them on the same street. Talking by telephone or in person almost every day, Mildred Cherryhomes Durham, Thomas Tipton Cherryhomes, and Robert Roy Cherryhomes were as alike and as different as the ubiquitous three peas in a pod.

Mildred, the oldest, held strong influence over her brothers to the end of their lives. She was the last word, the final determiner. Her life decisions were the family benchmark against which all others were measured.

Each sibling had a broad stubborn streak. Mildred worked to temper hers with calm self-control. Her brothers, not so much.

Tom, like his pa and grandpa before him, ranched, raised quality cattle, fished, and hunted quail, turkey, and dove. Keeping his guns clean and slick as a whistle, his powder dry, his bird dogs well-fed, he won awards for his prize Hereford cattle.

Roy Jr. thrived on being himself while living life with reckless abandon. Hiring managers to oversee his land and cattle, his raucous laugh echoed through many a public place in his little town. A loveable if sometimes caustic contrarian, he took pride in reinventing the meaning of the word *outrageous.*

They might criticize one another between themselves, but criticism from outsiders was not tolerated. Even their ranches were irrevocably joined by deep arteries of water, oil, and minerals.

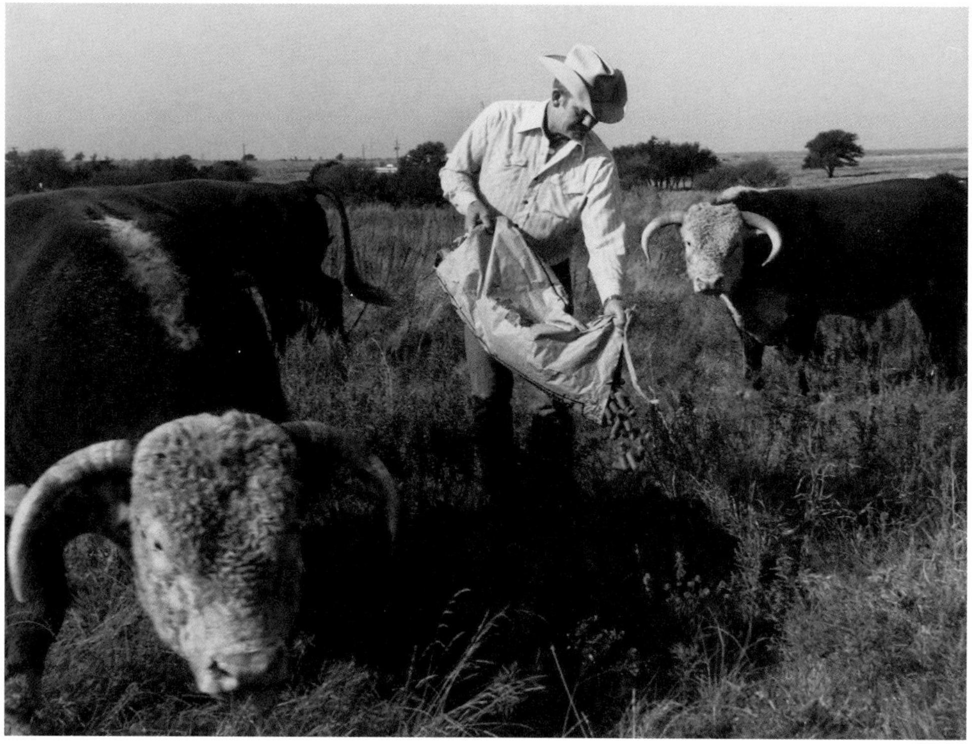

Ranch manager and part owner Monroe Henderson, circa 1982.
Family collection.

So true to each other, so deeply tied together, at the end of their lives the three siblings died within eighteen months of one another (1970-71). As usual, Mildred led the way, followed by Tom and then Roy.

But these and other stories are for another time and place. Suffice it to say that the dreams of a strong-willed, hard-driving, determined man came to fruition in ways that even he could not have imagined. And by the grace of God and untold hours of hard work, the dreams of T. H. Cherryhomes continue to this day.

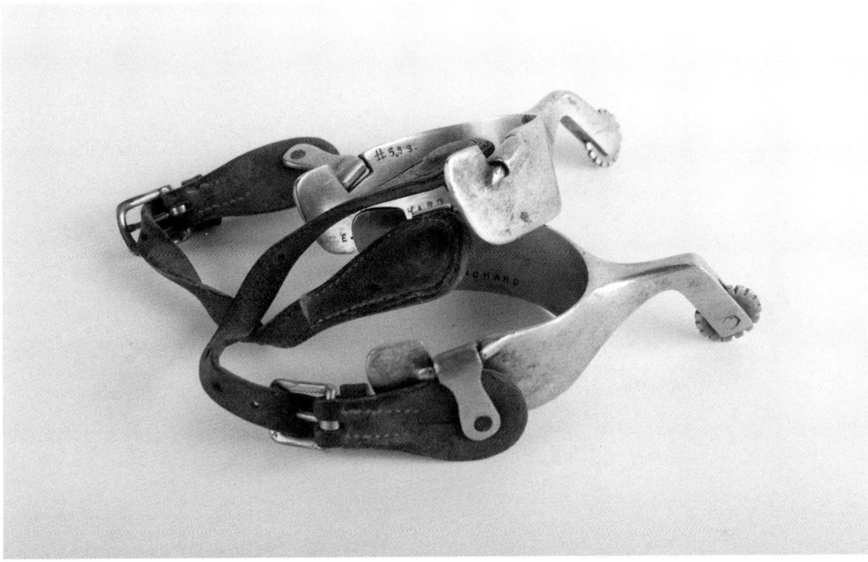

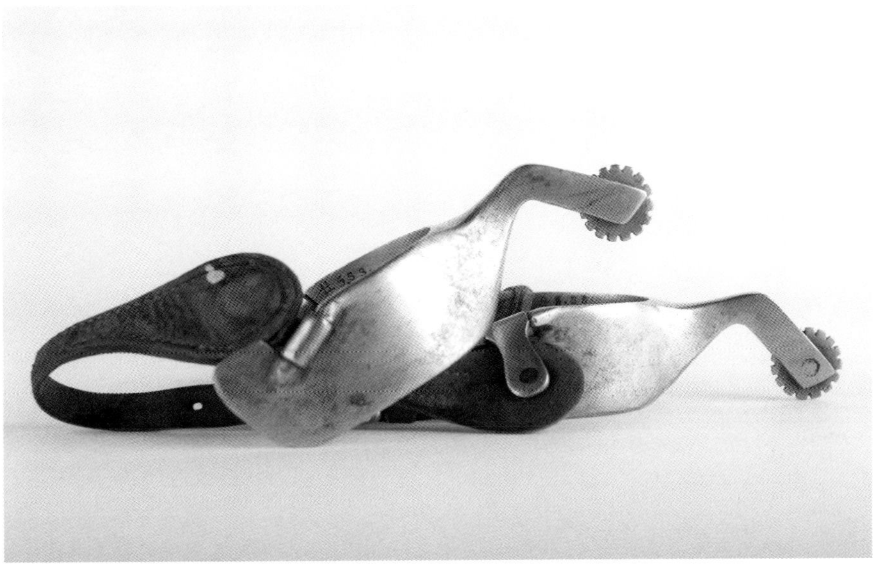

Necessary ranch equipment:
hand-forged spurs owned by Monroe Henderson. Photos by Jeremy Enlow.

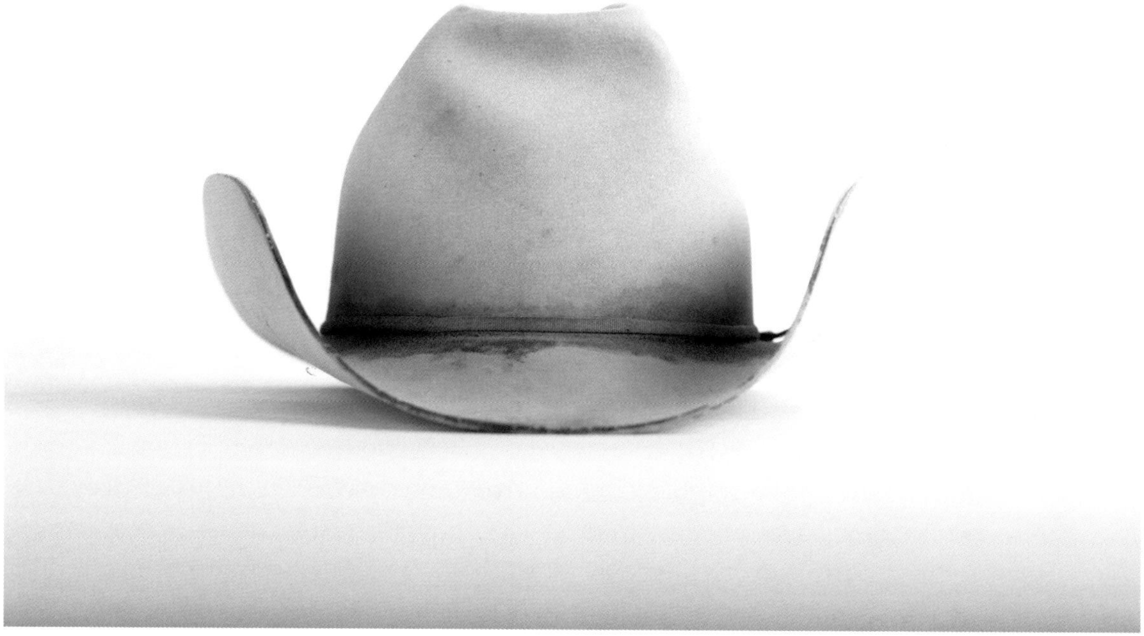

Stetson hat: Monroe Henderson.
Family collection.

CHAPTER 33

What of the Cherryhomes ranch land today? How has it fared? Still owned and operated by T. H. Cherryhomes's descendants, cattle graze its pastures, and the course of the West Fork of the Trinity River has changed little.

Where the Overland Stage line once ran, black Angus mother cows and calves now graze. Along the banks of the rivers and creeks, where campsites of the native Kiowa Indians once bustled with activity, white-tailed deer, wild hogs, and turkey live together in relative peace. When Mother Nature calls in thunderclouds, and rainstorms wash away the topsoil, a keen eye can still spot small shards of pottery and the occasional arrowhead.

Even though the fondly remembered horned lizard is close to extinction, rare sightings are reported from time to time, and more than one cougar sighting stirs the imagination, especially when its scream echoes through the hollows. Coyotes howl and shriek and chatter and make their dens while the eminent domains of public utilities compete with blue sky and billowing clouds across the horizons.

Unmarked burial grounds of long-ago pioneers remain undisturbed. Marking the gravesite of three Texas Rangers, the descendants of the Rozelle family have installed contemporary headstones.

Three of T. H.'s great-great-grandchildren have their own homes on the land he called the River Ranch, now called the Henderson-Durham Ranch. Their offspring celebrate springtime with turkey calls and fish for bragging

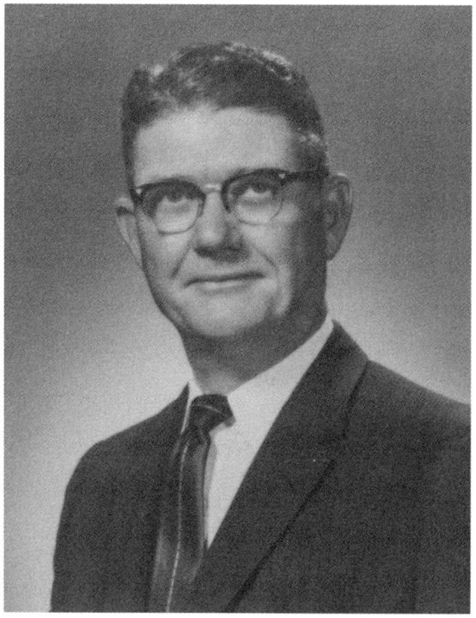

William Joseph (Joe) Durham, ranch manager 1944-1985. Family collection.

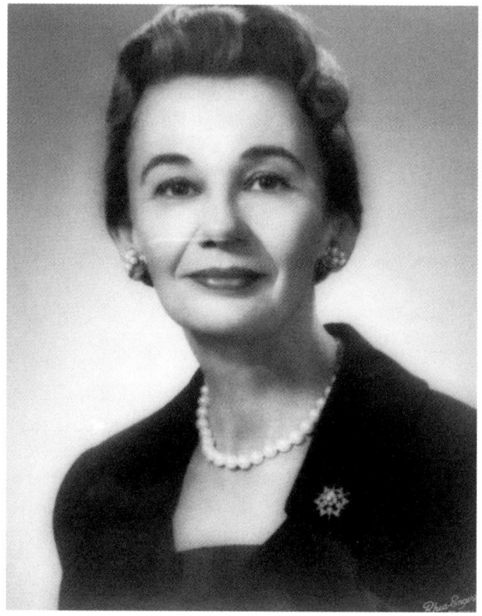

Mildred Cherryhomes Durham, granddaughter of T. H. Cherryhomes and owner of River Ranch 1943-1970. Family collection.

rights, declaring every year that the big mouth bass are getting bigger and better. Everyone pitches in during calving season, and when branding time rolls around, it's not unusual for hired hands and family alike to experience their own small version of a Wild West rodeo.

In general, the ranch remains relatively pristine. The family has taken great care to preserve its integrity, and everyone keeps an edgy eye on the weather maps for prospects of rain while acknowledging their low tolerance for anything gone amiss on the property. Trespassers are discouraged. Poachers draw the attention of the local game warden. And the locked front gate discourages unnecessary traffic.

The love of the land, the ranch, the heartbeat of the T. H. Cherryhomes legacy continues.

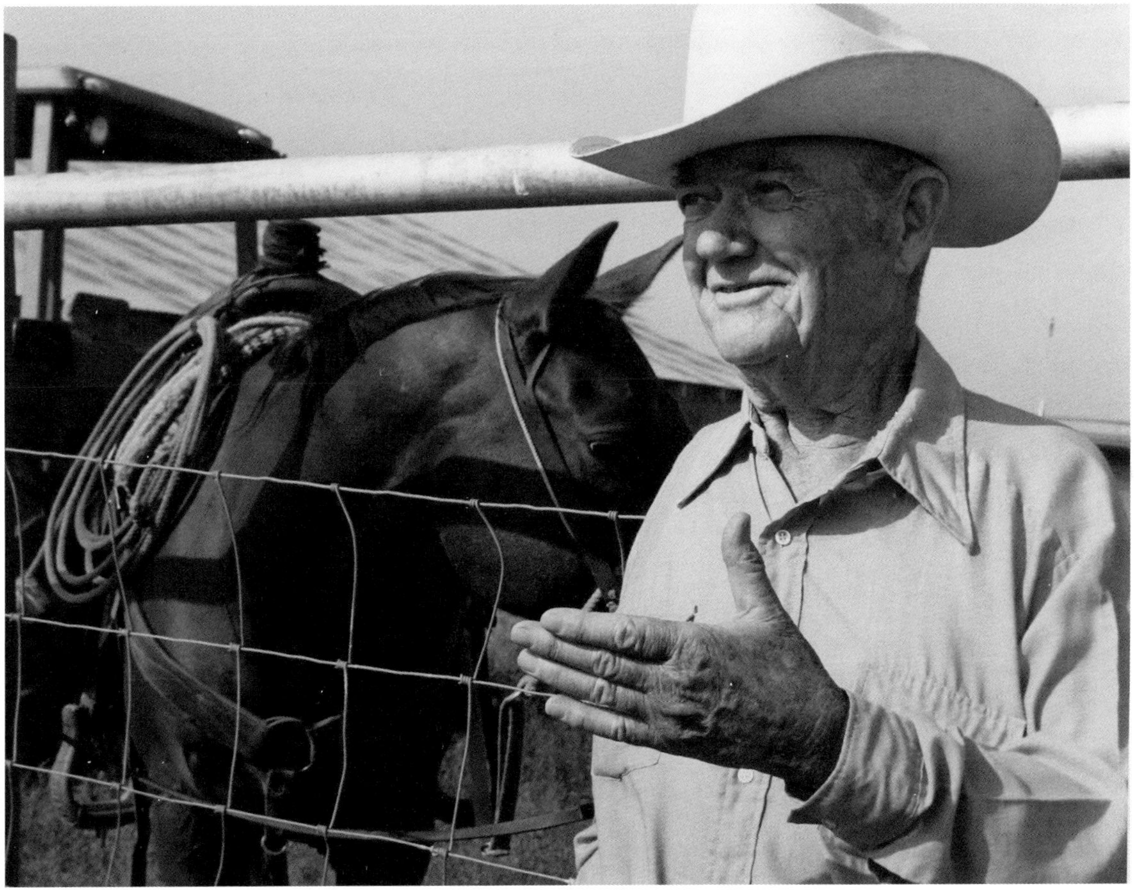

William Joseph (Joe) Durham, my father. Family collection.

I believe that my great-grandfather would be pleased with the condition of the land he once called home. Graveled roads, well-kept fences, cultivated fields, and one relatively small electric line runs through the heart of the old River Ranch. Two bridges span the West Fork, feed trucks honk, and cattle show up in the pastures eager and gentle. Where once ten thousand head of Angora goats kept briers at bay, T. H. would make note of the still-standing goat-wire fences, and he would be sure to smile at the water-filled tanks and the twenty-acre small lake stocked with bass, catfish, and the resident snapping turtles, bull frogs, and the inevitable water moccasins. The aggressive and venomous cottonmouth snake is nobody's favorite.

Perhaps, if T. H. were looking over the shoulders of his descendants and in-laws, he would puzzle over the continued absence of longhorn cattle, but likely would agree with one of the current cowboys who recently said, "If you see that old grey longhorn devil over on the south side, he broke through the neighbor's fence again and you better shoot him. He will flat kill you if he gets the chance."

Sometimes through the haze of family memory, I imagine T. H. overseeing his land, his life's work, and I think he might be amazed. Perhaps, he would muse out loud like he always did, clicking his tongue and muttering. "I knew that the dad-damned oil companies would make a mess, but all in all, it's not so bad. Too damned many roads, but they are all graveled, and looks like no more than two or three hired hands feed the entire herd of cattle. But damned if I can see a single paint horse. Them sorrels look sleek and fat, too fat for my likin', but maybe they're good cow ponies. Not one huntin' dog in sight unless you want to count them black labs. Never took a likin' to them myself, but some folks swear by 'em. And I'll be damned if I see a single windmill."

Sucking his teeth as he was known to do when perplexed and ladies were within earshot, limiting his urge to swear and spit, he might take a step back and declare. "Hell's fire. That old River Ranch where we used to live, it's a damned fine sight to see. A damned fine sight for these sore old eyes. Green grass, tall and ready for grazin'." Perhaps he would turn to some of his old cronies standing close by.

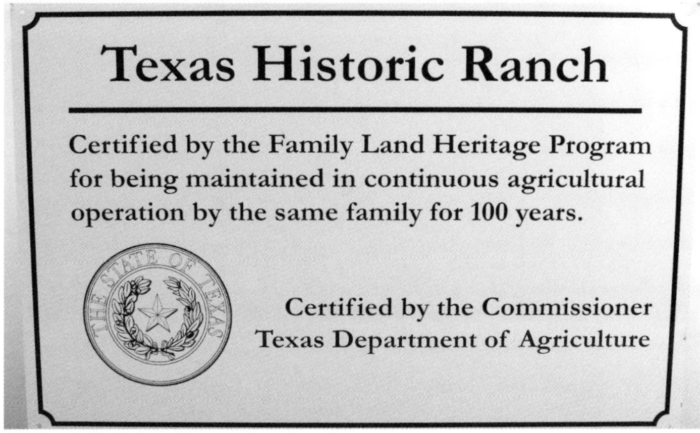

Texas Historical Ranch Award.
Family collection.

"…and look at them buck deer. Bet my bottom dollar, they're offspring of them we brought in. Big devils, ain't they. Feral hogs takin' over? The no good so and sos. Guessin' they came by way of them city folks in the north part of the county with their fancy huntin' lodge and them foreign animals. Russian boars, they call 'em. Any fool would know they tear up the countryside.

"Hee hee. Lookey there. My great-great-great-grandchildren catchin' ten-pound bass an braggin' on ever one. Humph. They shoulda seen the fifty-pound catfish we caught in the river.

"Hear tell them city slickers pay good money to the neighbors just to go out and shoot somethin'. Wouldn't have it. No sir-ree. 'I god, some of 'em'll take a shot at anythin' that moves. Can't trust 'em. Them fancy lookin' vehicles they drive, raisin' all kind of dusty hell. No, wouldn't have it."

In my mind's eye I see him slowly shaking his head in silent wonder, a twinkle in his faded blue eyes as his form blurs into the distance. I feel certain he's gone to do a little more bragging to his cohorts. "You should see that old land. A damned fine sight."

CHAPTER 34

The Ranch Today: An Album

Early Morning Round Up

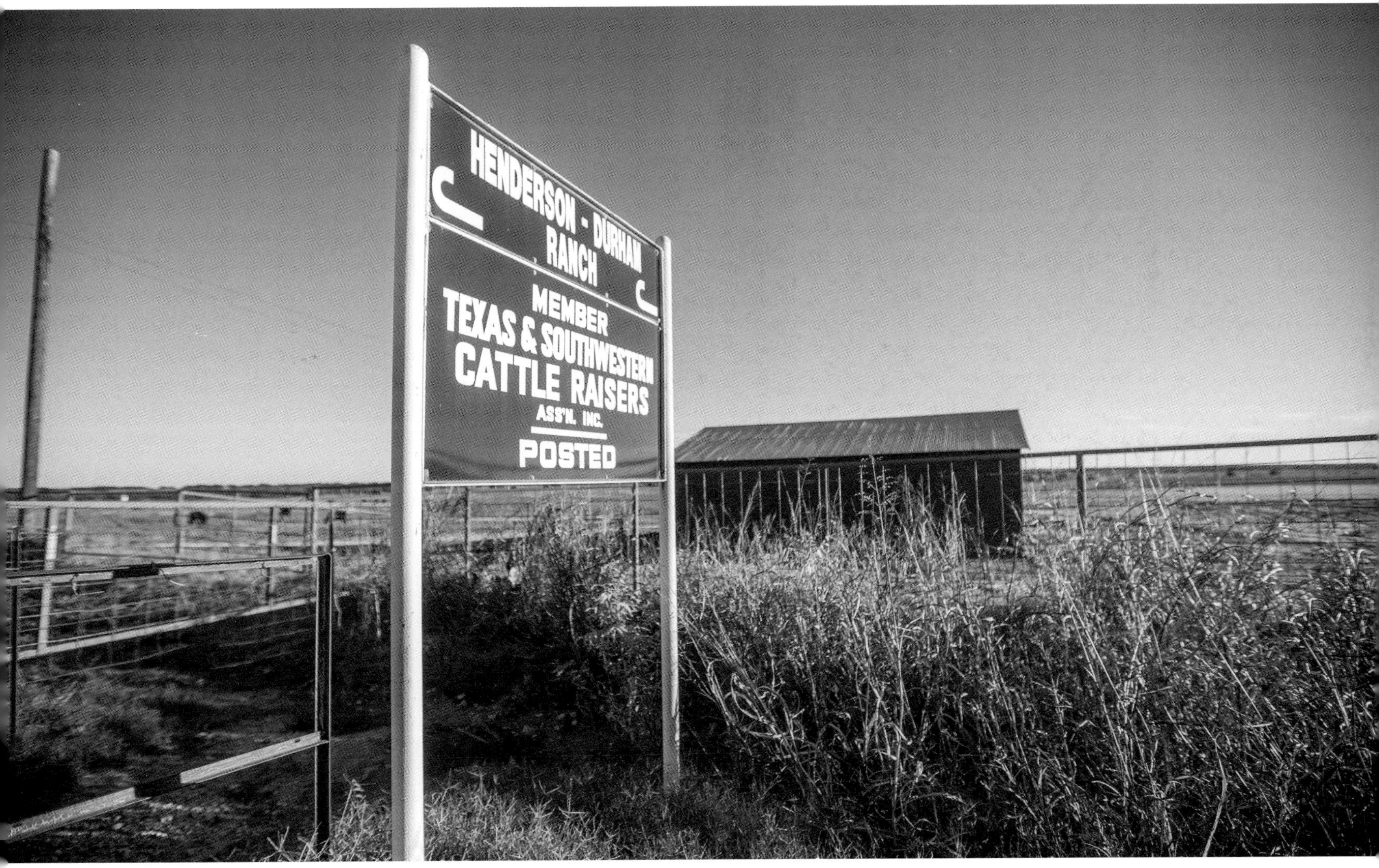

Sign at entrance to H&D Ranch.
Photo by Jeremy Enlow.

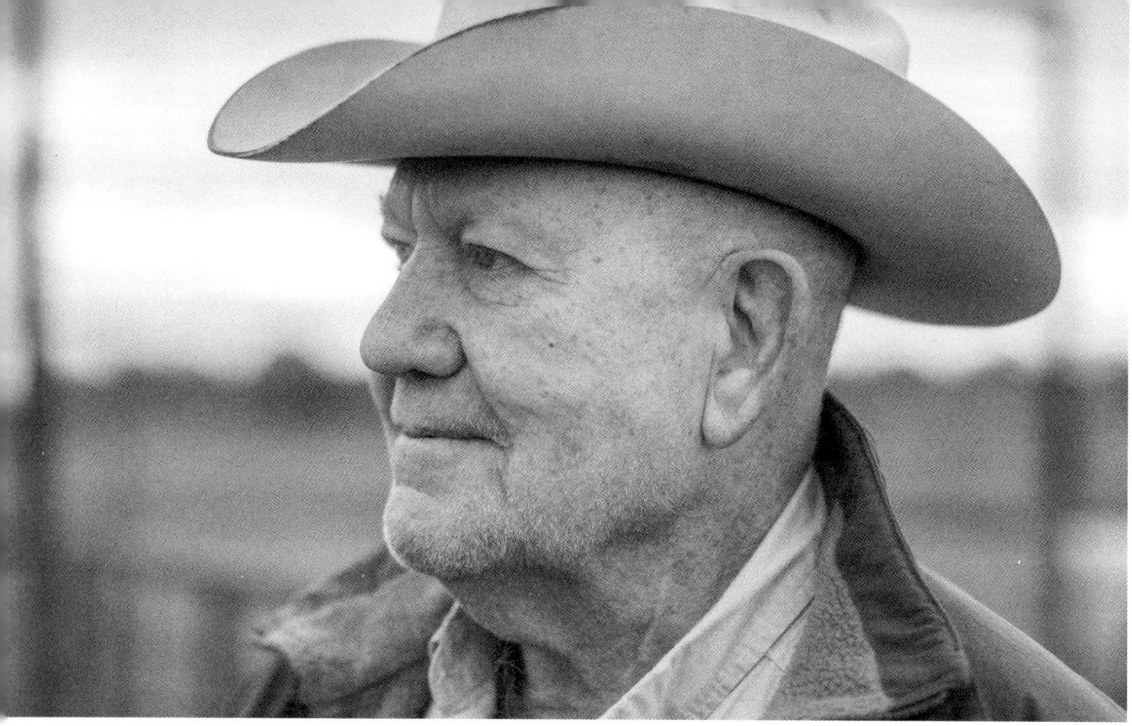

Monroe Henderson, managing partner, husband of Carol, 2016. Photo by Jeremy Enlow.

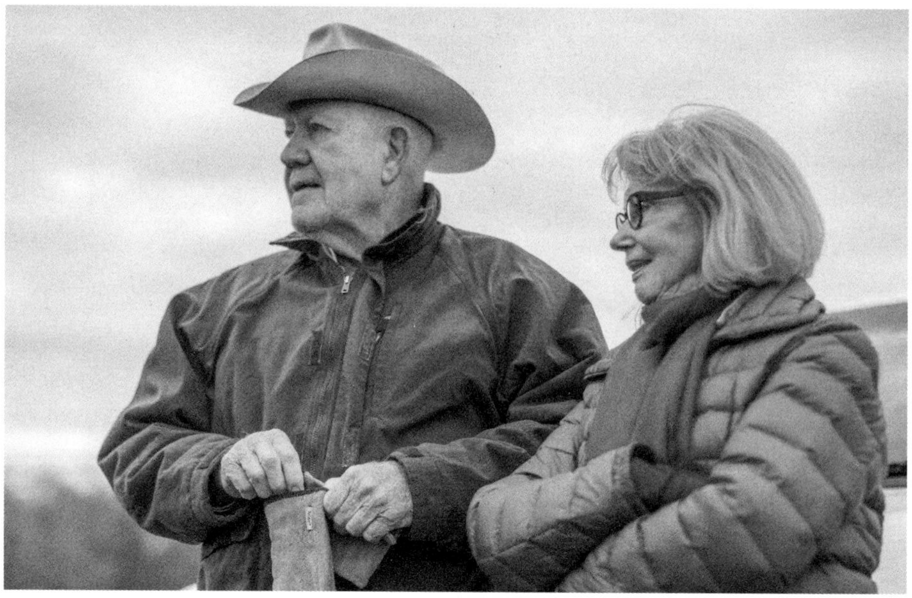

Monroe and Carol Henderson. Cattle working day, 2016. Photo by Jeremy Enlow.

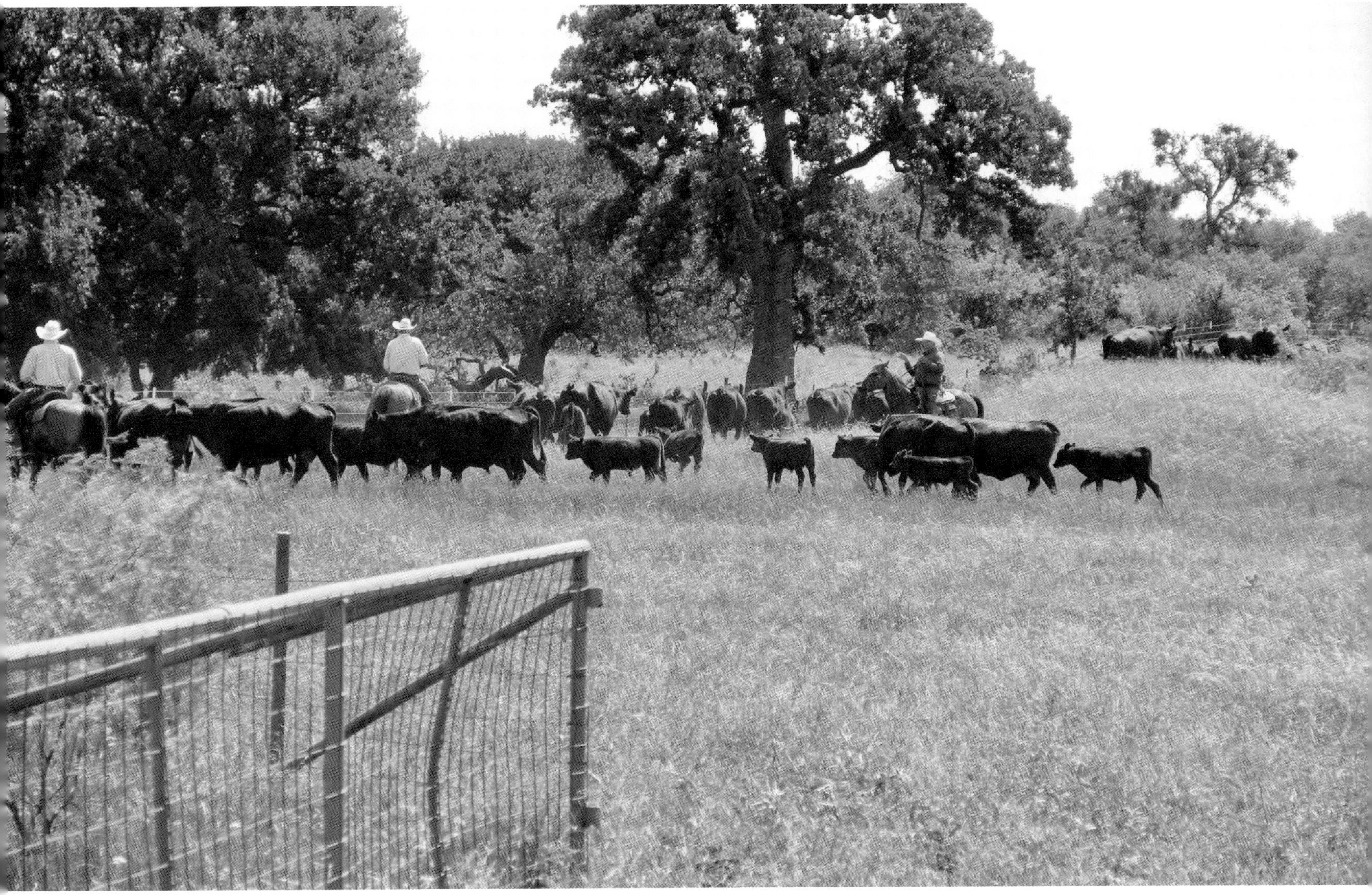

Round up, 2020.
Photo by Donna Henderson Craft.

PAGES 198-199
Break time, Henderson-Durham Ranch, 2020.
Photos by Donna Henderson Craft.

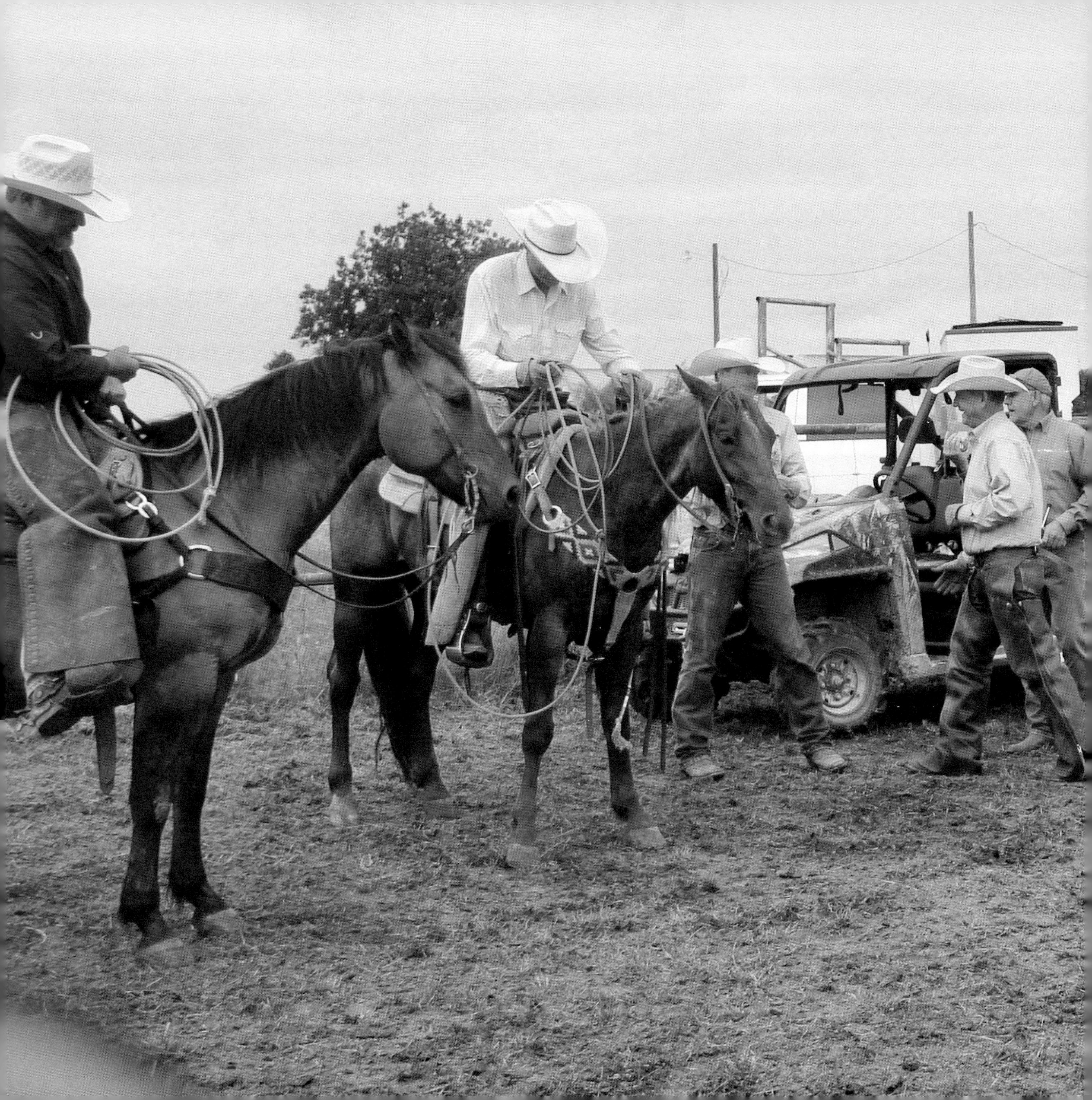

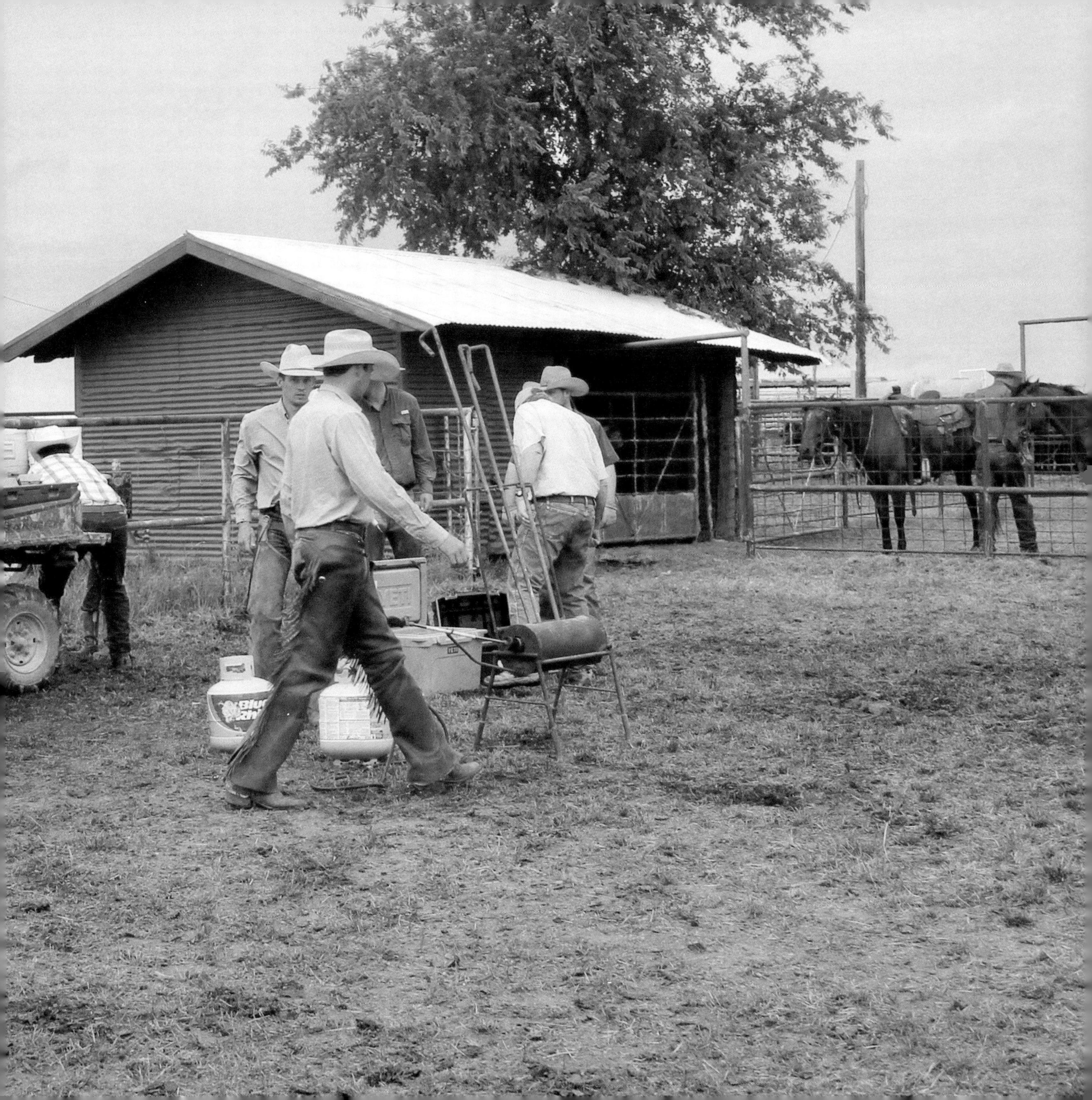

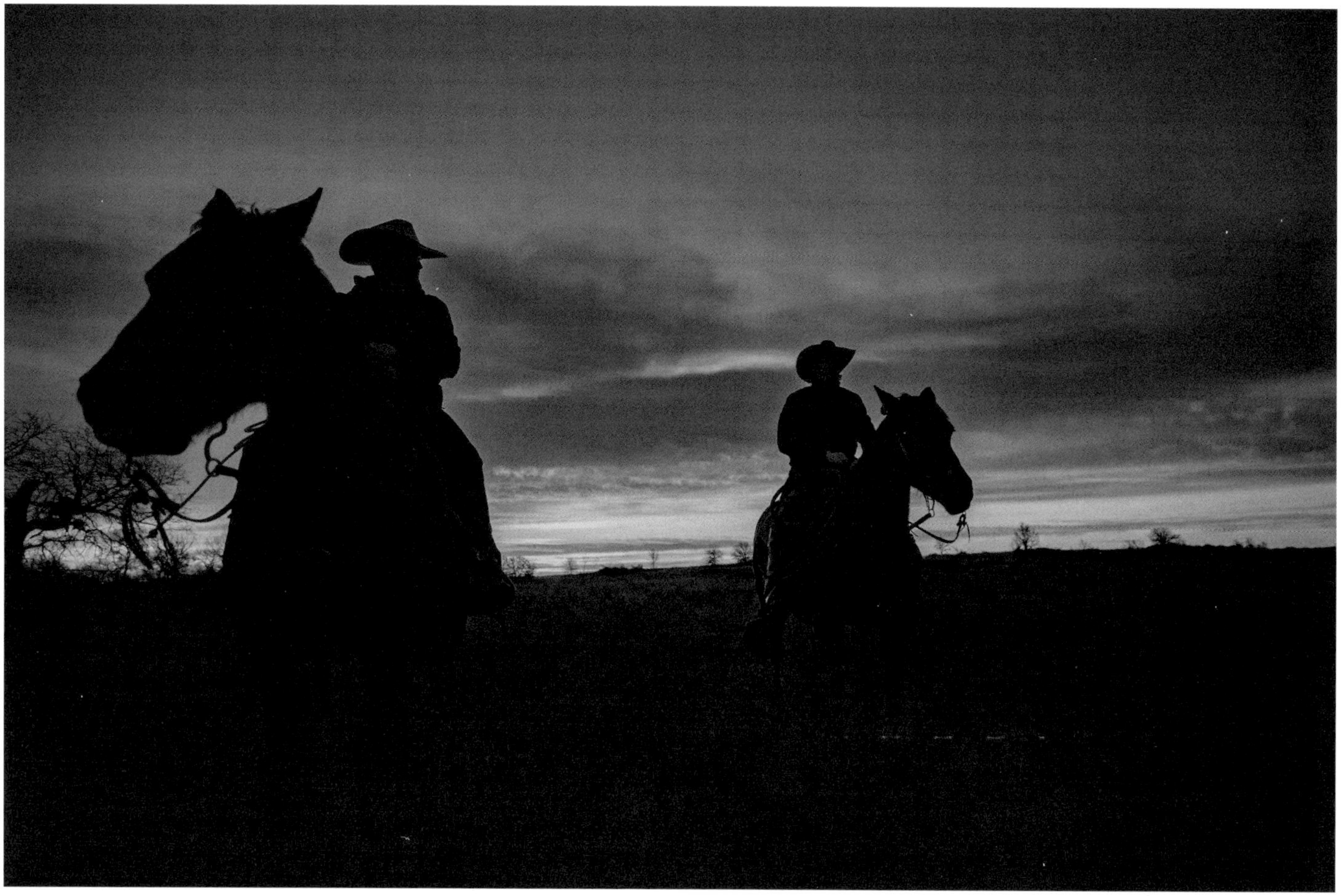

PAGES 200-203
Early morning round up, January 2021,
Henderson-Durham Ranch.
Photos by Jeremy Enlow.

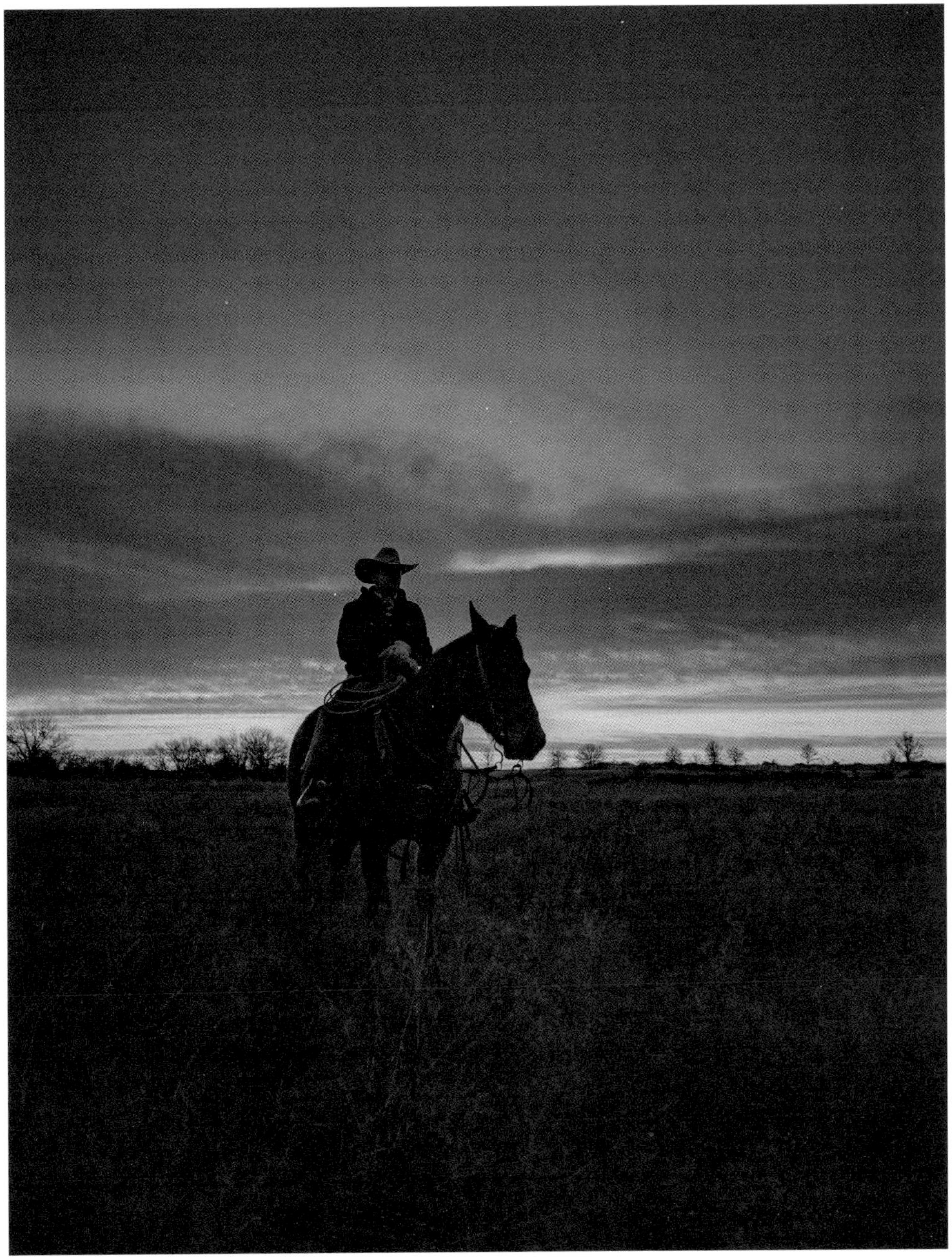

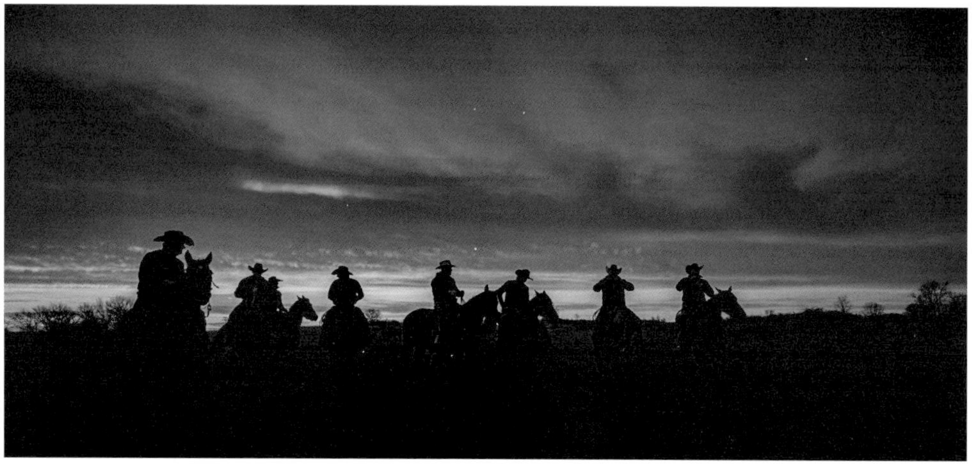

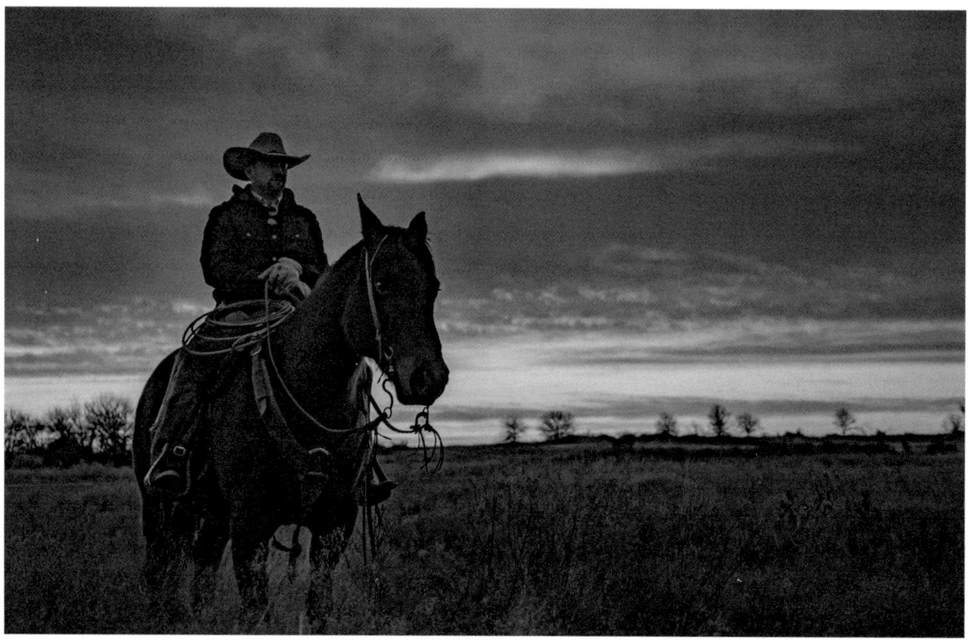

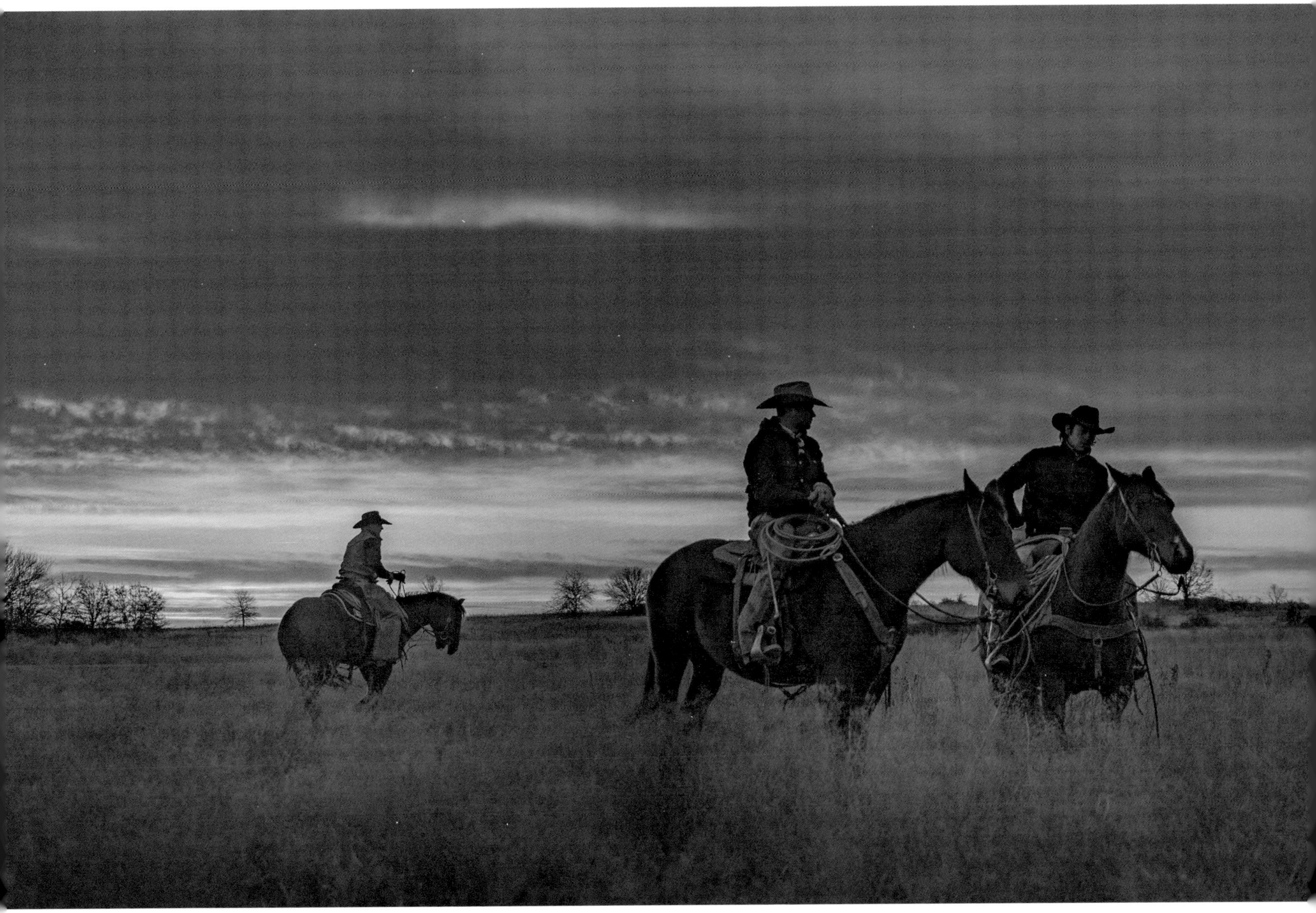

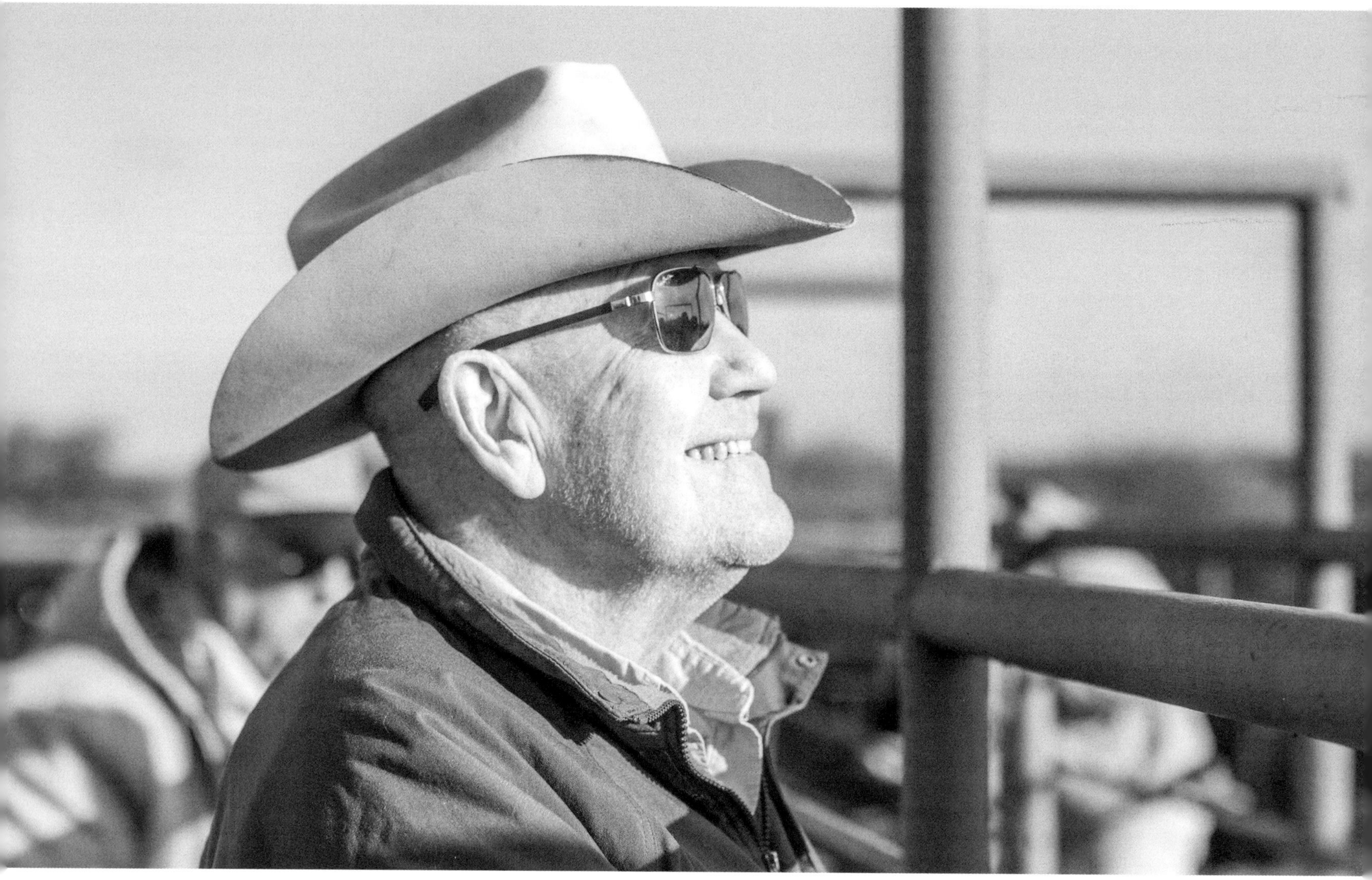

Monroe Henderson, managing partner, pleased with the day's work, 2016.
Photo by Jeremy Enlow.

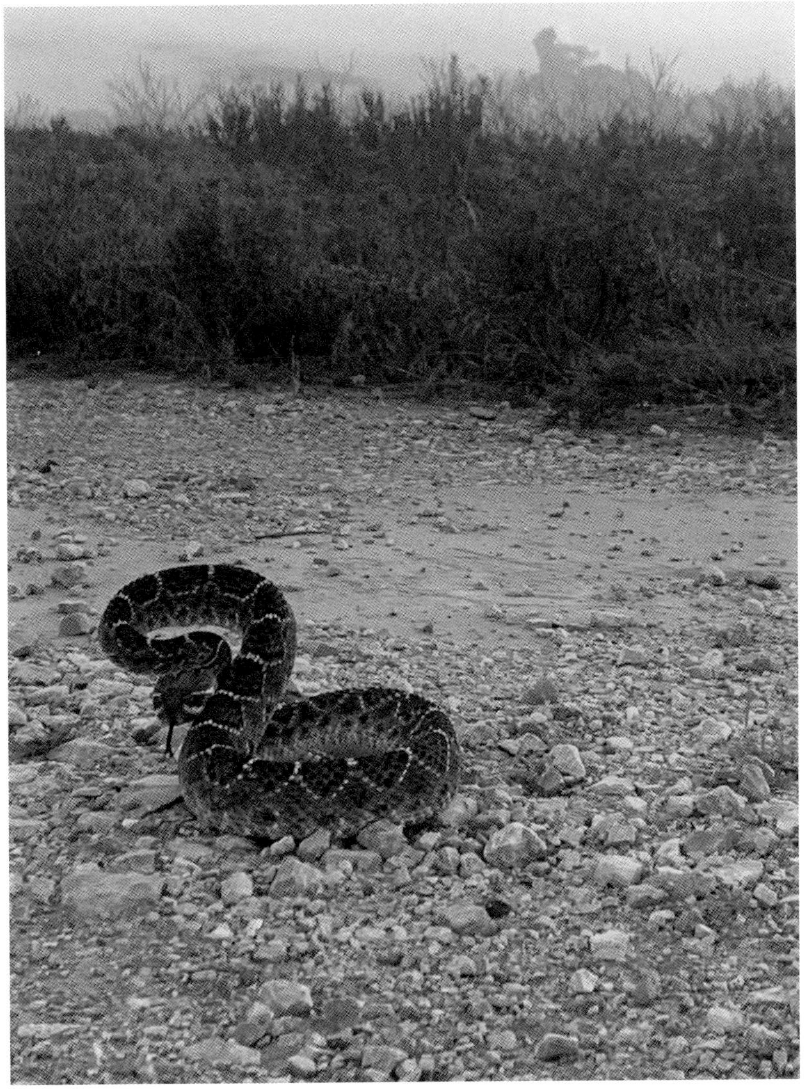

Rattlesnake on the ranch, 2020.
Photo by Ross Craft.

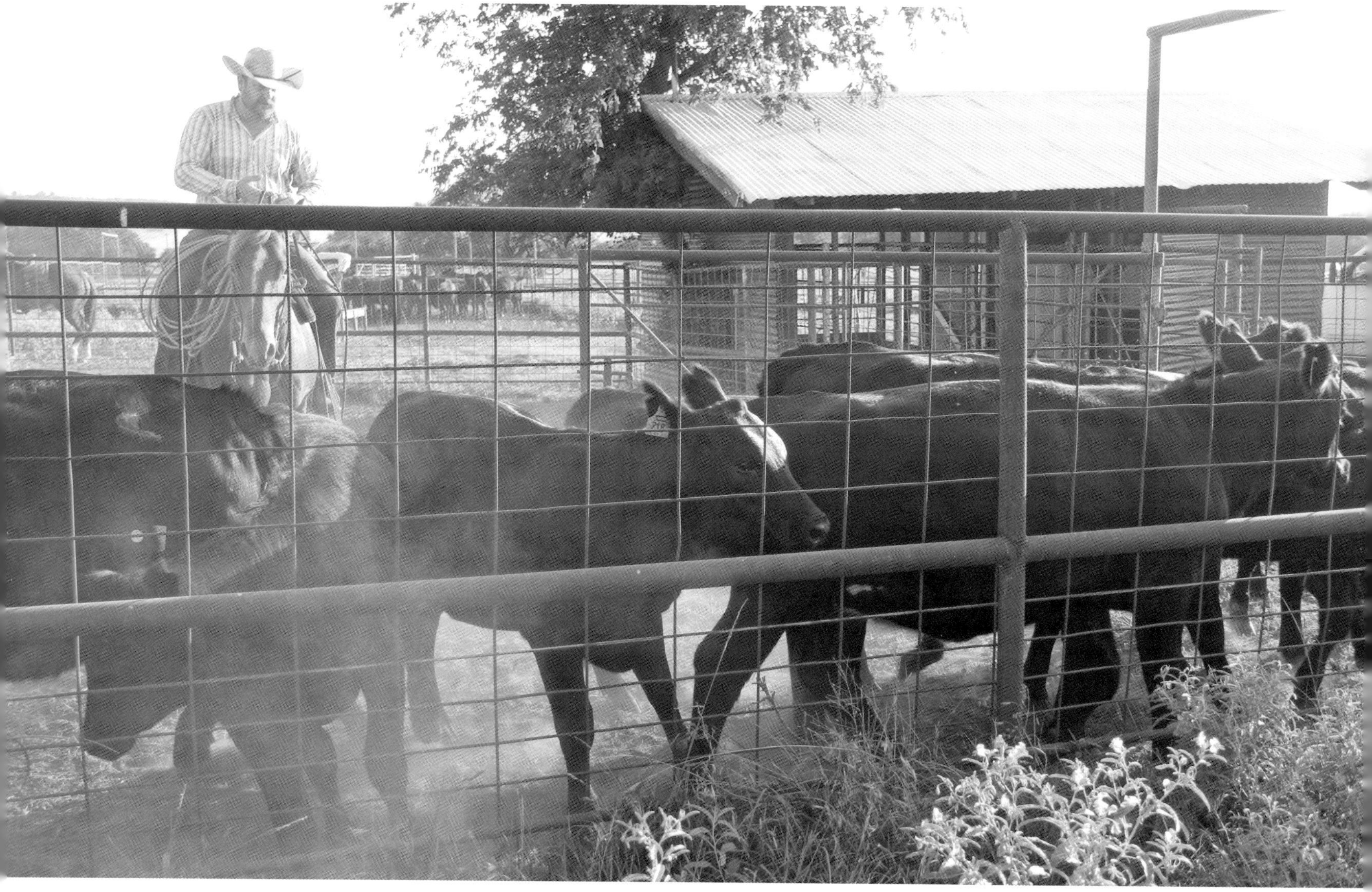

Calves waiting to be weighed and loaded into truck, 2020, Henderson-Durham Ranch.
Photo by Donna Henderson Craft.

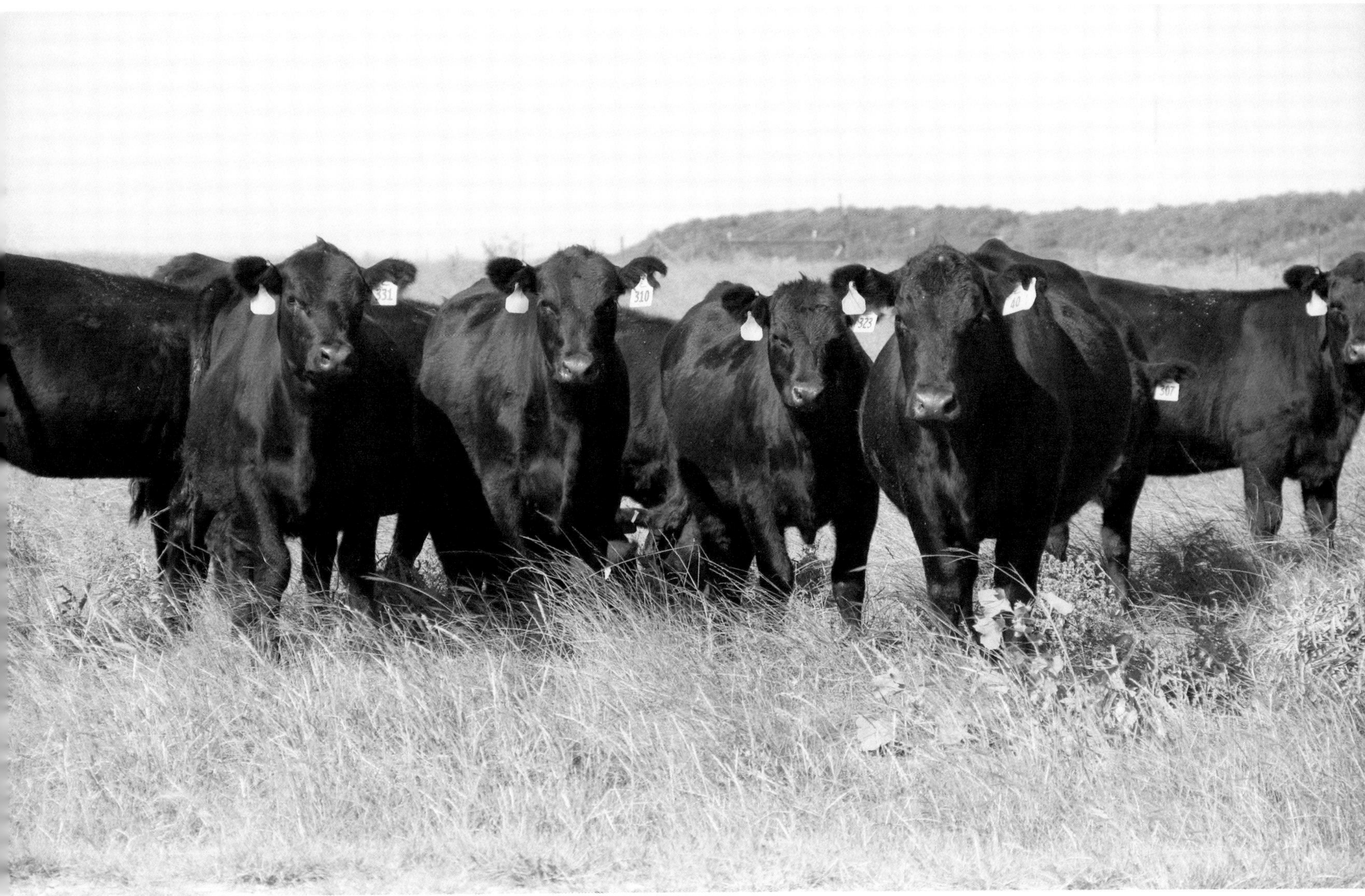

Angus cows, new ear tags, 2020, Henderson-Durham Ranch.
Photo by Curtis Henderson.

Missing Calf

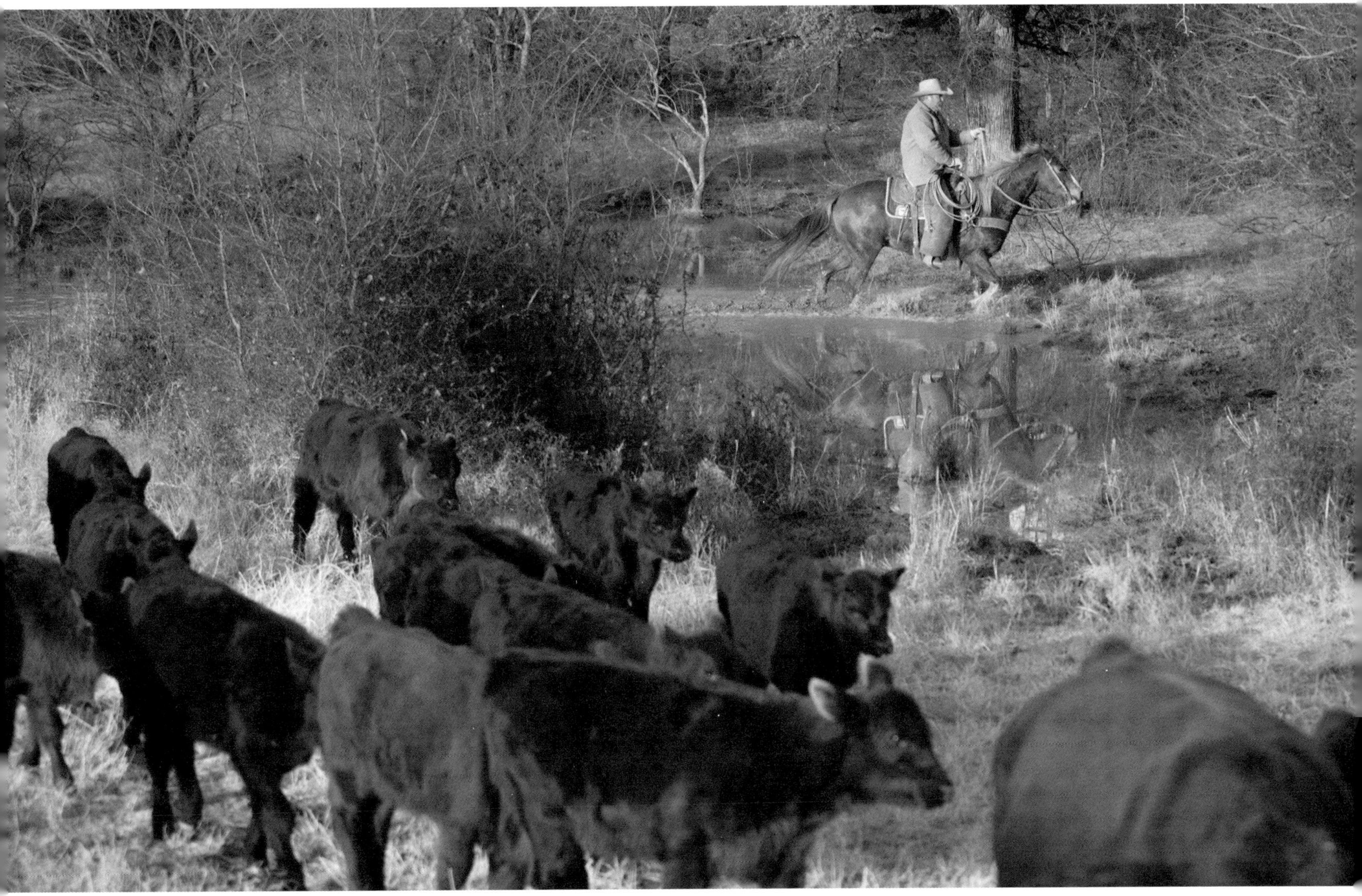

PAGES 209-210
Cowboys looking for missing calf, January 2021.
Photos by Jeremy Enlow.

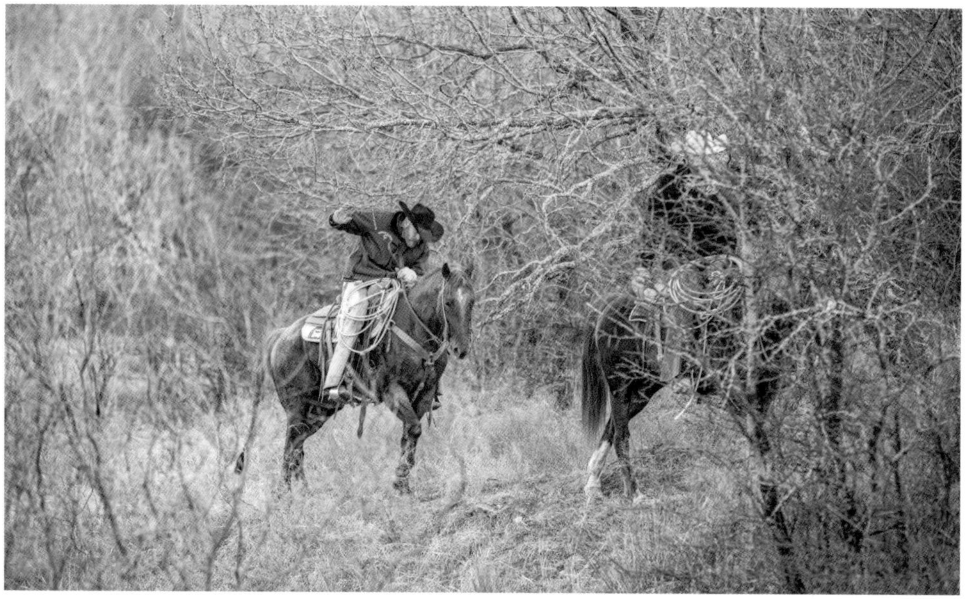

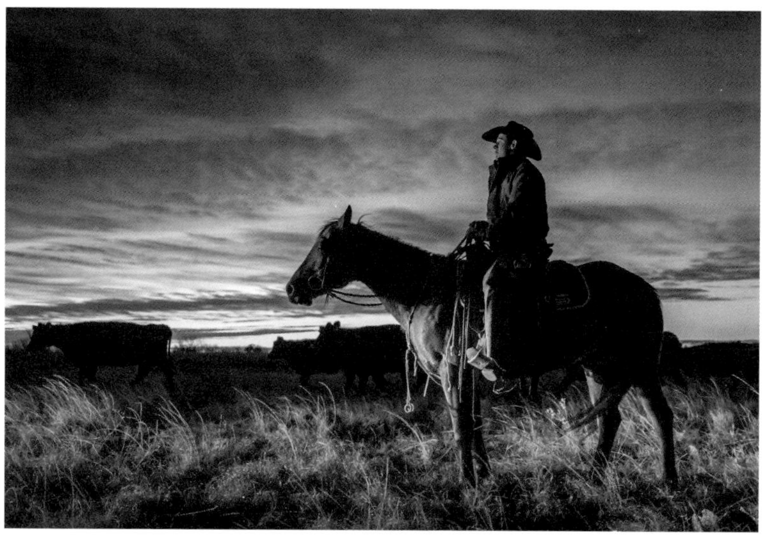

Ranch Foreman Cory Pippen, at sunrise, 2021.
Photo by Jeremy Enlow.

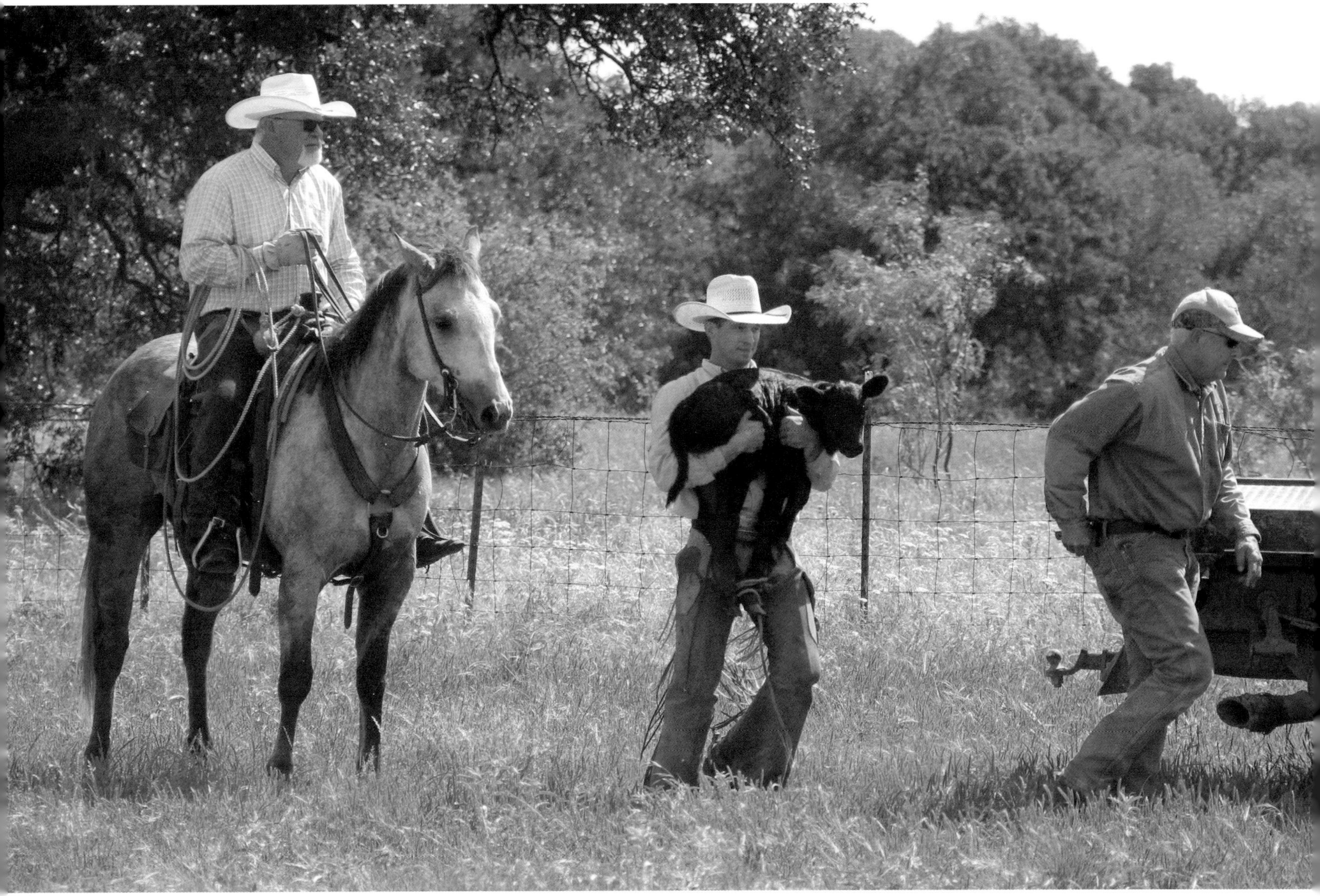

Cory Pippen with lost calf, 2020.
Photo by Donna Henderson Craft.

A Family Business

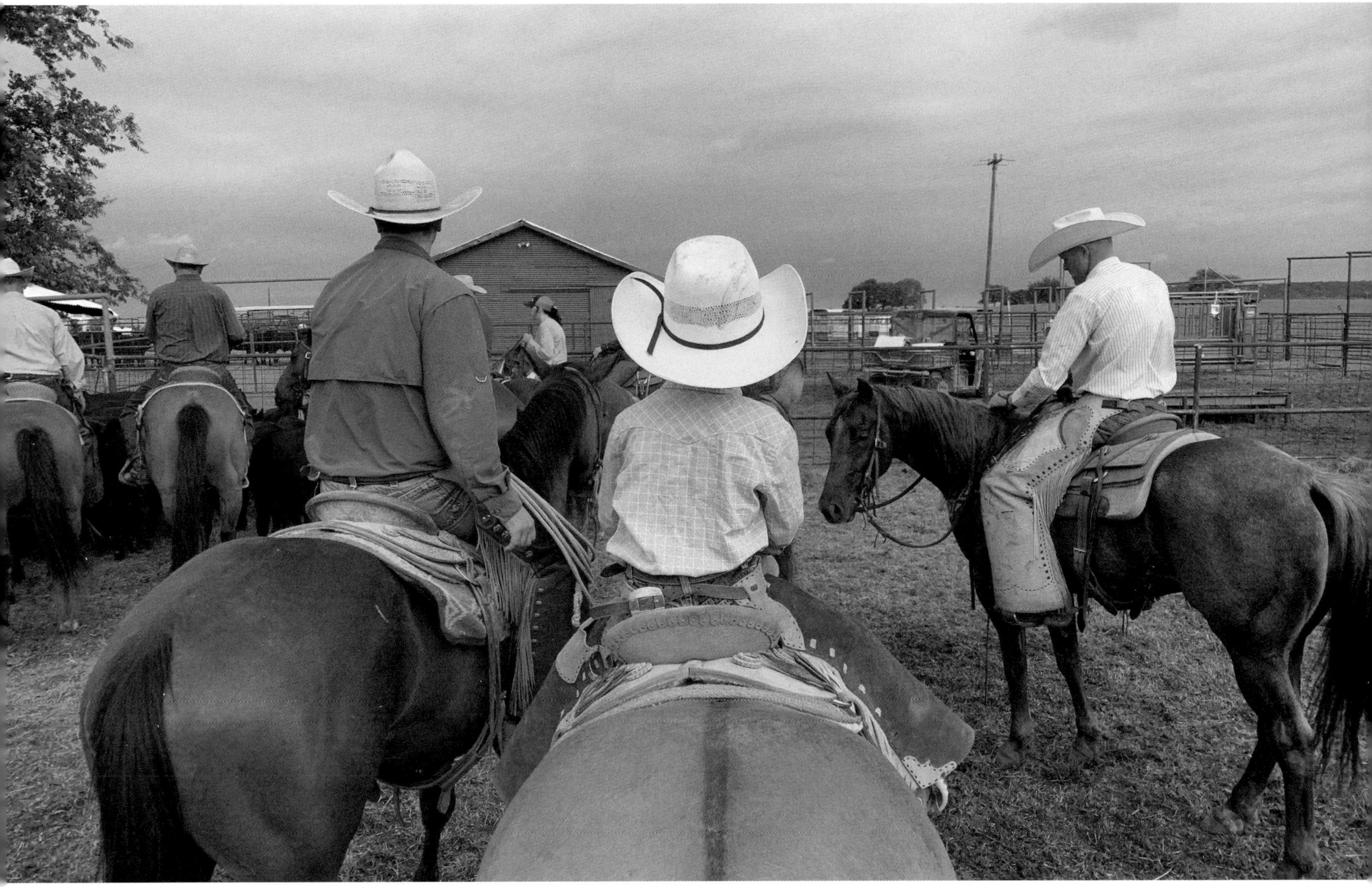

Littlest cowboy with his grown-up buddies, 2020.
Photo by Donna Henderson Craft.

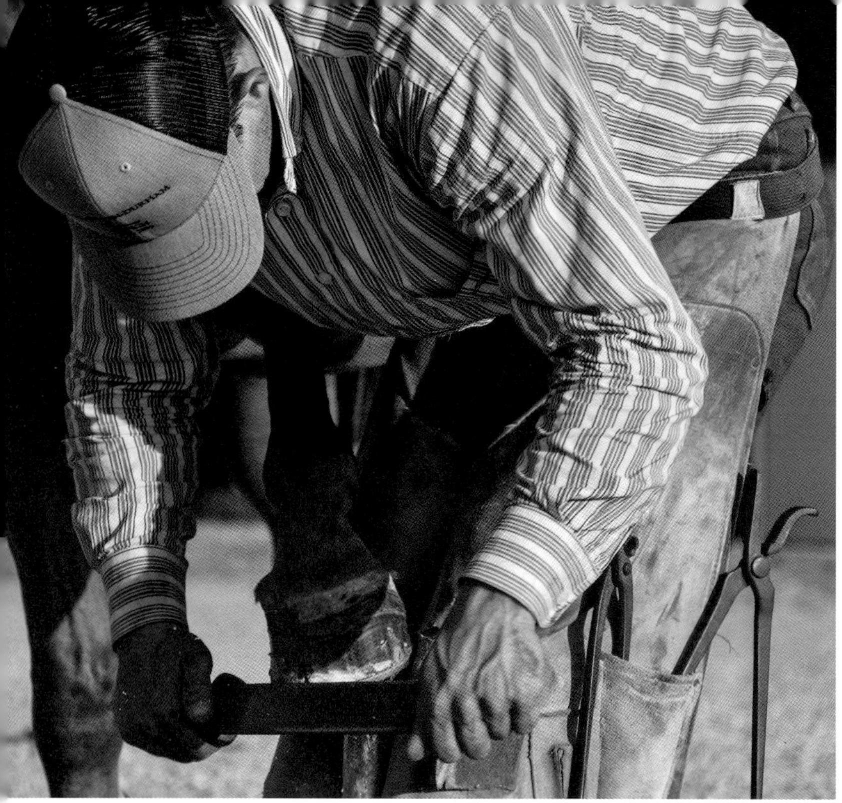

Shoeing a horse, 2020.
Photo by Curtis Henderson.

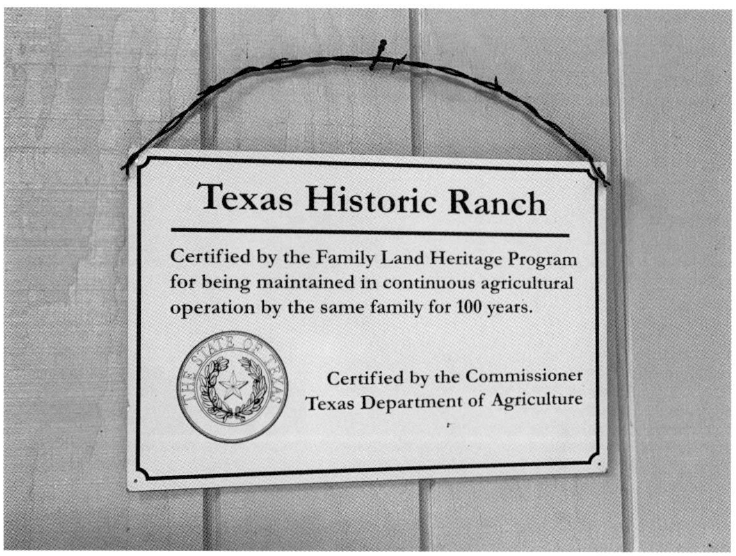

Historic Ranch designation sign at H&D Ranch.
Photo by Jeremy Enlow.

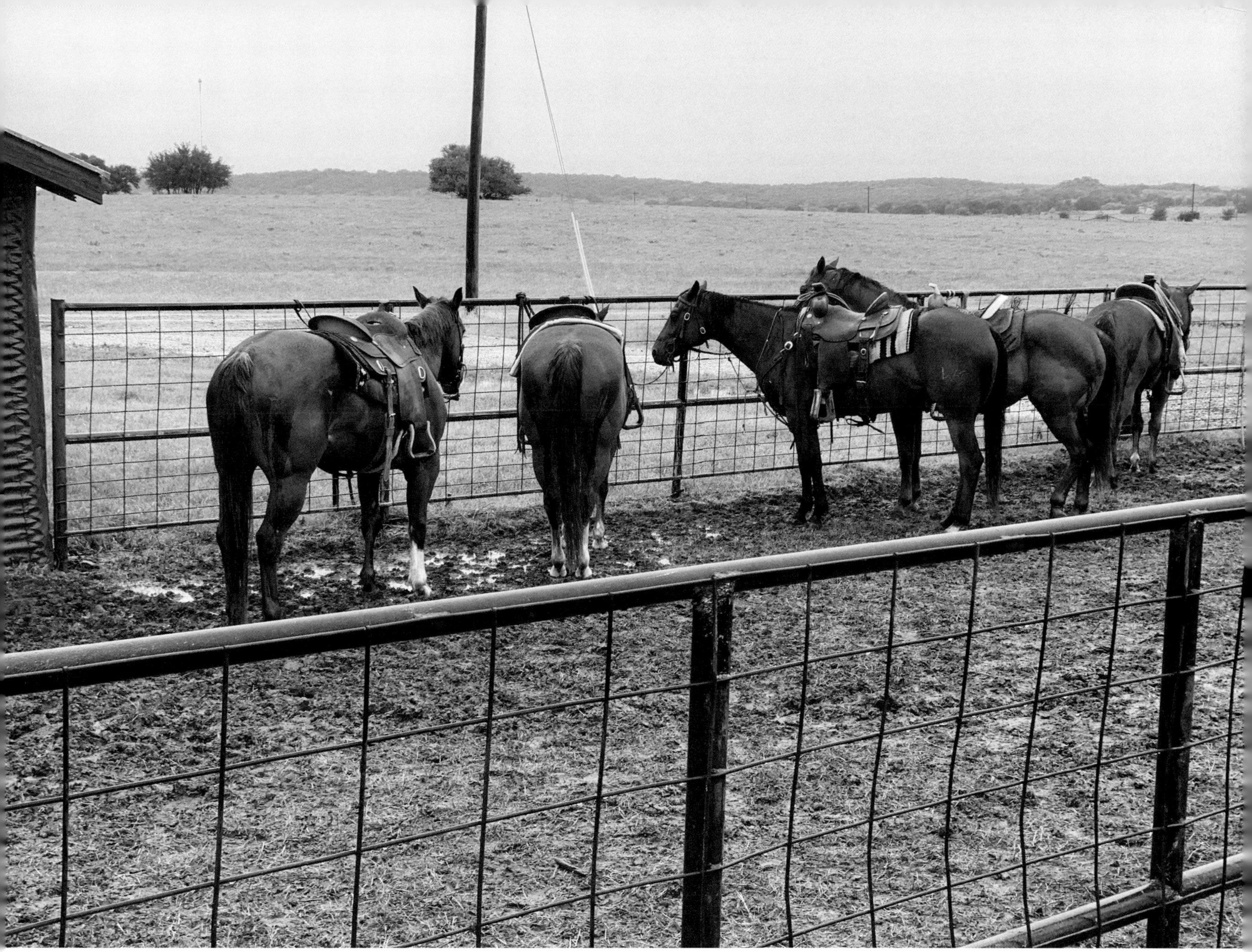

Hardworking horses take a break, circa 2020.
Photo by Donna Henderson Craft.

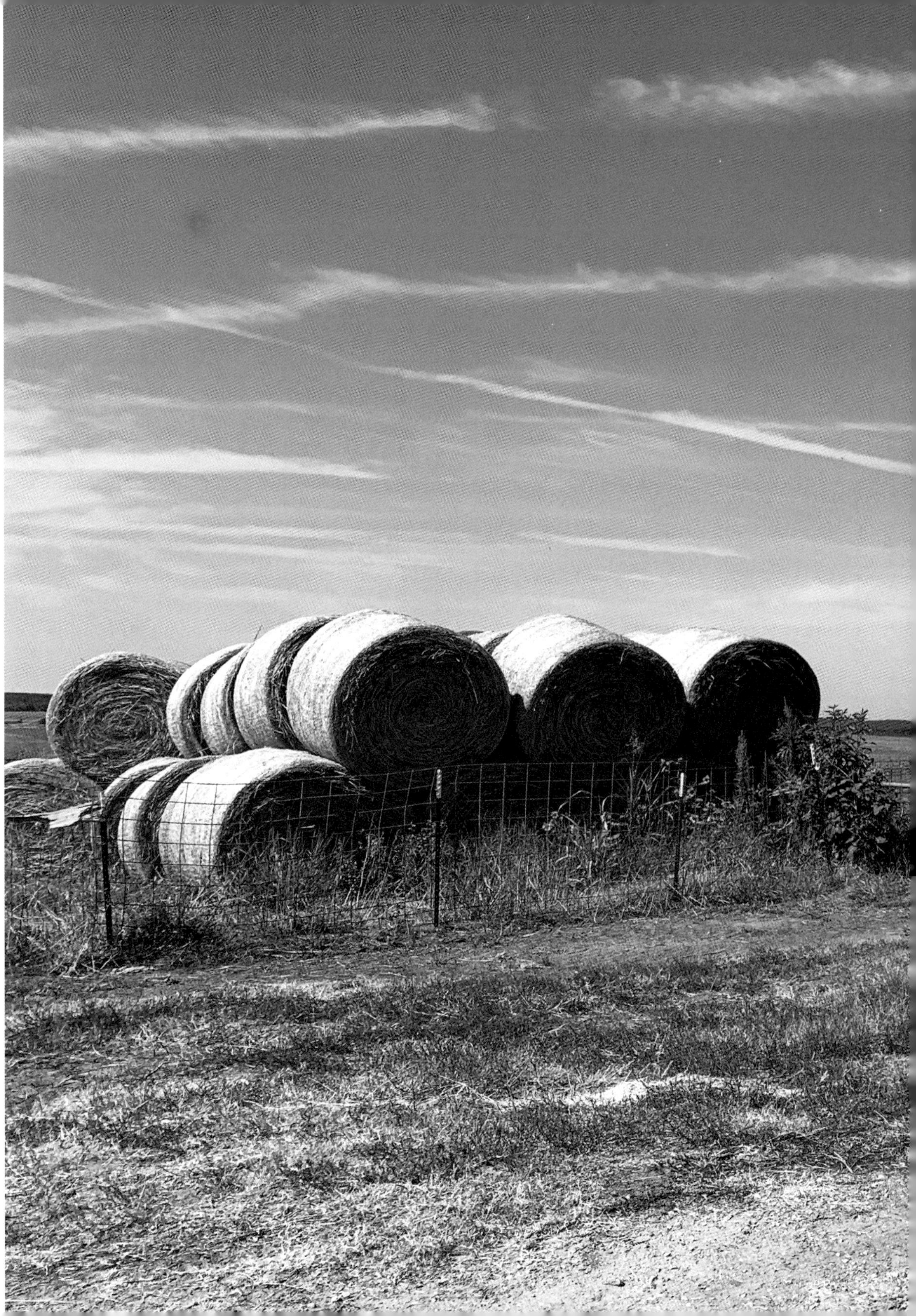

Hay barn is full, 2020.
Photo by Jeremy Enlow.

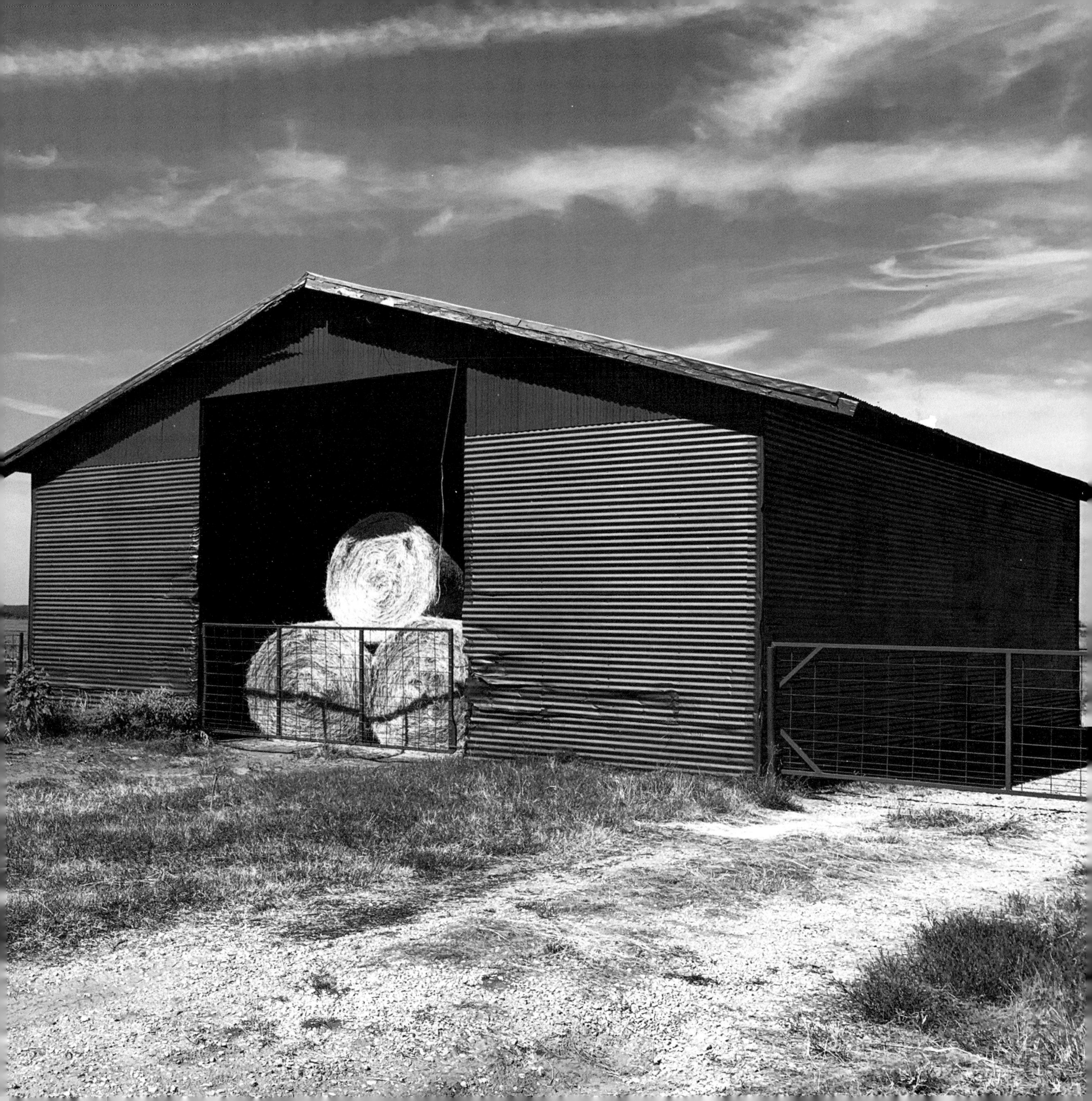

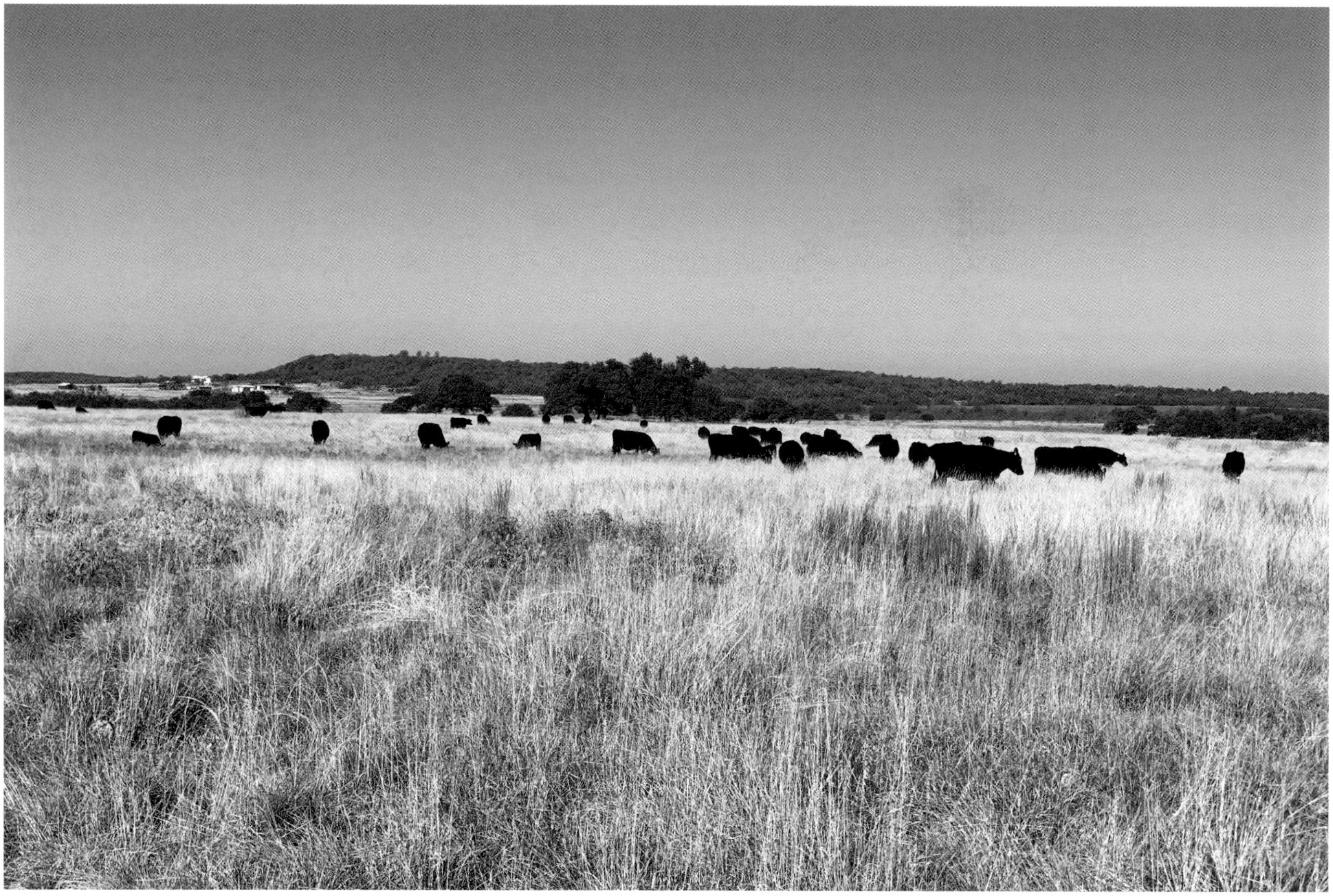

Good pasture land at H&D Ranch, 2020.
Photo by Curtis Henderson.

OPPOSITE
Sign at ranch entrance, 2020.
Photo by Jeremy Enlow.

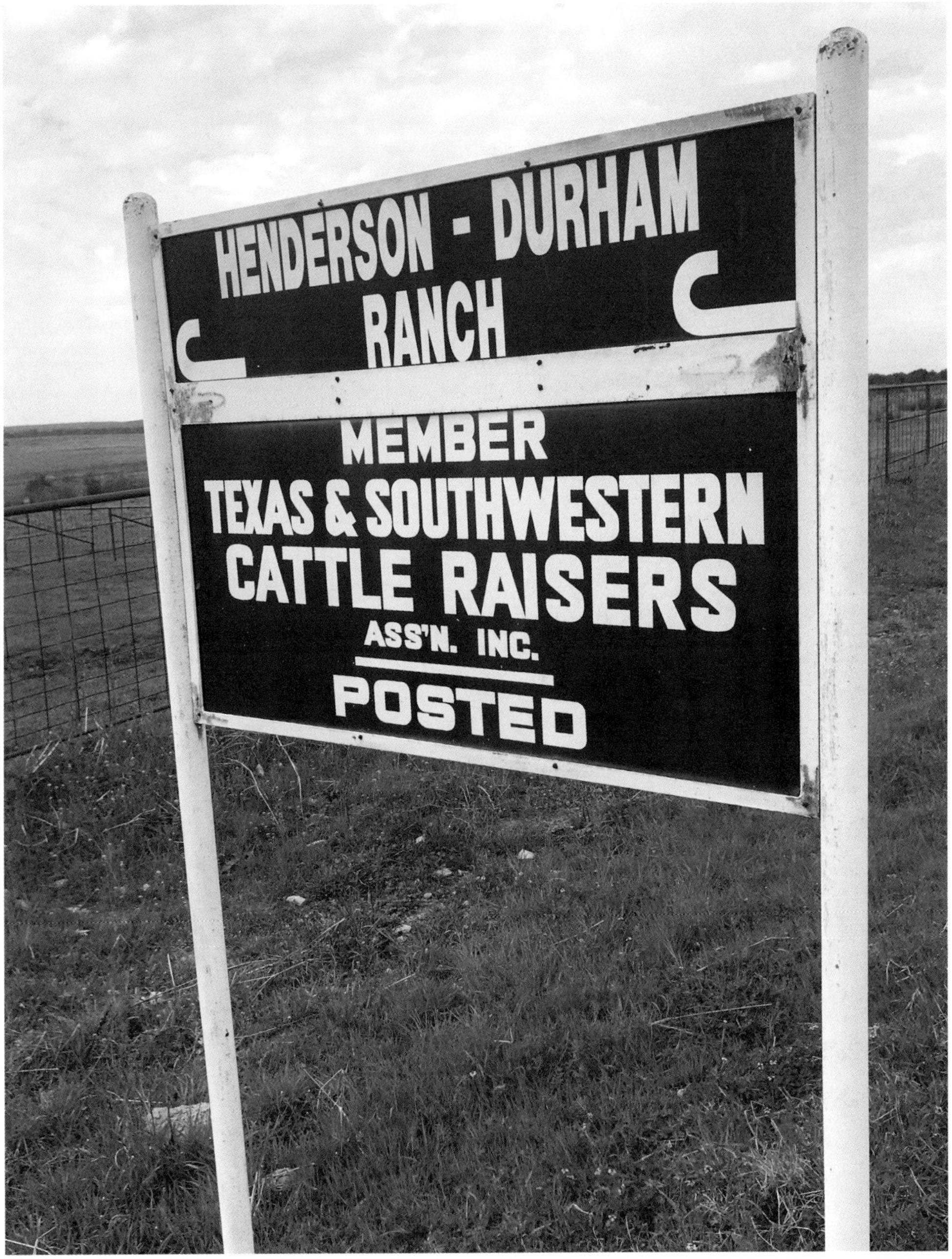
HENDERSON - DURHAM
RANCH
MEMBER
TEXAS & SOUTHWESTERN
CATTLE RAISERS
ASS'N. INC.
POSTED

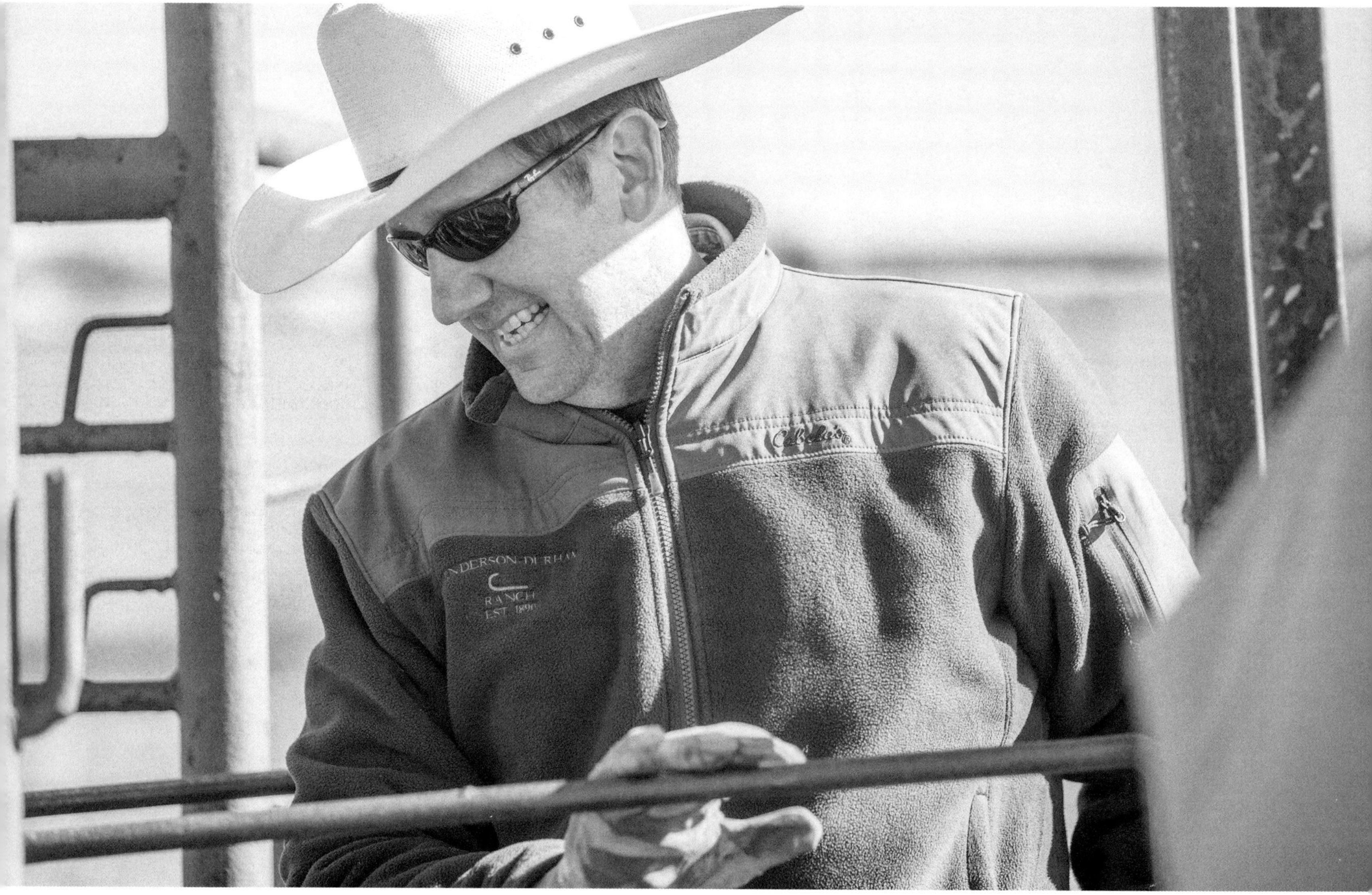

Curtis Henderson: "We've got this." Great-great-grandson of T. H. Cherryhomes, 2020. Photo by Jeremy Enlow.

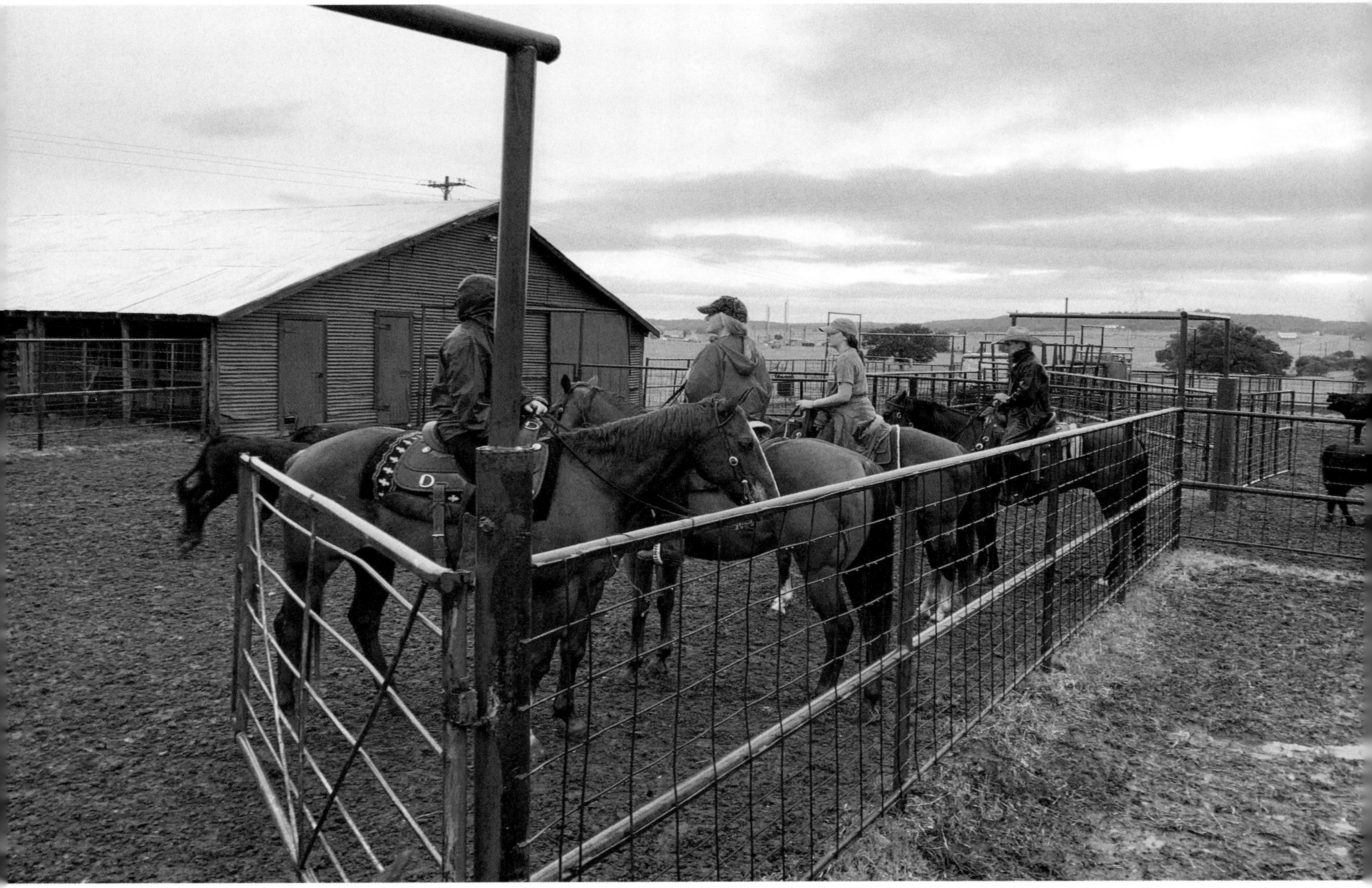

Cowgirls fit right in. Ranch hands ready for action. First shown rider, Kate Henderson, great-great-great-granddaughter of T. H. Cherryhomes. Photo by Donna Henderson Craft.

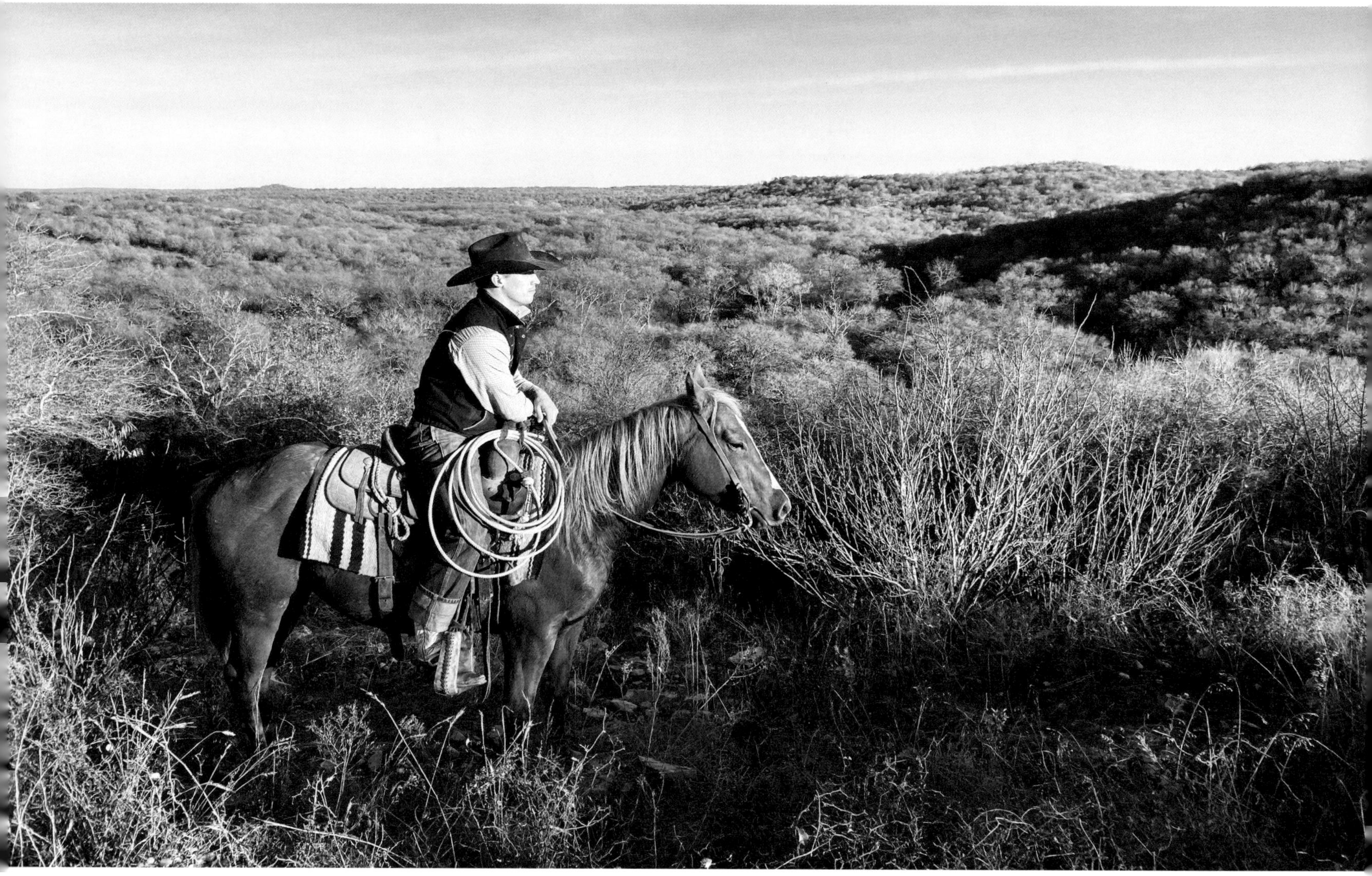

Cory Pippen on a regular work day, 2020.
Photo by Jeremy Enlow.

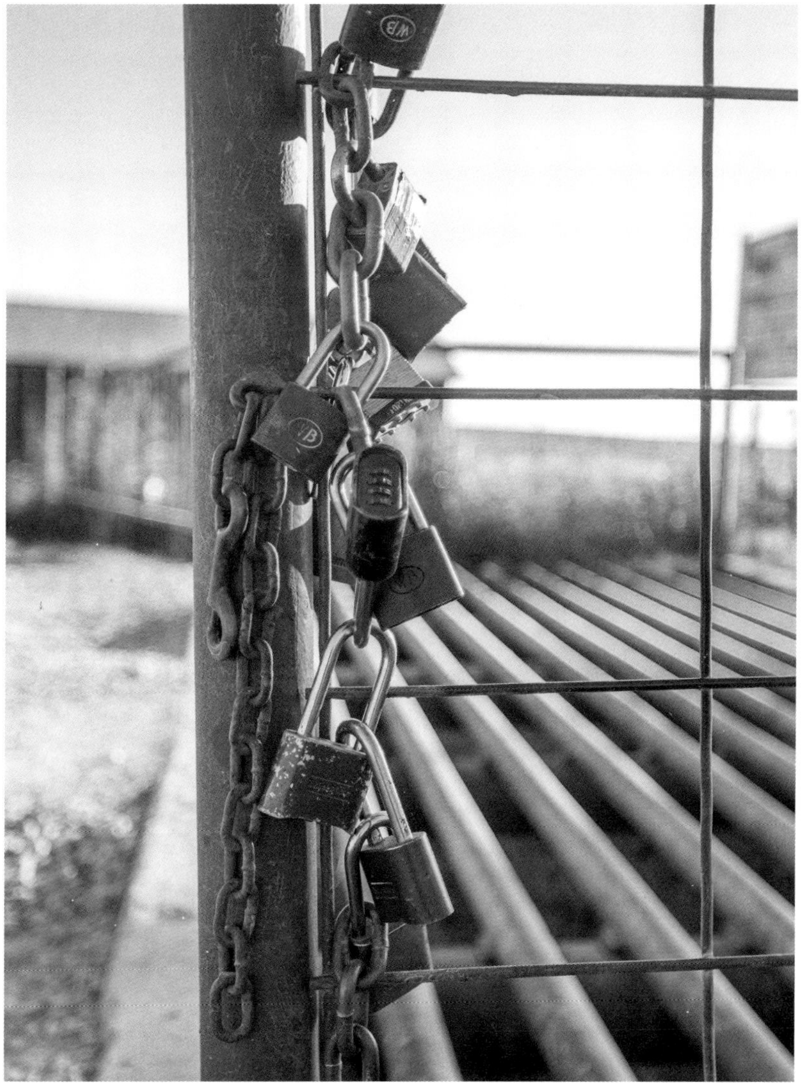

Gate at ranch boundary, 2016.
Photo by Jeremy Enlow.

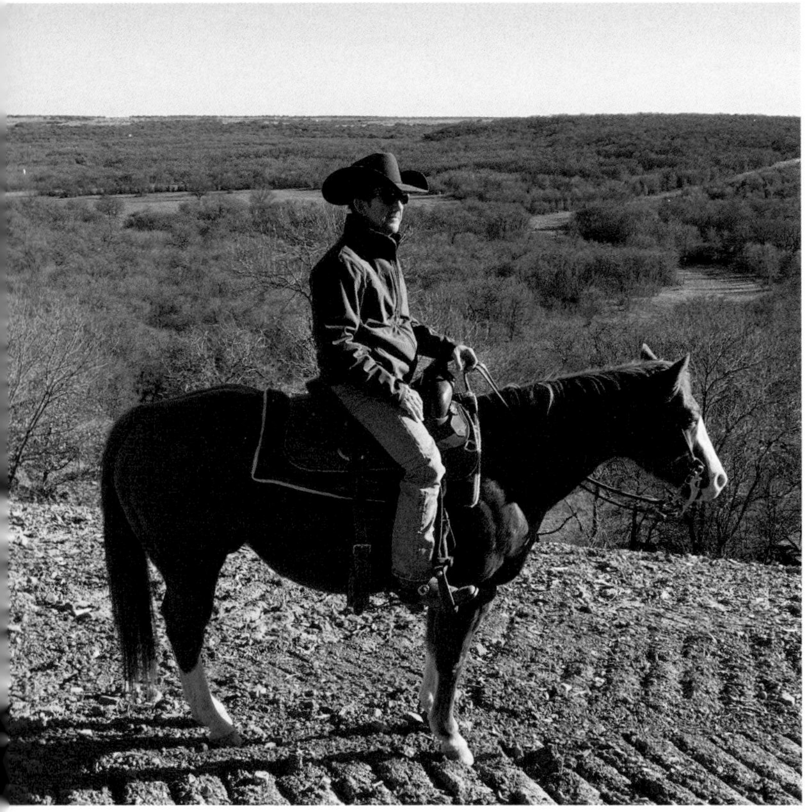

Curtis Henderson, 2020.
Photo by Jeremy Enlow.

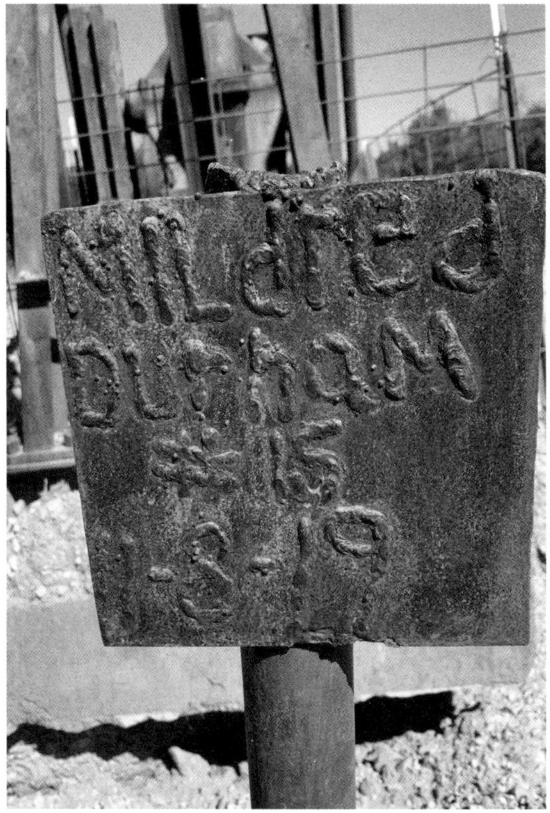

Handmade sign identifying well site of Mildred Durham #15 well, 11-8-19.
Photo taken in 2020 by Jeremy Enlow.

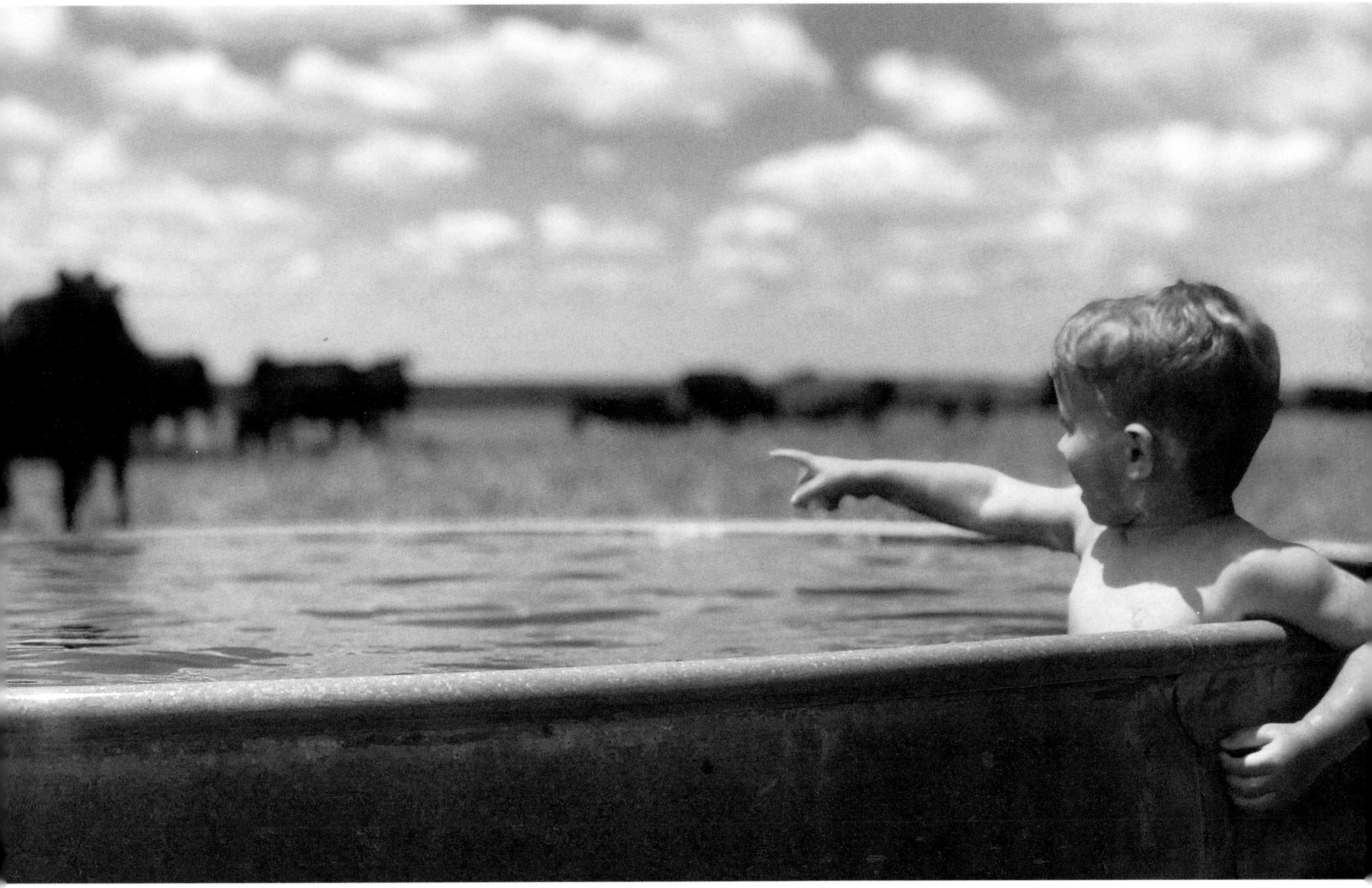

Baker Pippen, age two, son of ranch manager, Cory, cooling off in a water trough. H&D Ranch, 2021. Photo by Cory Pippen.

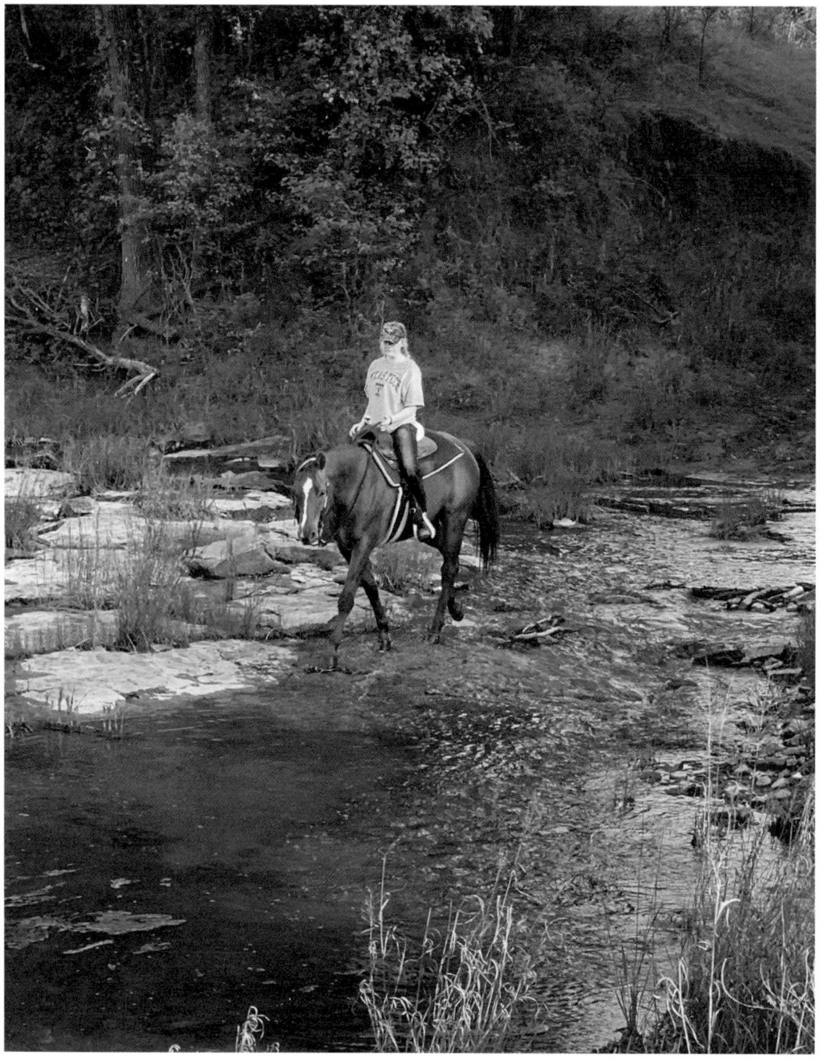

Kate Henderson, great-great-great-granddaughter of T. H. Cherryhomes, 2020. Photo by Curtis Henderson.

OPPOSITE
Roping another calf to work, 2020. Photo by Jeremy Enlow.

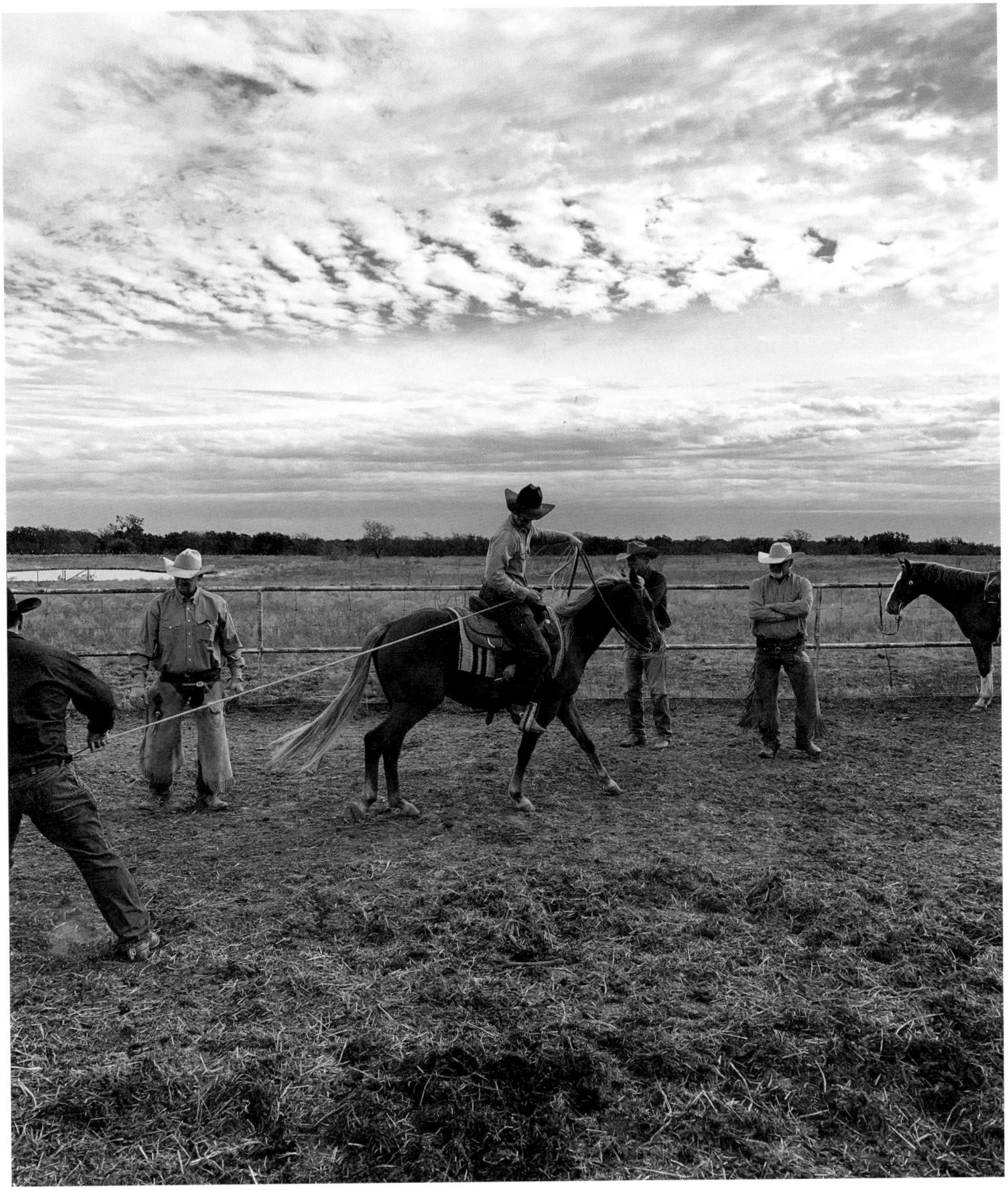

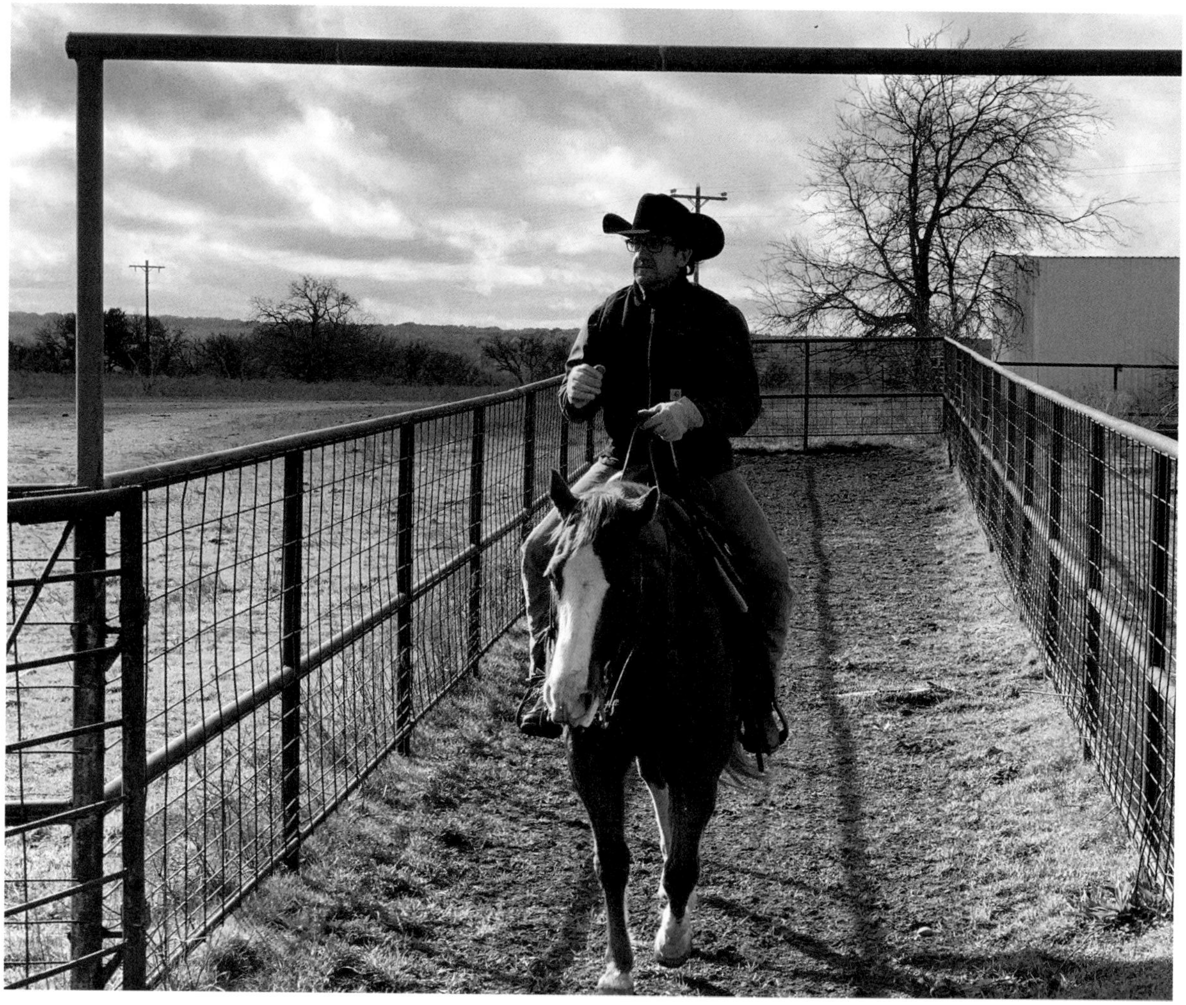

Curtis Henderson, ready to work, 2020.
Photo by Jeremy Enlow.

OPPOSITE
Kate Henderson, horse whisperer, 2020.
Photo by Curtis Henderson.

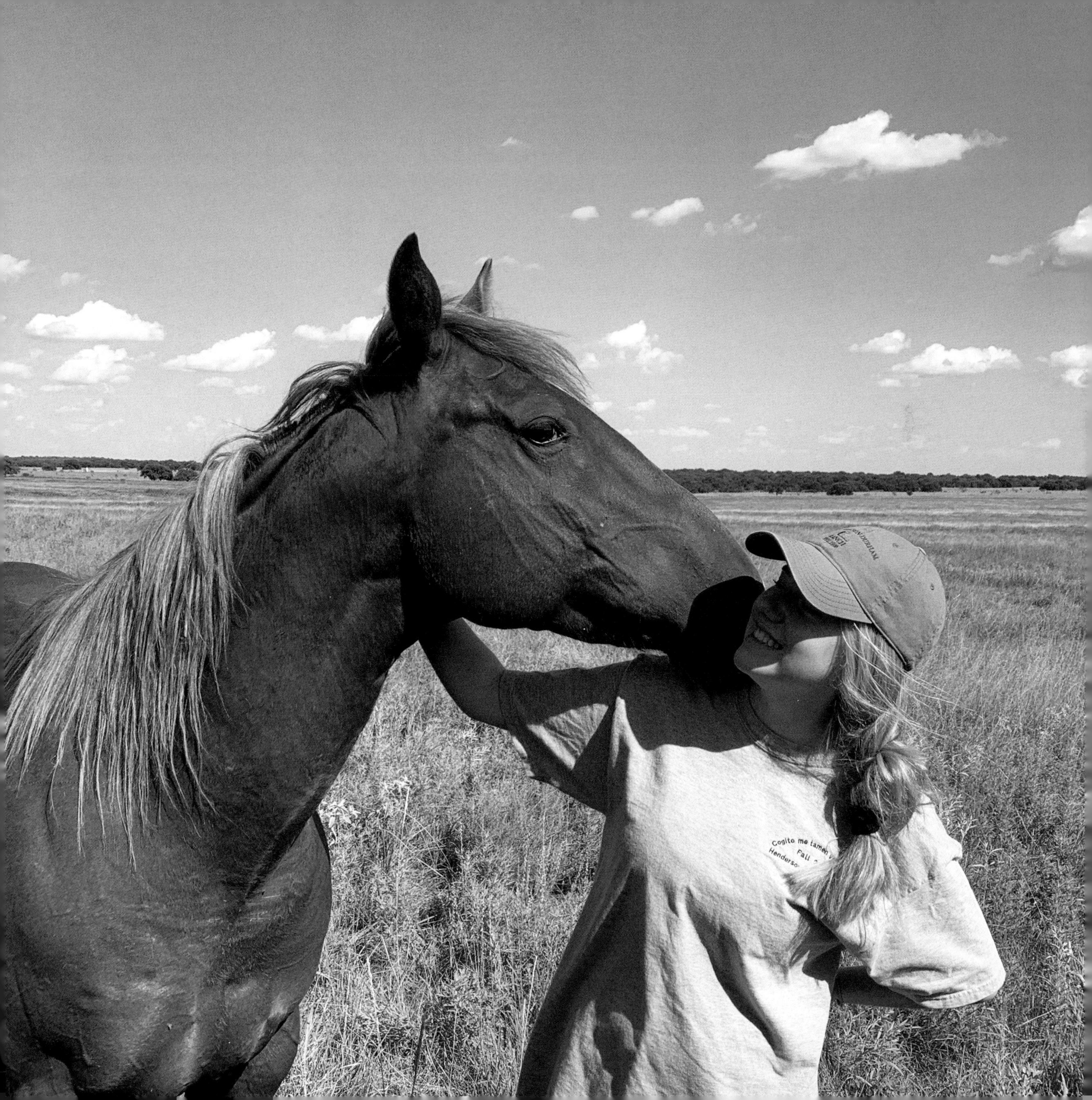

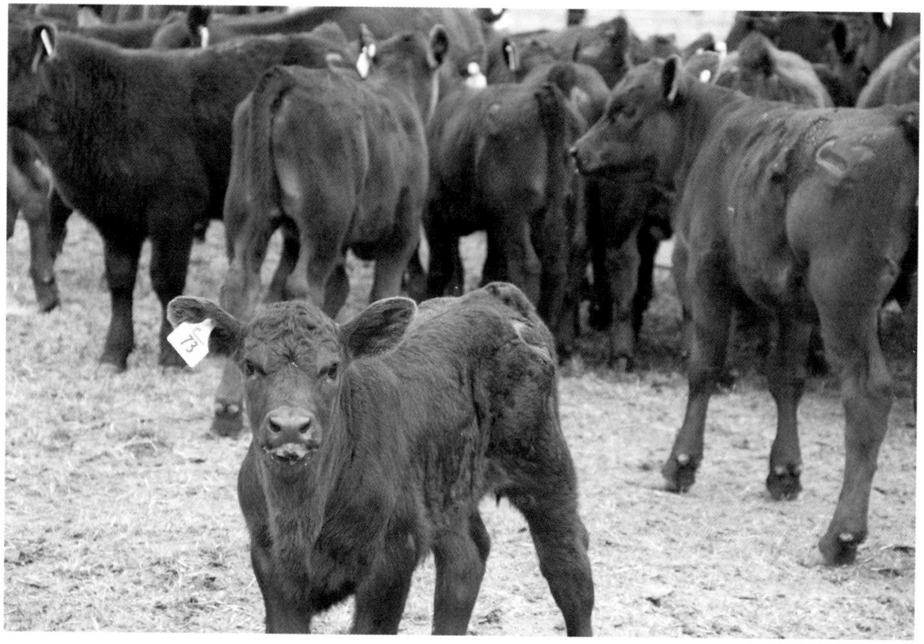

Not a bit happy, 2020.
Photo by Donna Henderson Craft.

OPPOSITE
Kate Henderson, loving the warm day, 2020.
Photo by Curtis Henderson.

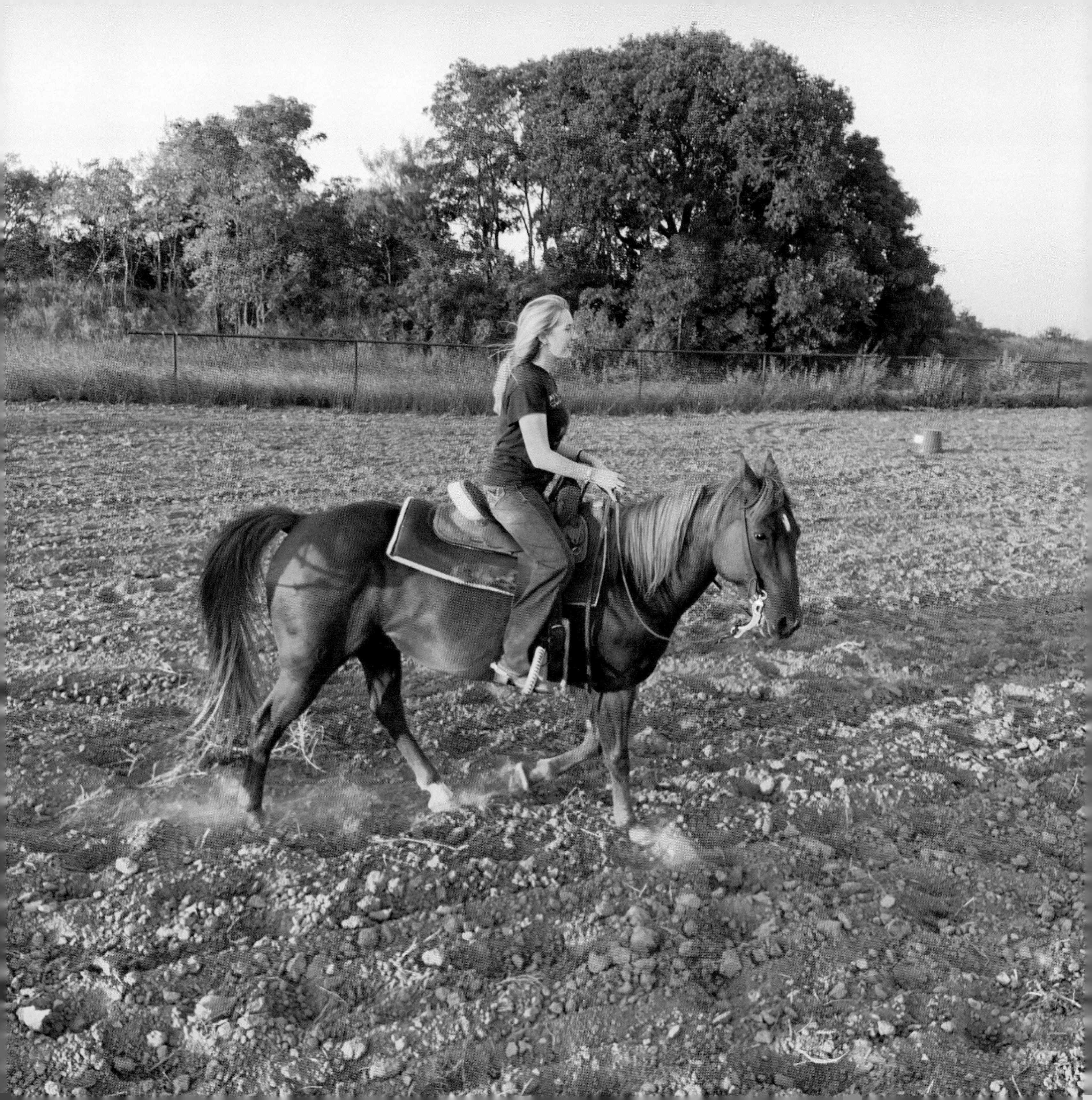

Branding Time

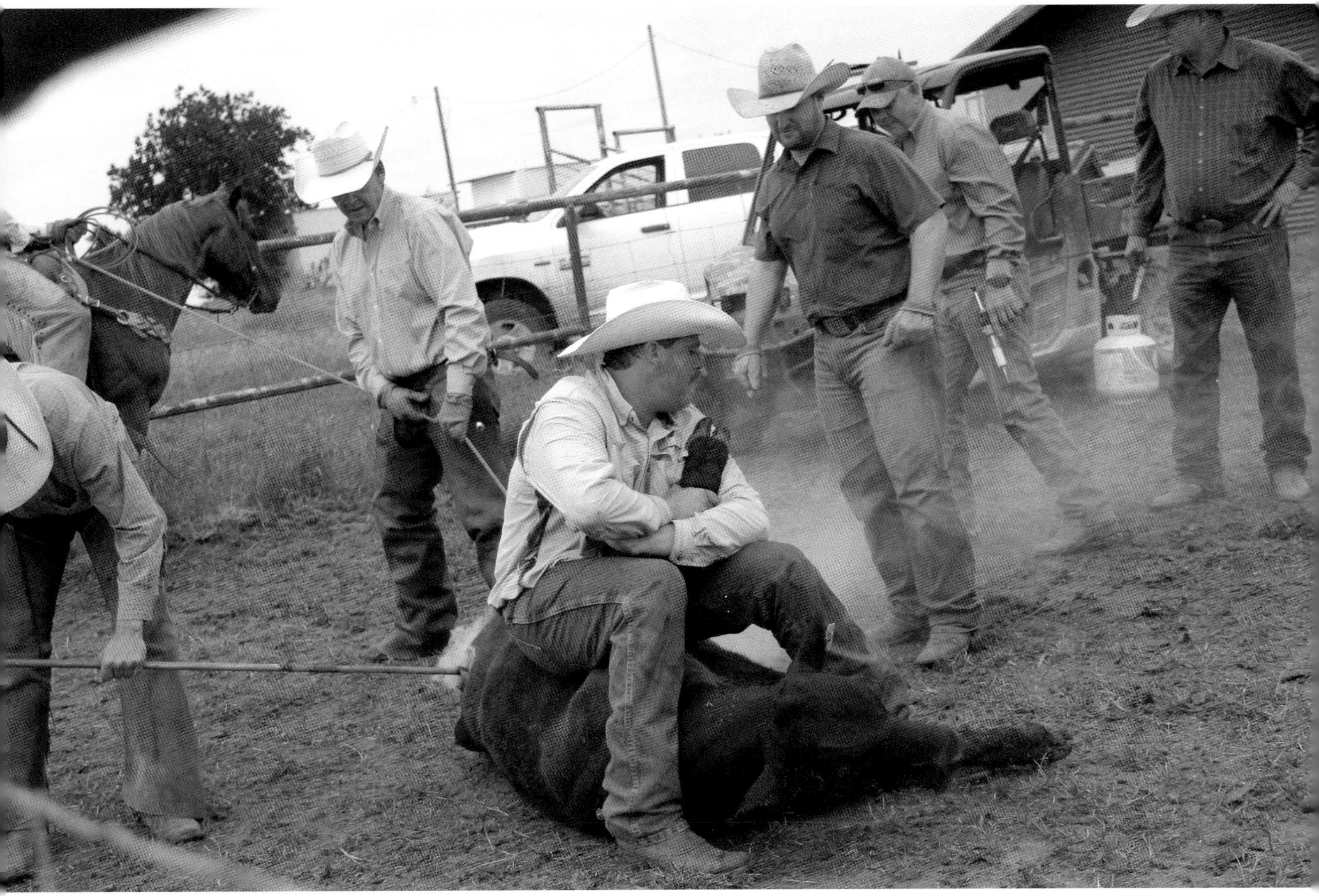

Branding, 2020. Corbin Monroe Craft, T. H.'s great-great-grandson holding down calf. Photo by Donna Henderson Craft.

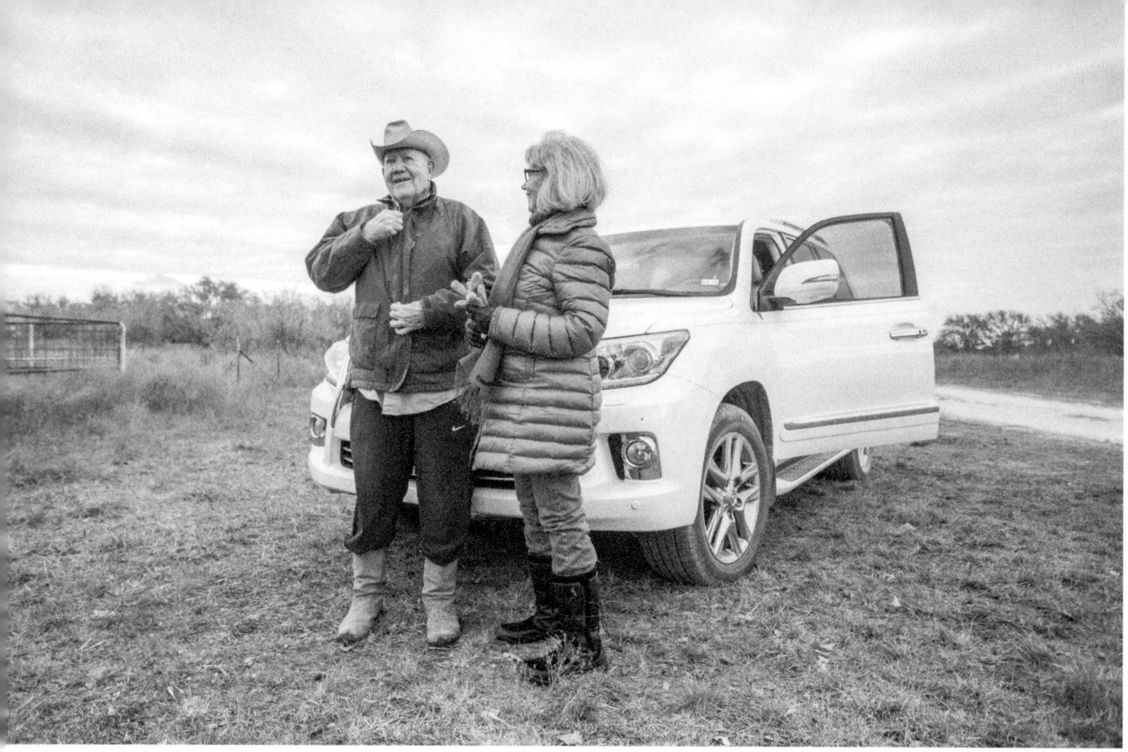

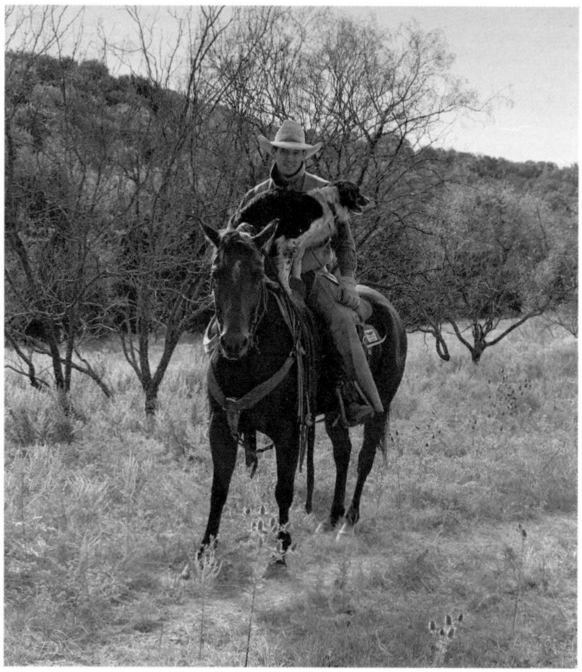

Monroe and Carol Henderson, cattle working day, 2016.
Photo by Jeremy Enlow.

Cory Pippen and dog, Kirby, 2020.
Photo by Curtis Henderson.

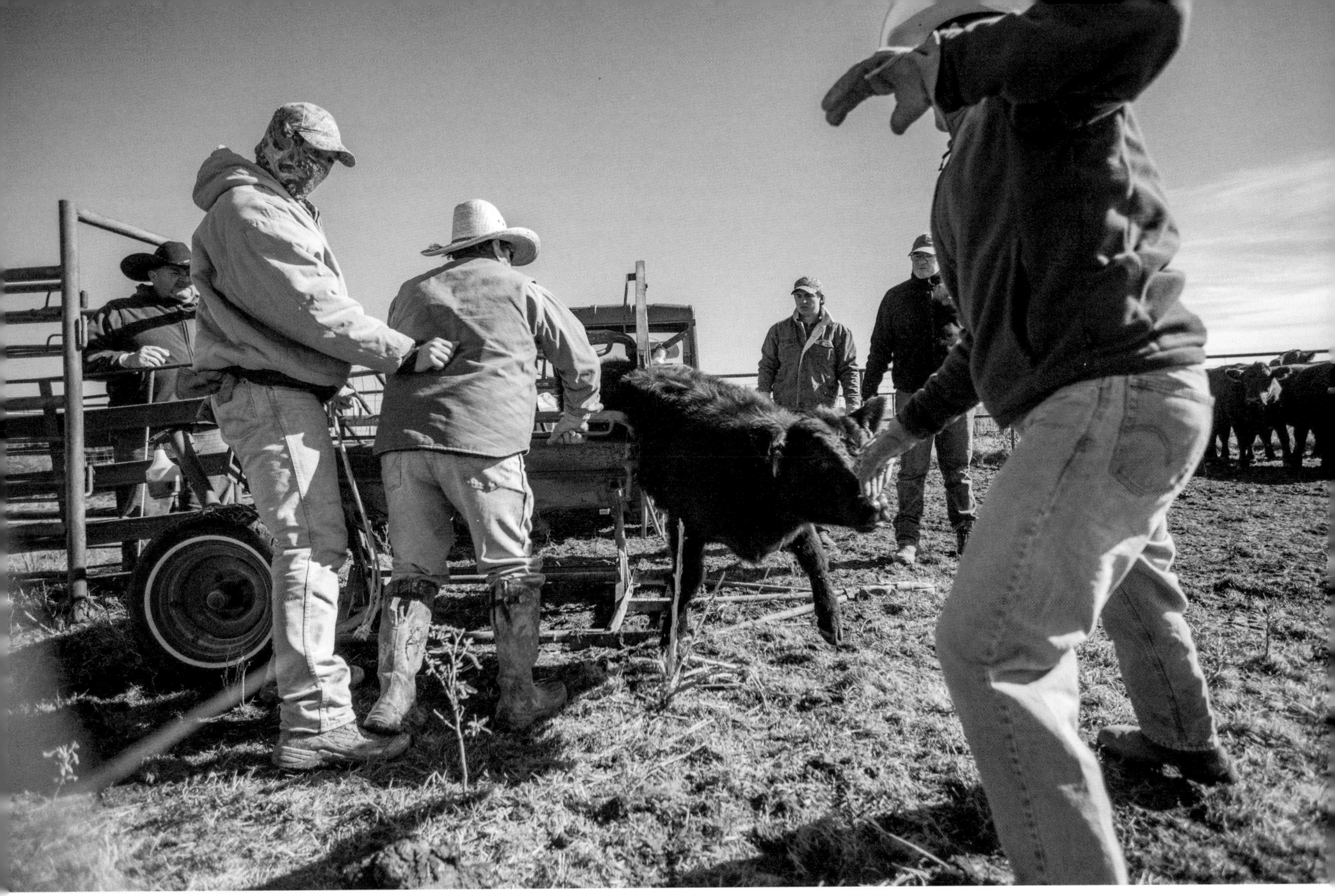

Angus calf looking for escape, 2016.
Photo by Jeremy Enlow.

PAGES 236-237
Grandson Corbin Monroe Craft, great-great-great-grandson of T. H. Cherryhomes, roping calf, 2017. Photo by Donna Henderson Craft.

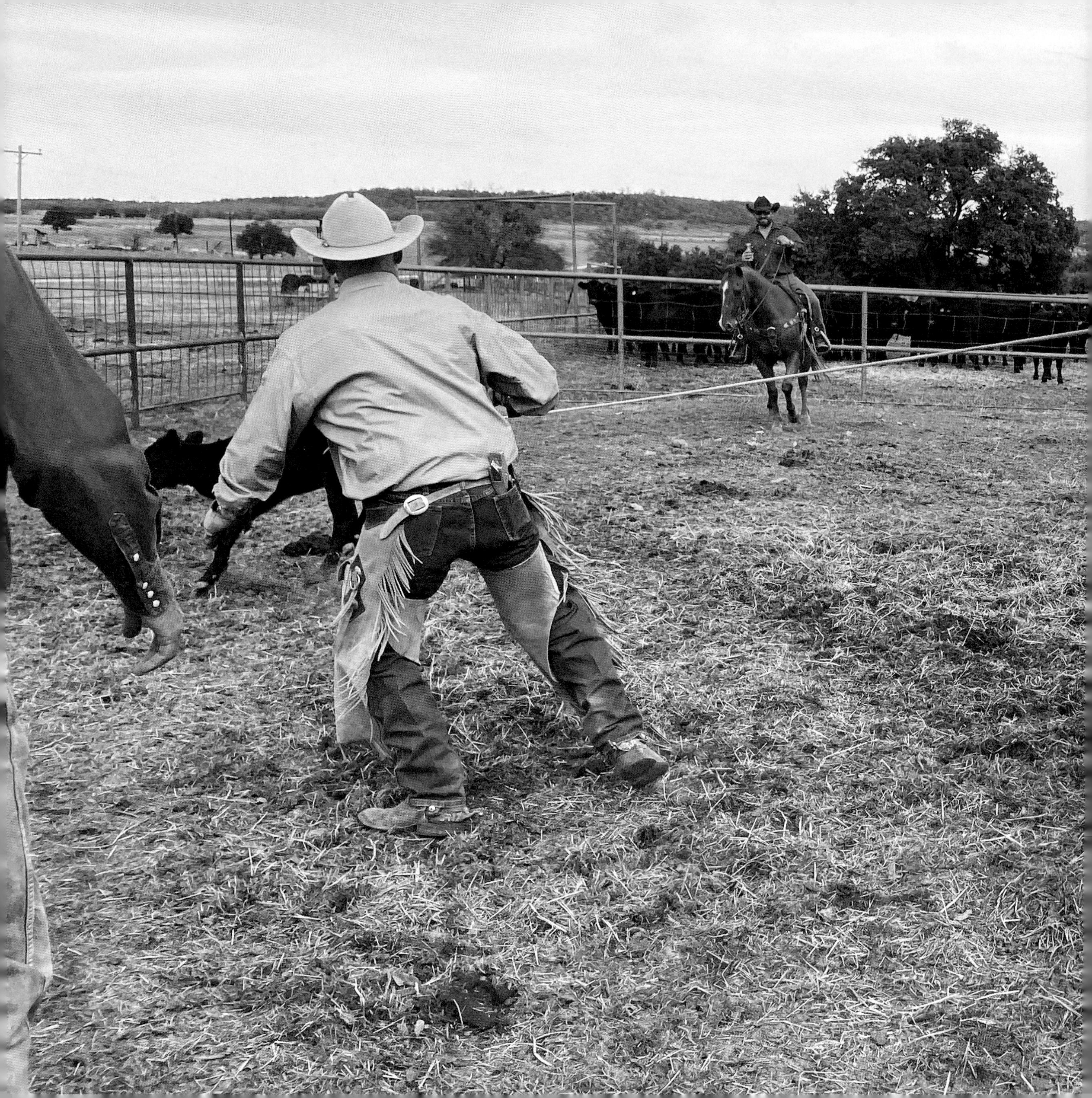

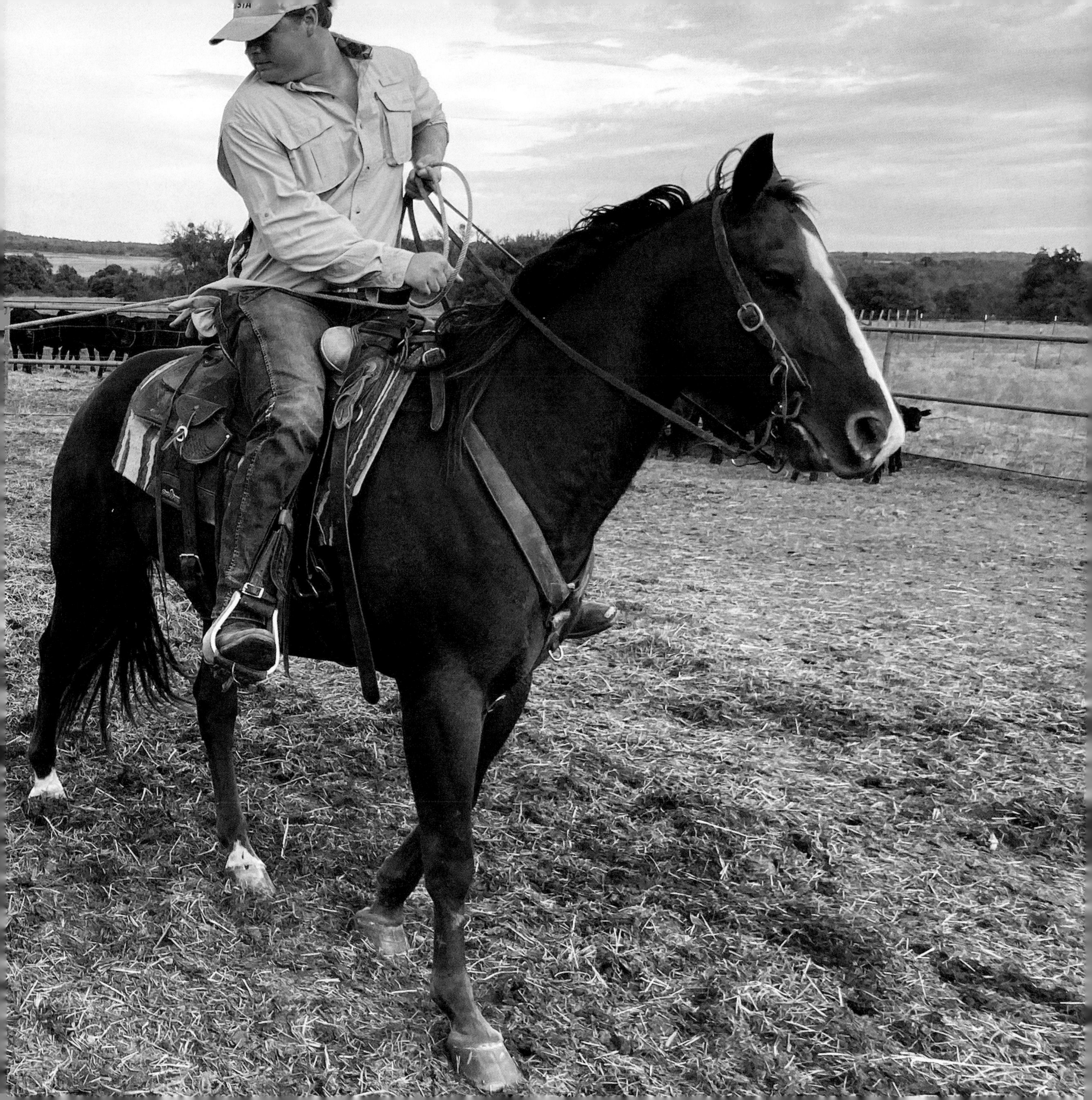

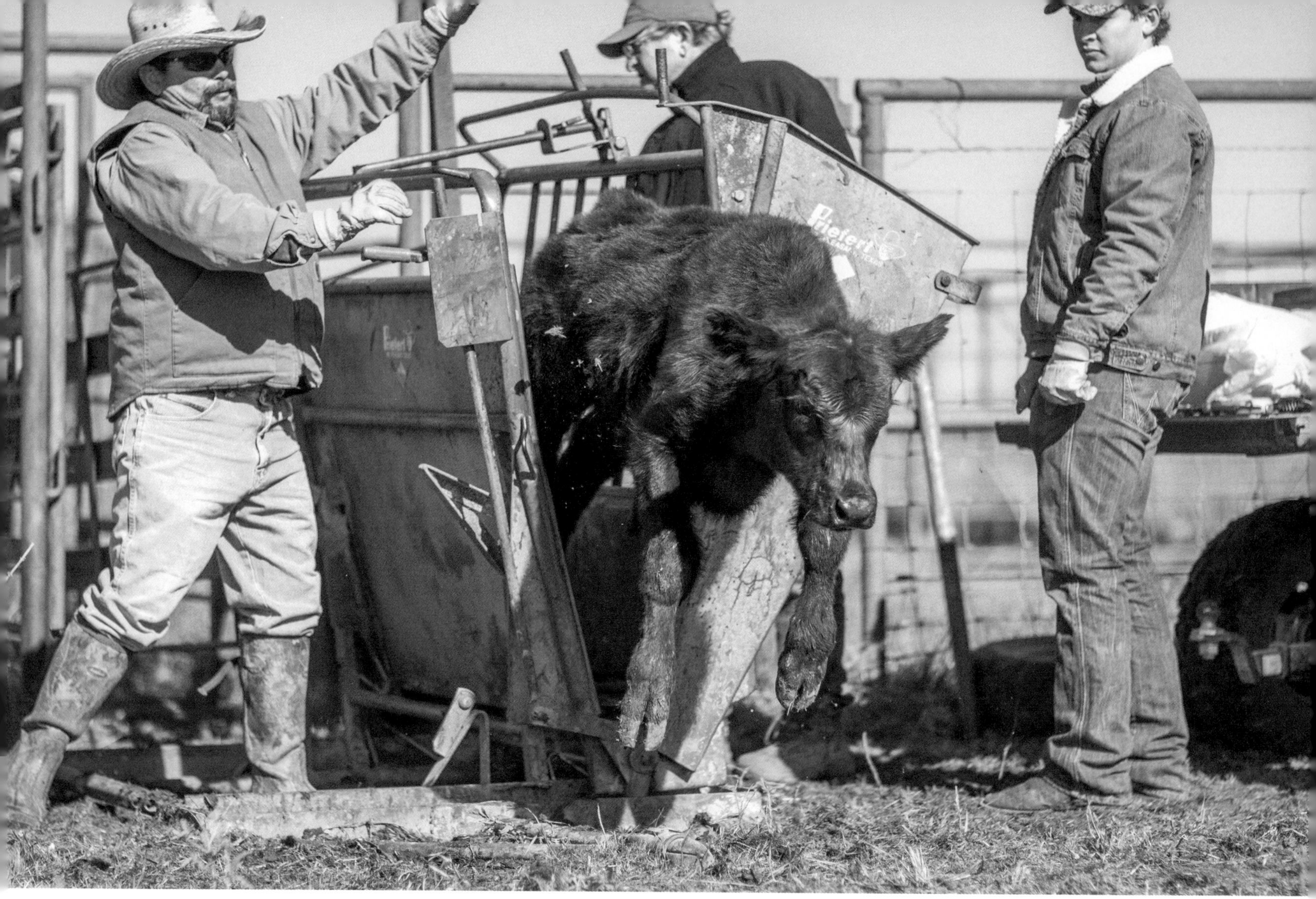

PAGES 238-239
Get out of the way! Calf breaking free, 2016.
Photos by Jeremy Enlow.

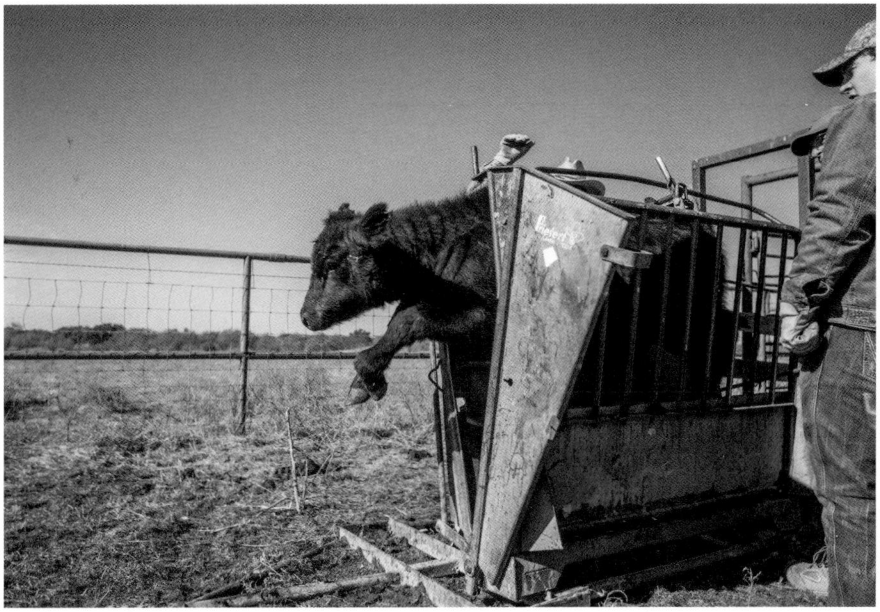

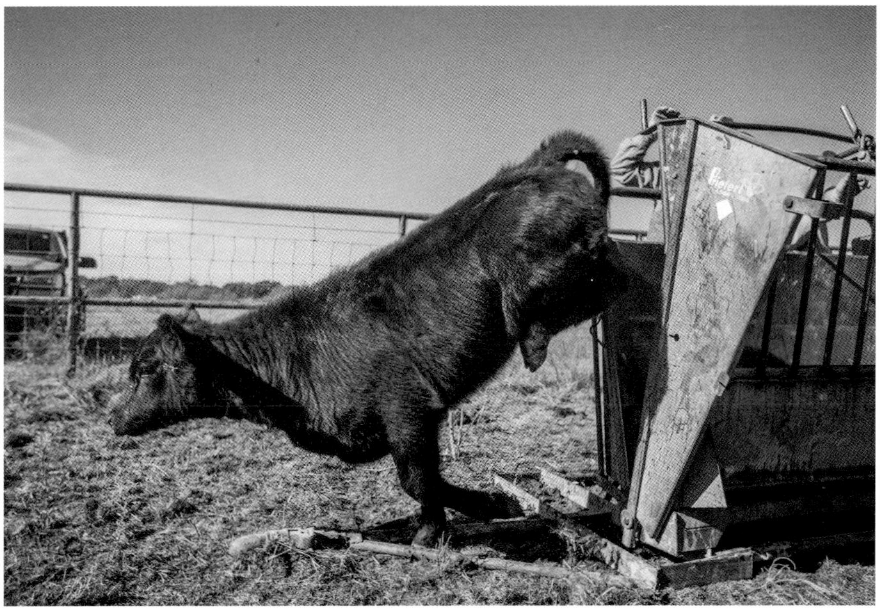

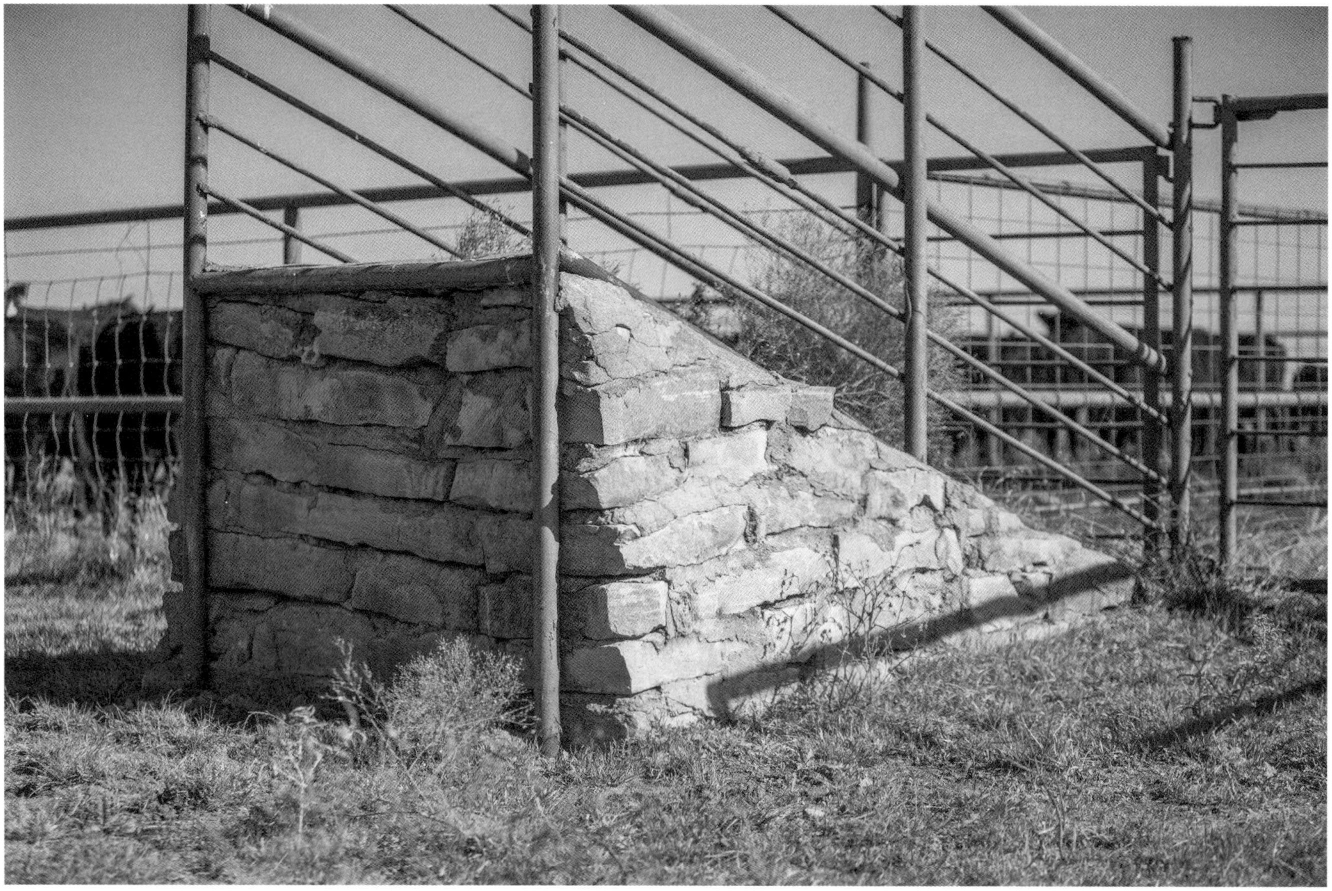

Cattle loading shoot. Rock base circa 1895.
Photo by Jeremy Enlow.

OPPOSITE
Branding time, 2020.
Photo by Jeremy Enlow.

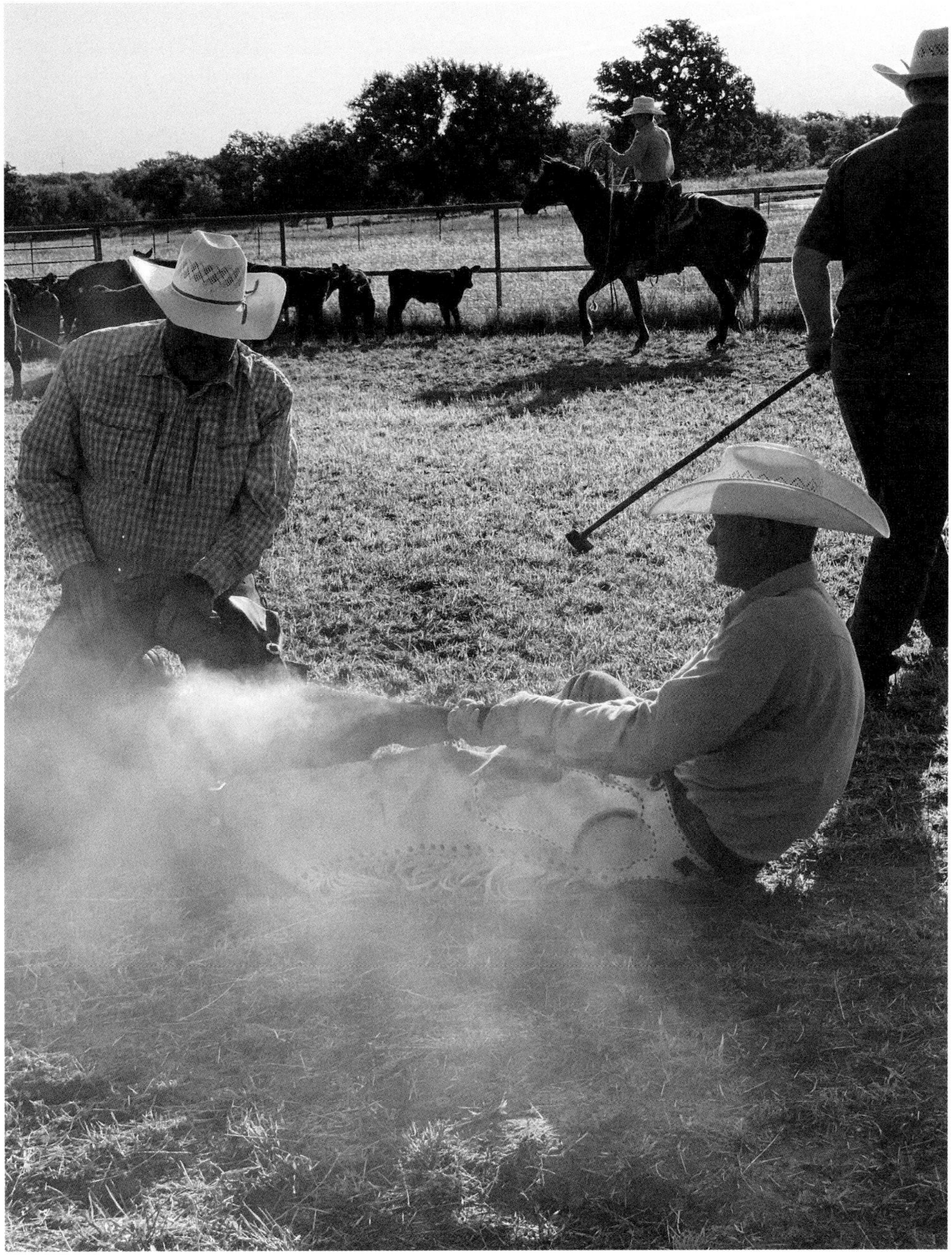

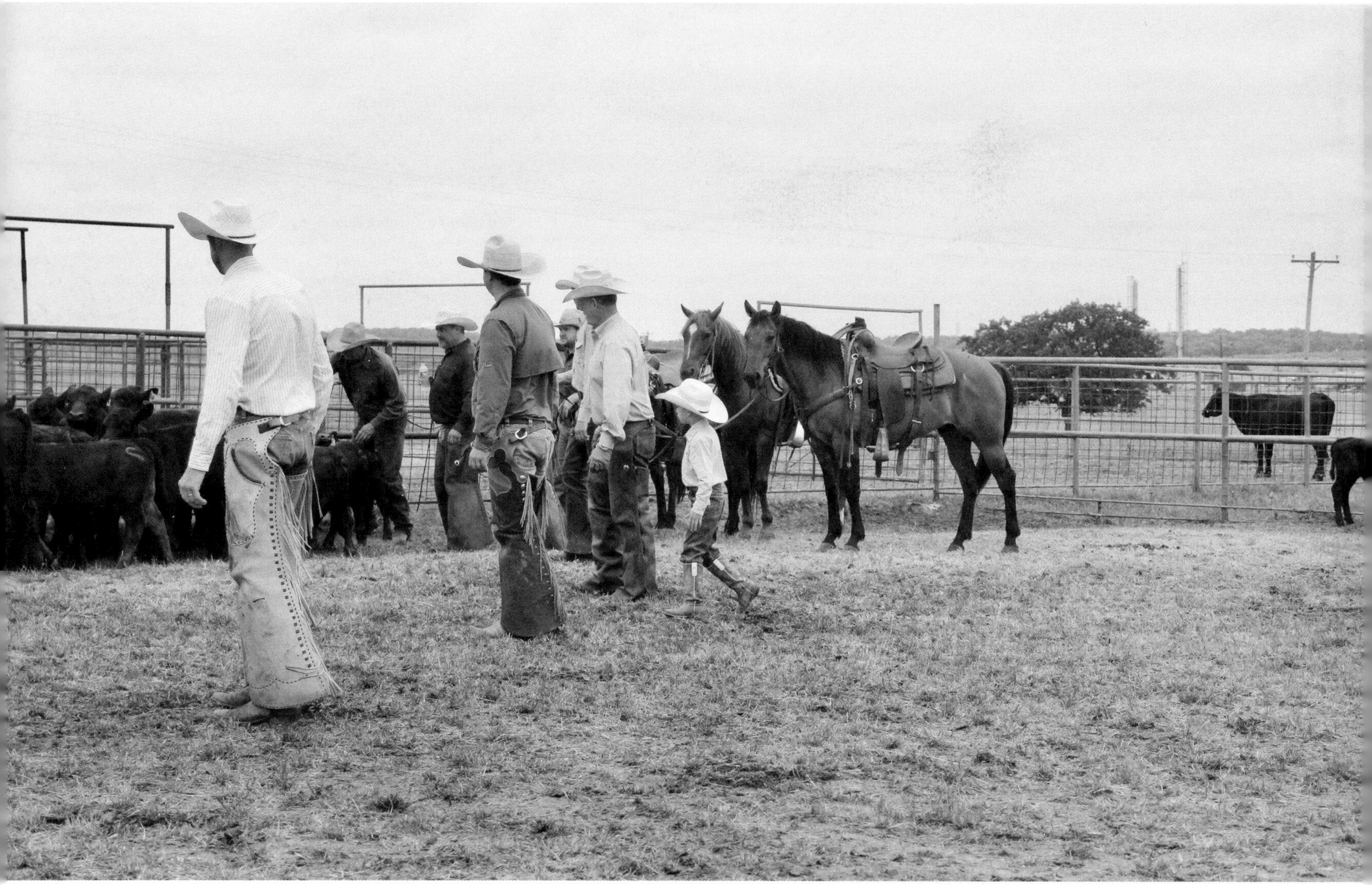

Little guy wants a closer look, 2020.
Photo by Donna Henderson Craft.

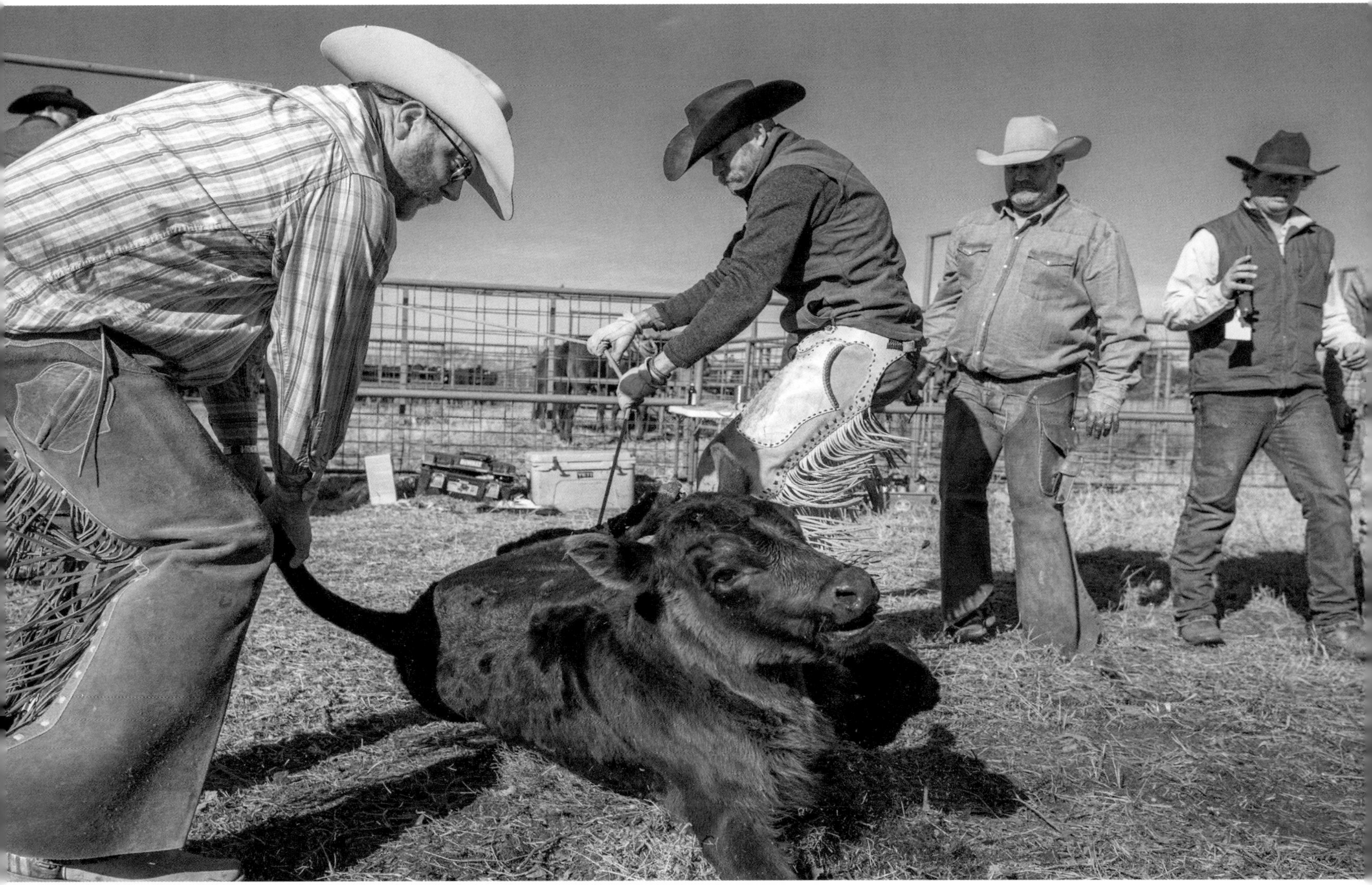

Cowboys branding a calf, January 2021.
Photo by Jeremy Enlow.

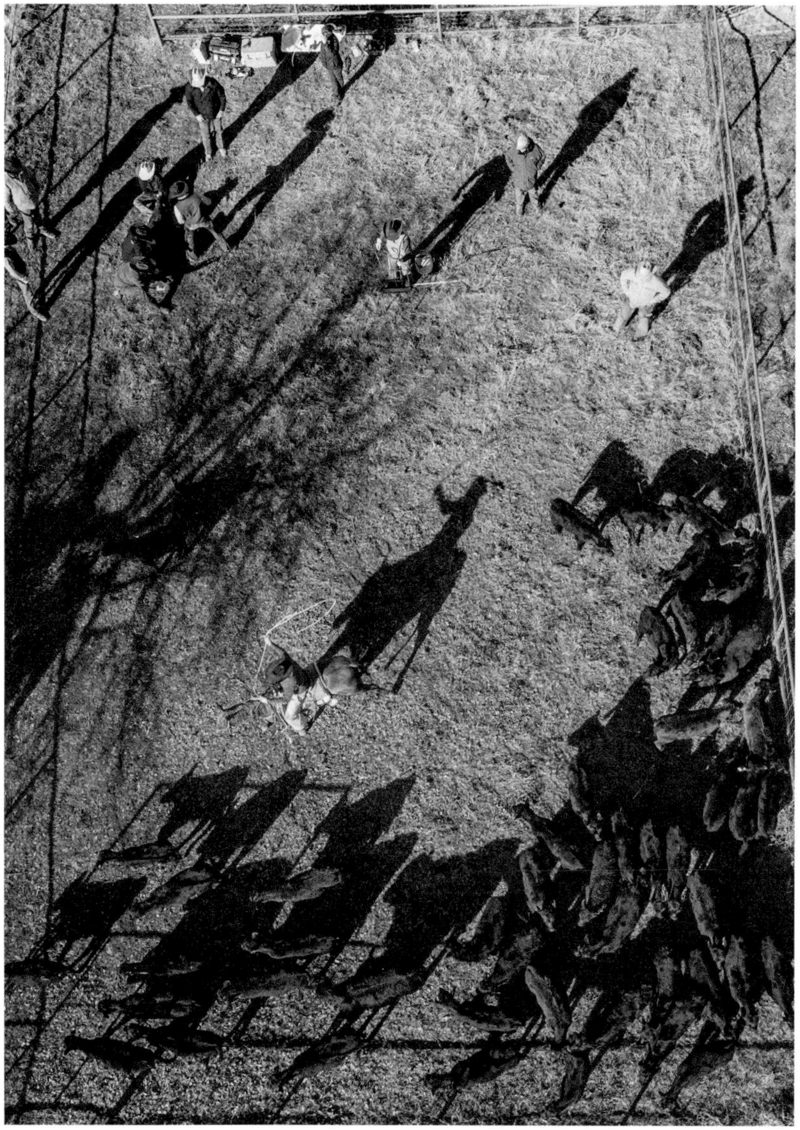

Cowboys choosing calves to brand, January 2021.
Photo by Jeremy Enlow.

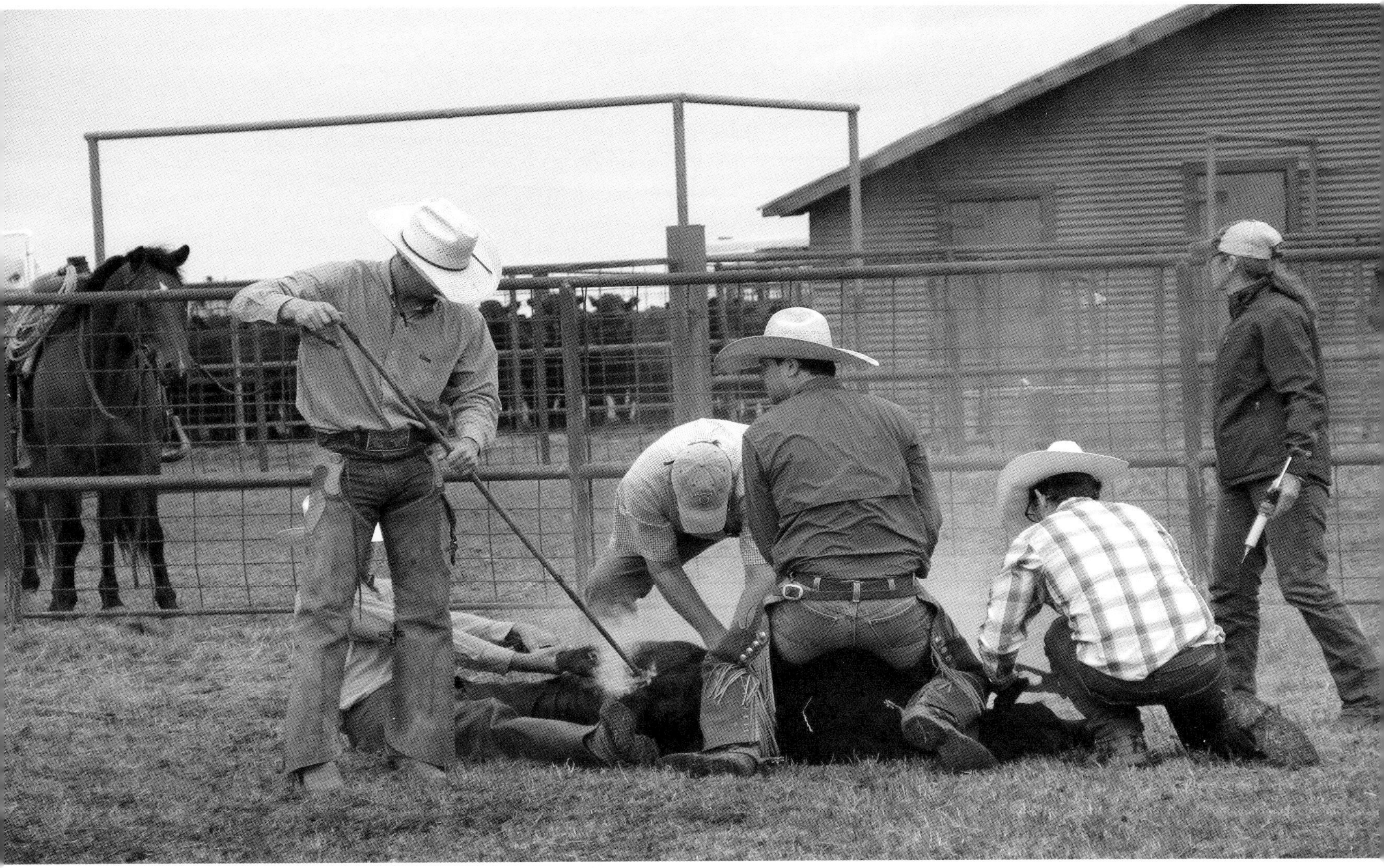

Branding, 2020.
Photo by Donna Henderson Craft.

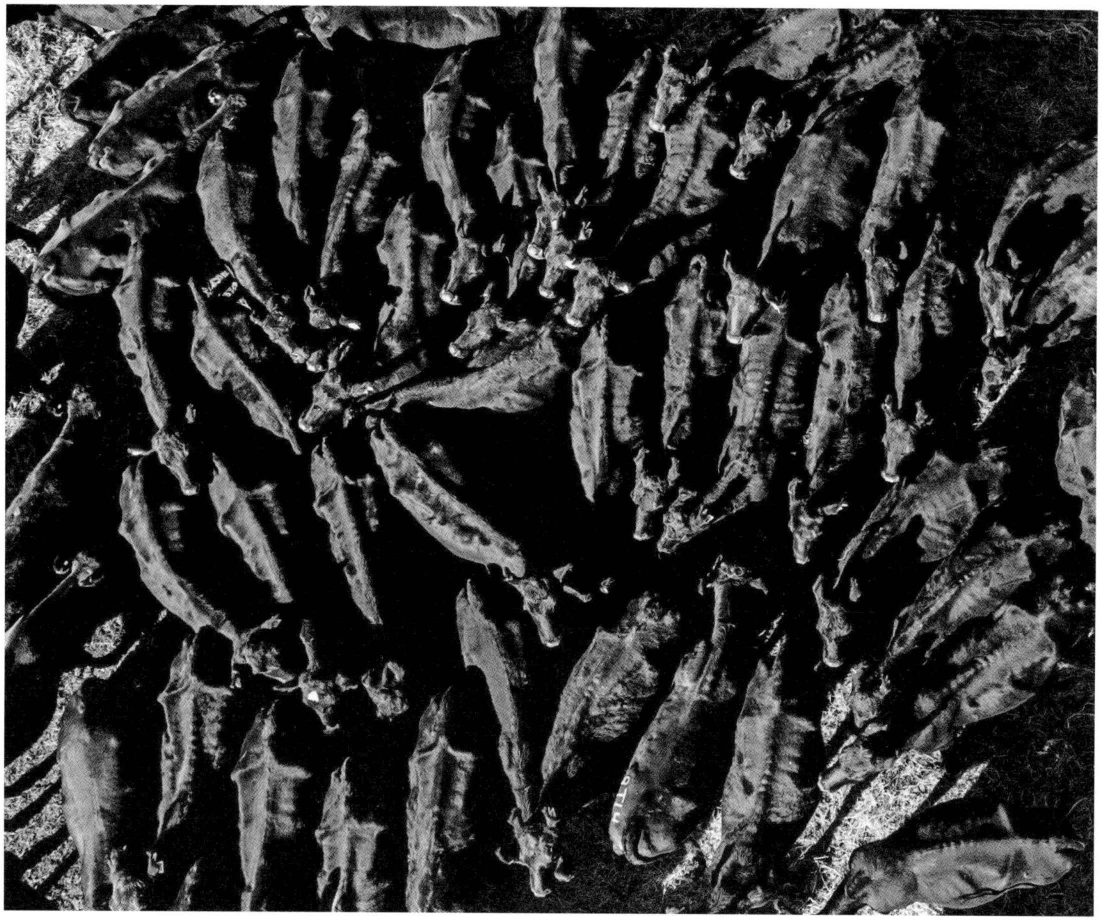

Aerial view of cattle gathered in corrals, January 2021. Photo by Jeremy Enlow.

OPPOSITE
Roping a calf for branding, January 2021. Photo by Jeremy Enlow.

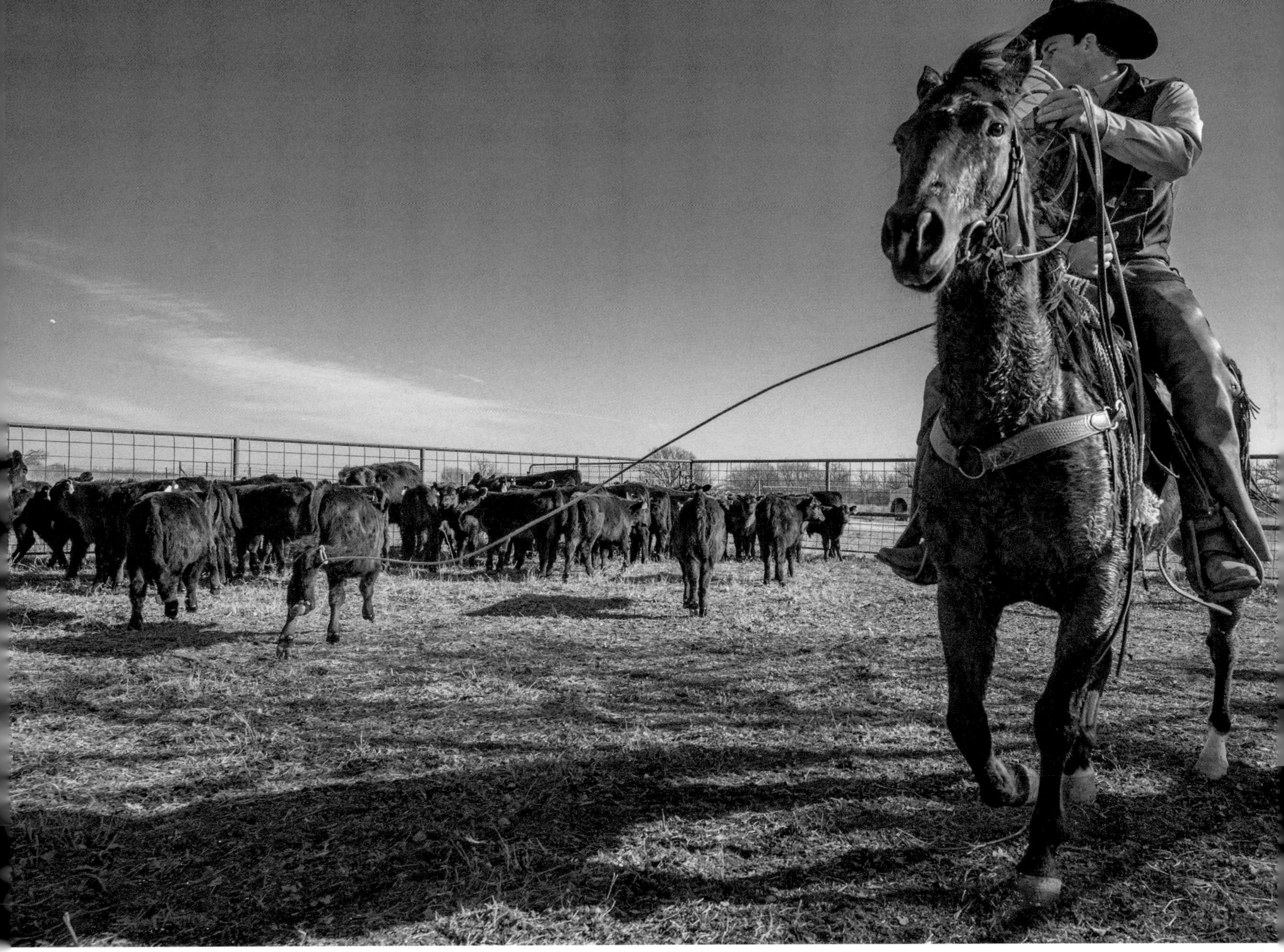

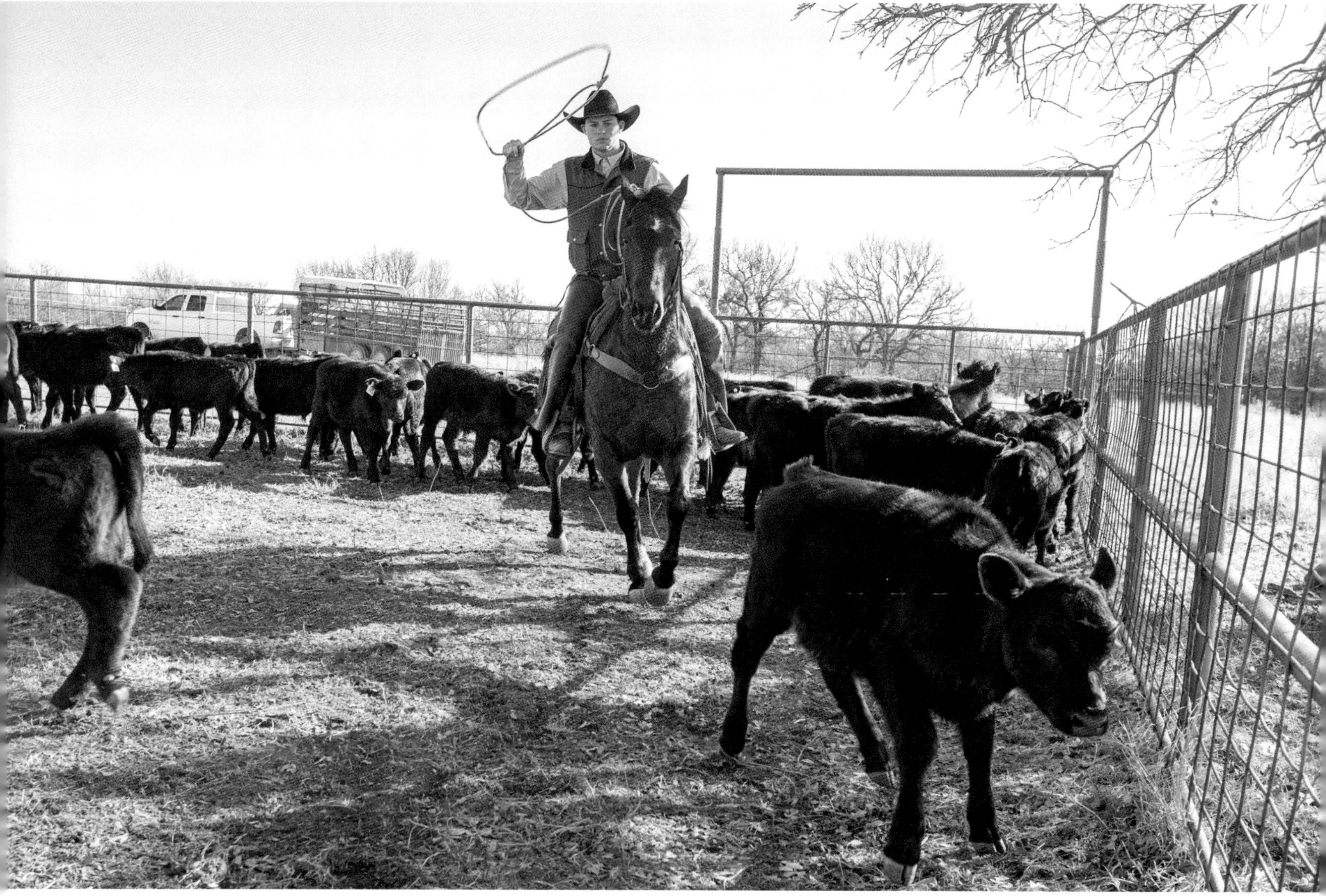

Cowboys roping calf for branding, January 2021.
Photo by Jeremy Enlow.

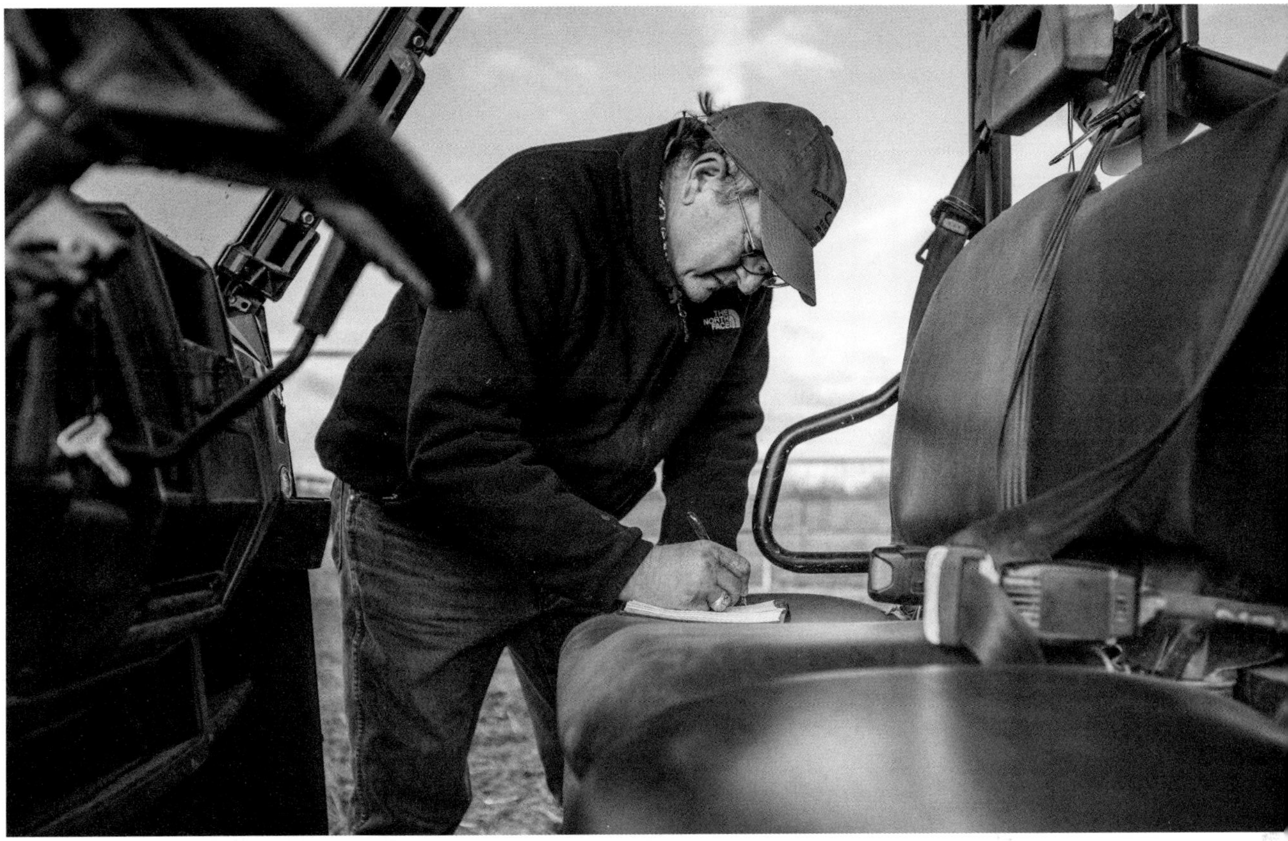

Ross Craft, son-in-law of Monroe and Carol Henderson, writing in tally book. Photo by Jeremy Enlow.

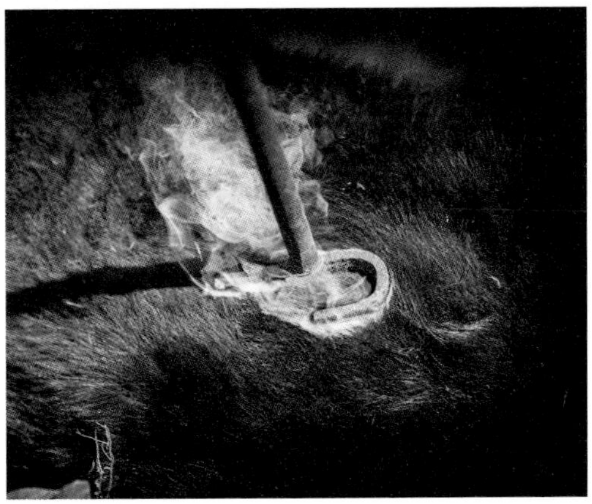

Branding Iron "Lazy J." Photo by Jeremy Enlow.

Chow

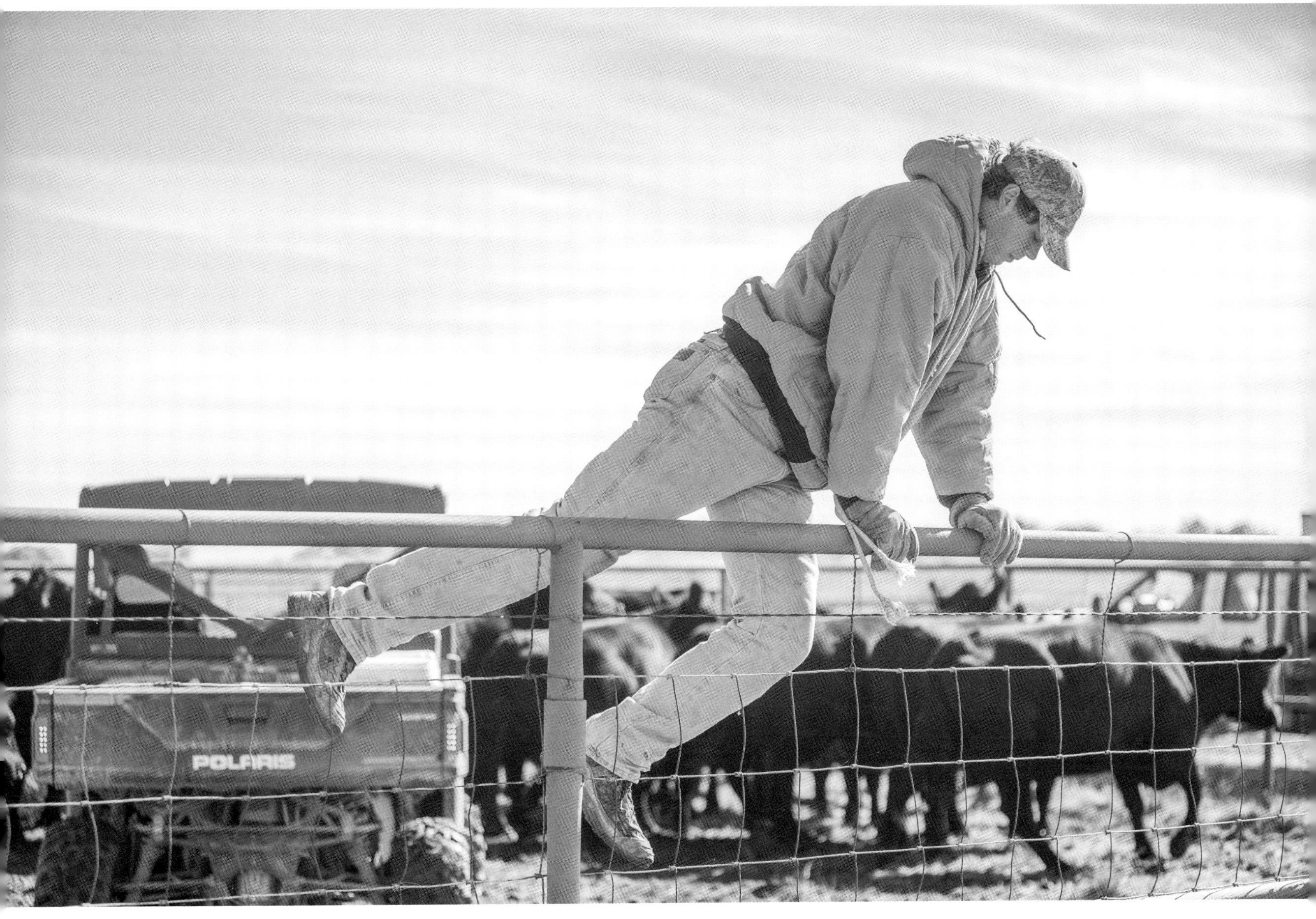

Corbin Monroe Craft, great-great-great-grandson of T. H. Cherryhomes, 2017. Photo by Jeremy Enlow.

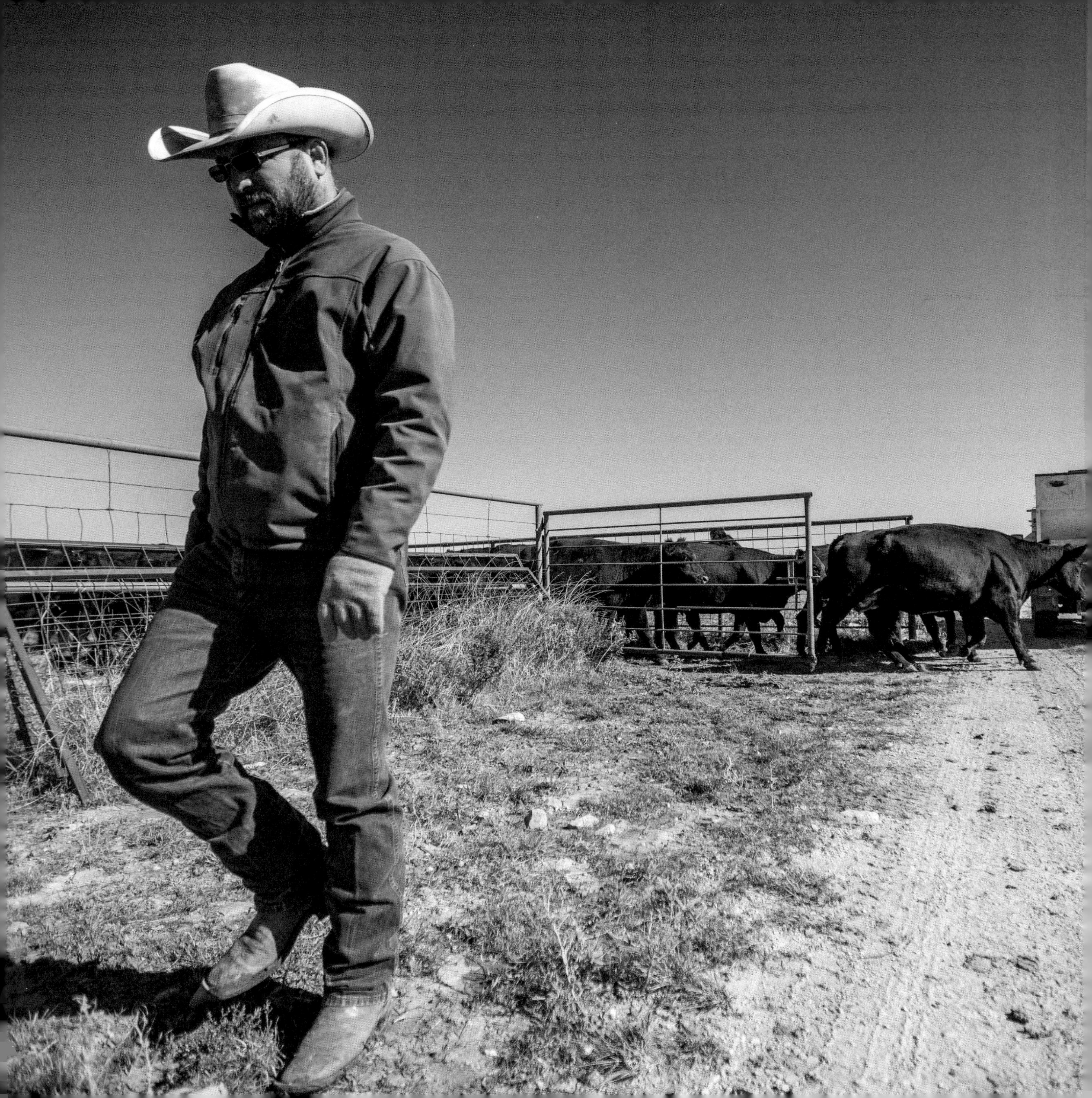

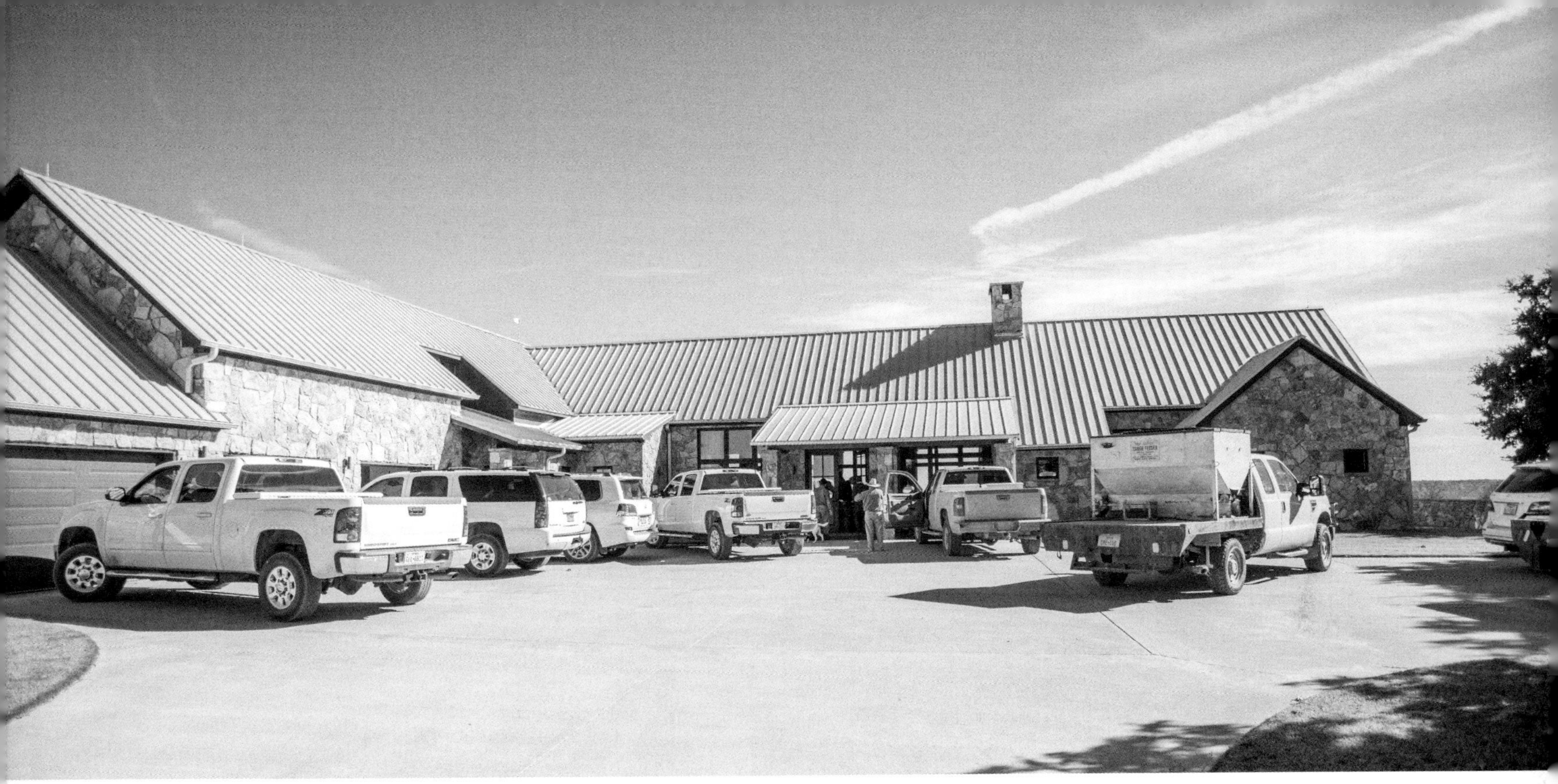

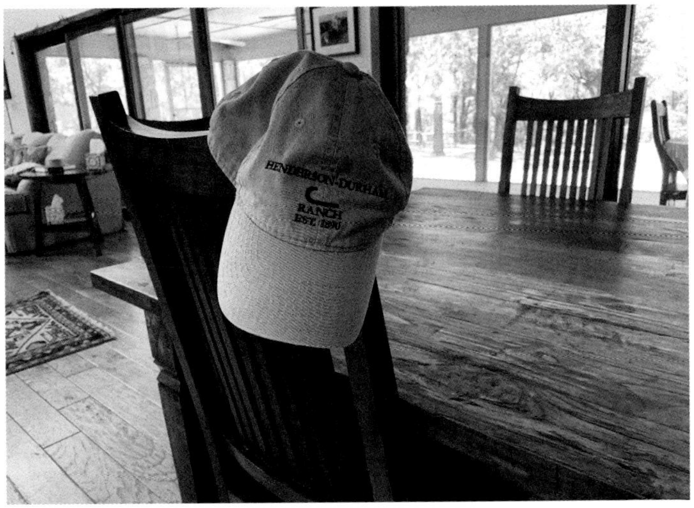

Lunchtime at H&D Ranch, 2016.
Photo by Jeremy Enlow.

Cap with H&D Ranch logo.
Photo by Jeremy Enlow.

OPPOSITE
Getting close to quitting time, 2016.
Photo by Jeremy Enlow.

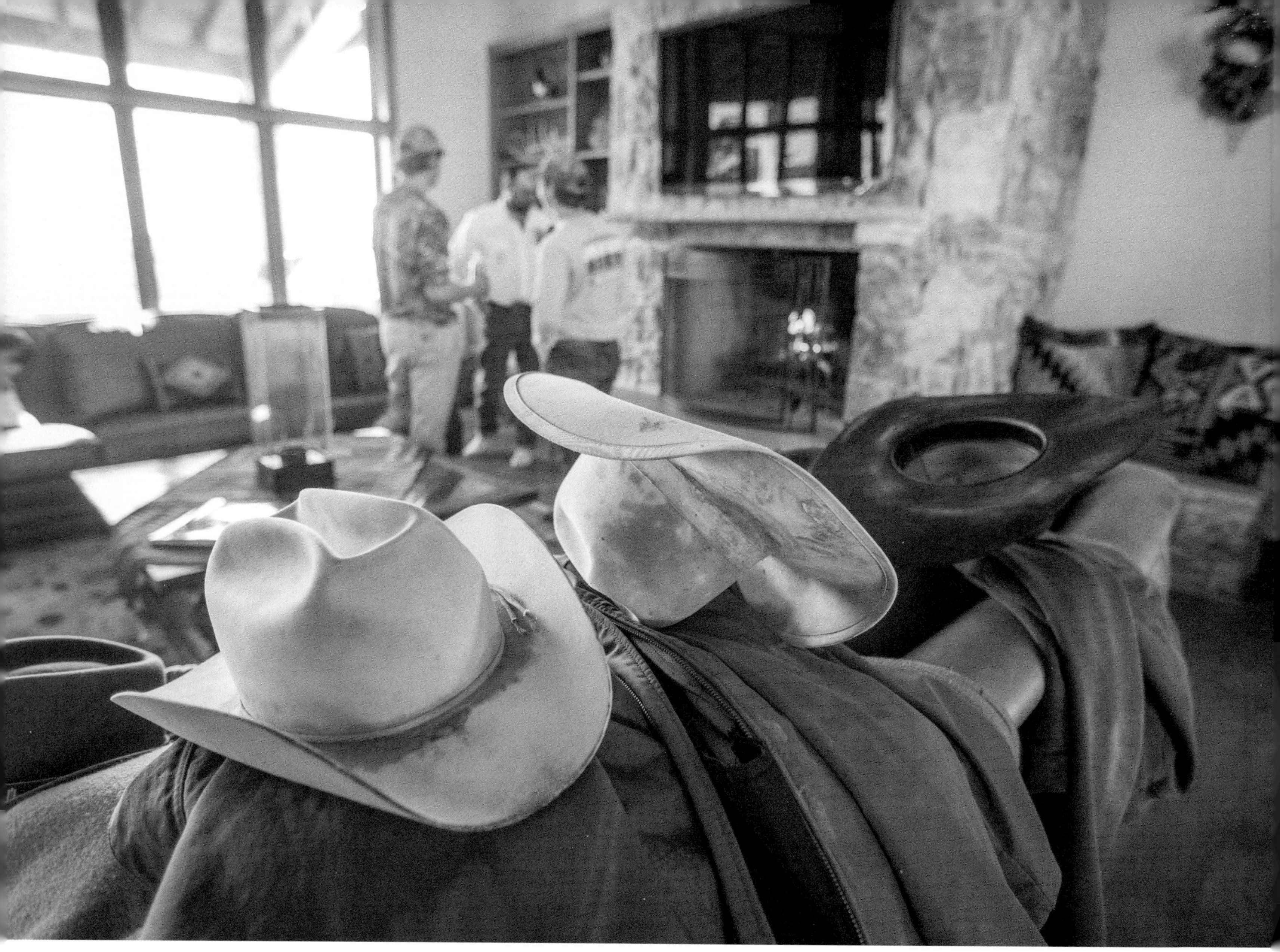

Lunch break, 2016.
Photo by Jeremy Enlow.

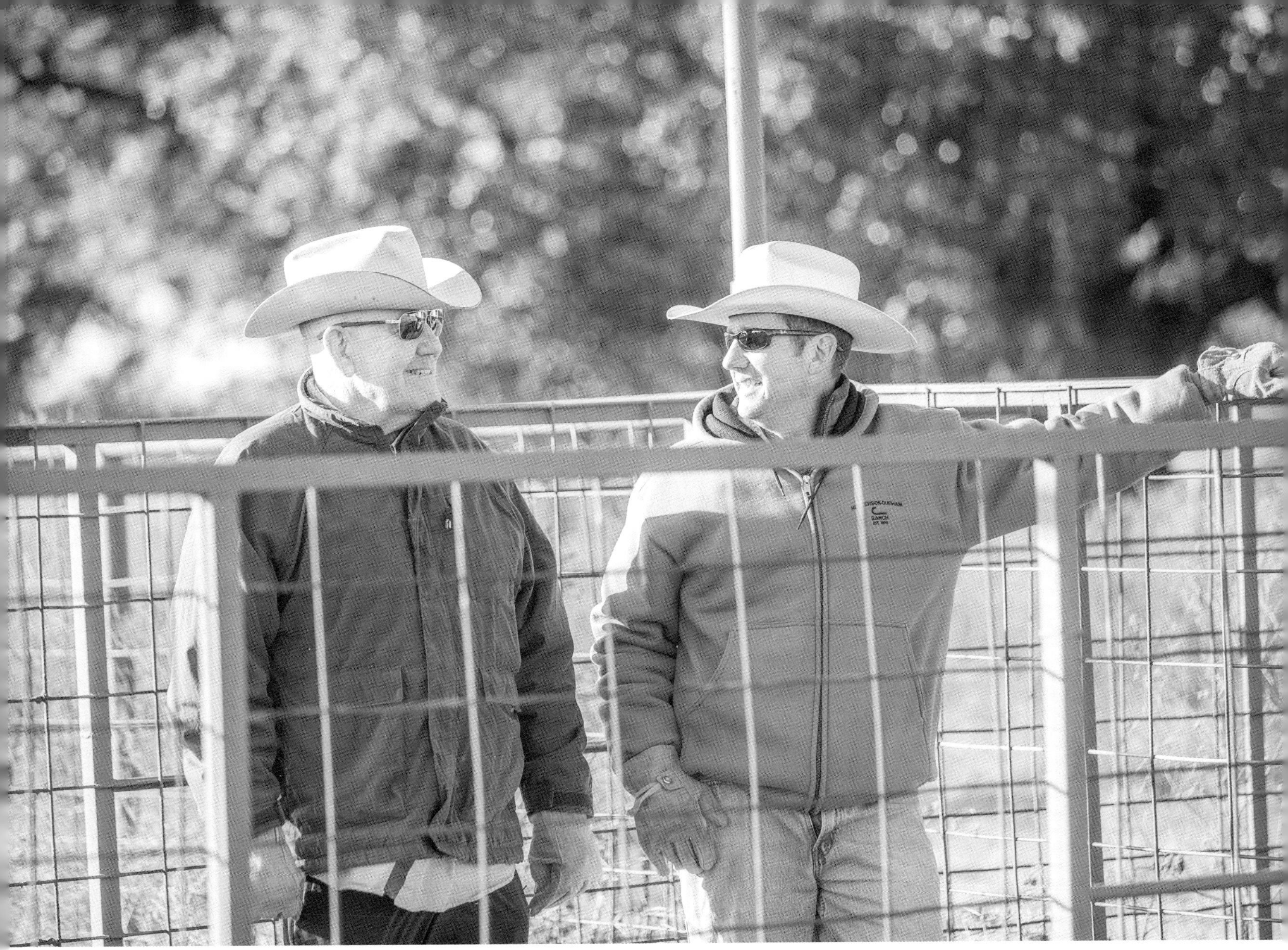

Monroe Henderson and son, Curtis Henderson, 2016.
Photo by Jeremy Enlow.

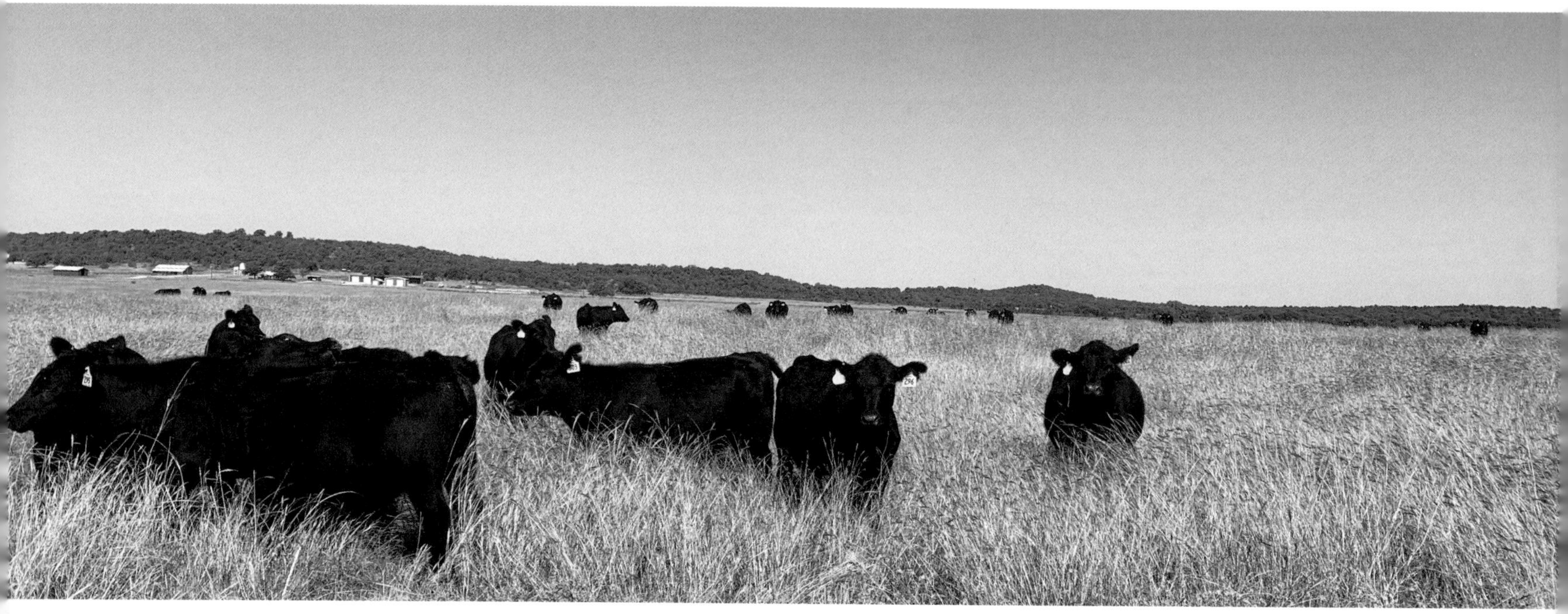

Good grazing, 2020.
Photo by Curtis Henderson.

"Leave your muddy boots on the porch," 2020.
Photo by Jeremy Enlow.

OPPOSITE
Waiting for feed truck, 2020.
Photo by Donna Henderson Craft.

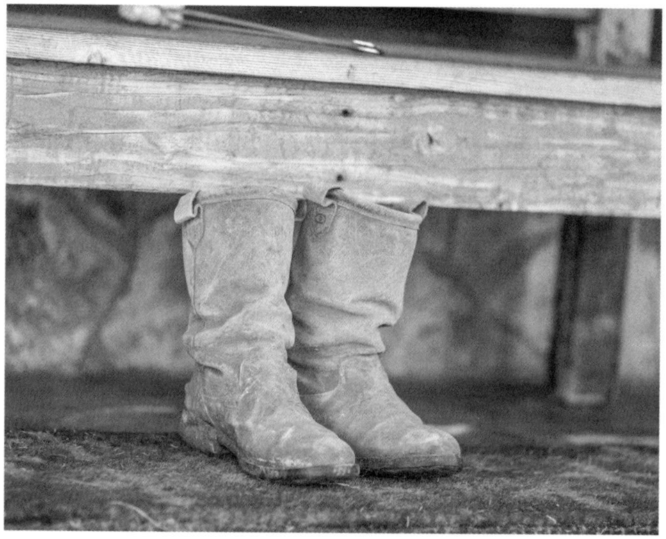

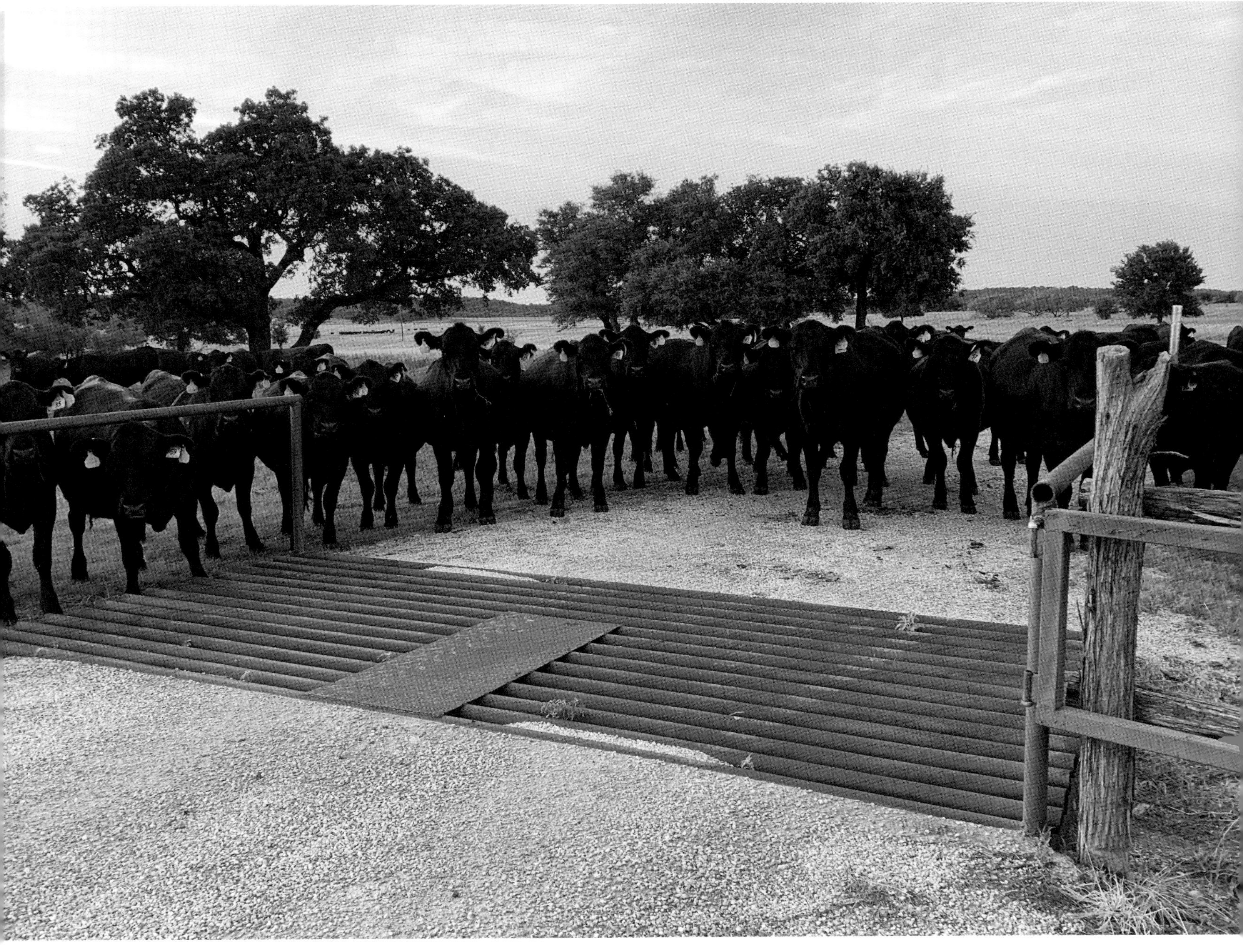

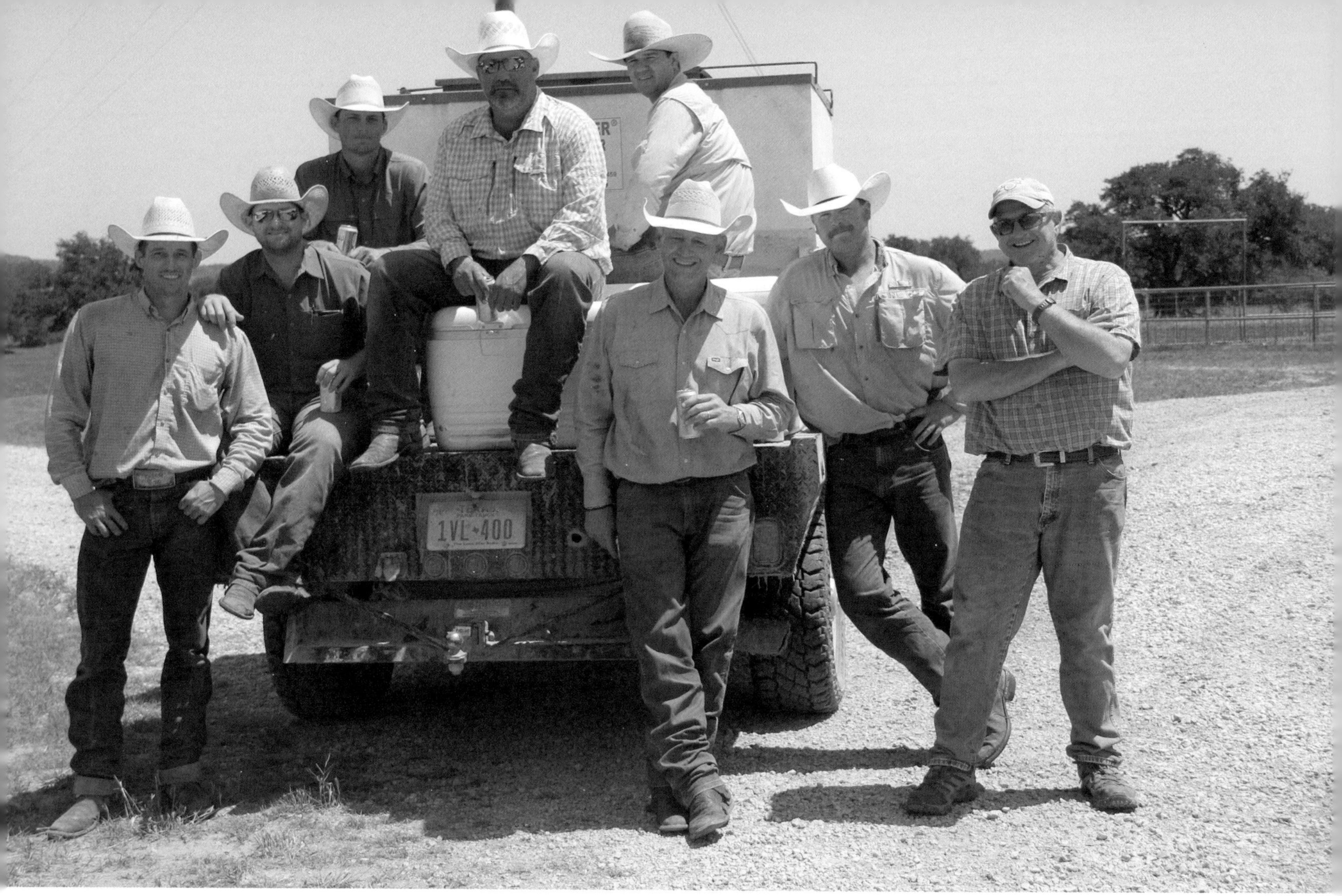

End of the day's work, 2020.
Photo by Donna Henderson Craft.

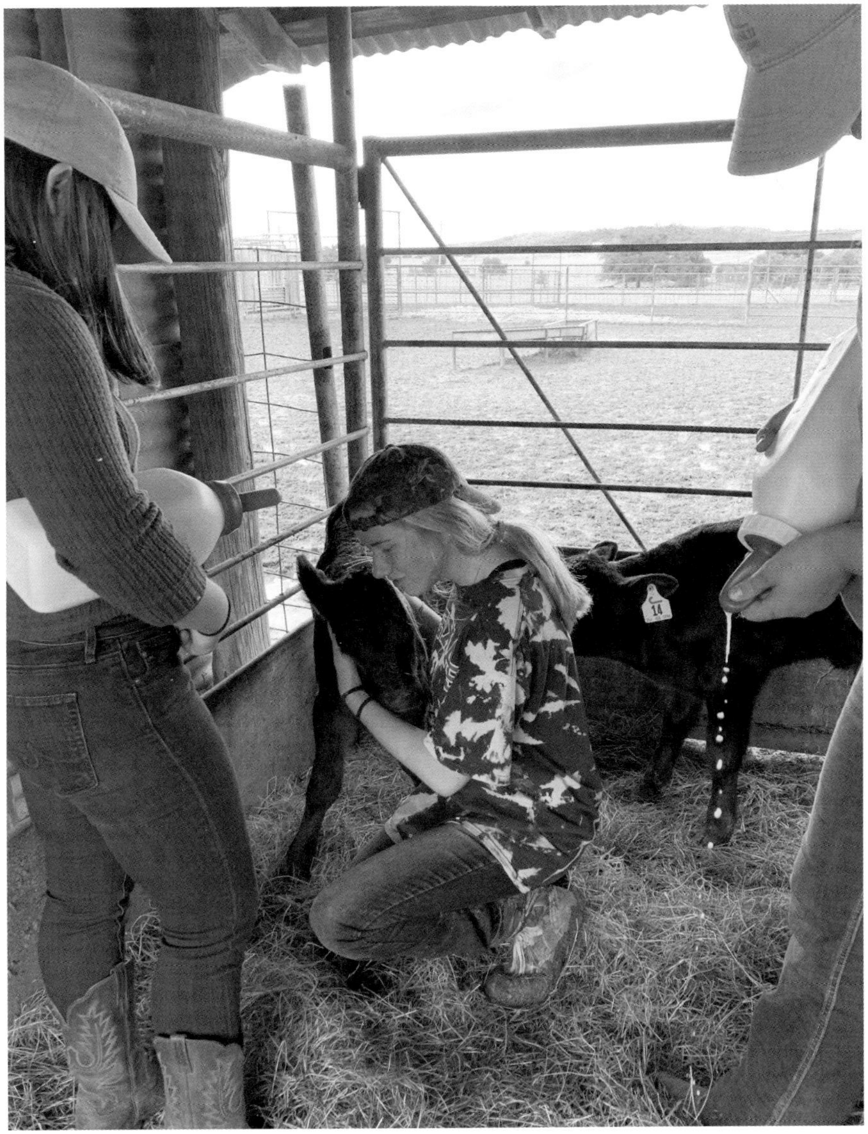

Kate Henderson, time to bottle feed the orphan calf, 2020.
Photo by Curtis Henderson.

AFTERWORD

A friend who knew the Cherryhomes family well and clearly remembered stories of T. H. and his exploits asked me a question: "Was T. H. a man of God?"

A curious thing to ask, I thought, and maybe a bit arrogant, but a straightforward question to which T. H. himself might have answered, "None of your damned business."

My honest reply was, "I don't know."

I think it's doubtful that he frequented prayer meetings or Sunday church services, and yet.

I do know this. My great-grandfather's personal beliefs and guiding principles expanded beyond the walls of any church or man-made dogmas. He believed in the land and its natural ways, which he knew as well as he knew the back of his own hands. Hard work, determination, and profound love and respect for the land guided and nourished the depth of his soul.

It's a fact that if you know how and where to look, if you take to heart what you see, if you live with the land and accept the truths it offers, watch the behavior of its wildlife, you will know that the land never lies.

Straightforward and honest, each slice of land, even the land on which you stand, is as unique as any human who ever lived. And more predictable. Like the humans who inhabit it, the land has its own face and stubborn needs. When honored and respected, cultivated and cherished, it will thrive.

When over-worked, over-planted, neglected, or ignored, its native plants will roam with abandon reclaiming homestead, garden, or cultivated field. Caretakers who dare to push the land into becoming something that does not suit its nature will suffer. Crops will refuse to thrive, and barren soil will show its face where seeds refuse to grow.

T. H., carving out a life for himself, was not naïve or ignorant. This new way of life was not his first rodeo. Humbled more than once by storms, crop failure, cockleburs, and drought, he took note of everything he saw, everything he experienced, and correcting his mistakes, adjusted his plans to suit the terrain, the expected weather, the seasons, and worked in tandem with them all while he pushed ahead with his dreams.

Was he a man of God? I would suggest this: his God was a living one who blew in the north, east, south, and west winds. A God who brought rain and drought and who gave strength and stubbornness to soil, plants, animals, and humans alike. And somewhere in that mysterious plan of all life, T. H. Cherryhomes stood tall and sure and strong.

OPPOSITE
Some of T. H.'s quotes and stories he told, which I found in his leather-bound scrapbook.
Family collection.

SOME COWBOY STORIES THAT WERE EXPERIENCED AND TOLD BY---

T.H. CHERRYHOMES

AT a cow round up a fellow came accusing the boys of stealing the cattle and driving them off while doing this kind of cattle work. He was riding an old grey mare and had a quilt doubled under him for a saddle, and was carrying an old army gun."He said-"By gol,something has to happen. Them cattle men have to have something done to keep from taking cattle".

The boys were sitting on the ground drinking coffee. One fellow pulled his 45 six shooter out and stirred the sugar in his coffeee . The old man said,"By gol-"and went to doubling up his quilt. As he jumped on his nag he said"I'll see you fellows again before you leave this country." Hewas soon out of sight.

ROCKING CHAIR ROUND UP

The boys got in the habit of running to grab the cups and plates before the cook hollered chuck.He told them several times not to do it any more,but they continued the practice.He finally got him a 45 six shooter,laid it up on the chuck box.He wanted the boys to wait until he hollered chuck.On this occasion he said "CHUCK" but at the same time he turned around,pointed his six shooter at them and said-"Not quite ready,you sons a'bitches!"

Deaf John was cooking for the Rocking Chair. Any of the range boys who were there will well remember when this happened,but I would not know where to find a single living man who was in Collingsworth county when it was organized.Martin Lane was Mr.Goodnight's nephew.He died about two years ago.He told me he did not know but two men who were left and that was he and myself.

CLIPPER

About 1907 Clipper was foaled.When he was lotted to brand,he got excited and jumped over the fence,which was six feet high.It would'nt do to let him outlaw so, one by one we went after him on good horses.After so many hours of pursuit, we opened the gate and finally put him in the same lot.He began giving good service at that time and is still clear footed and good life and almost as good race horse now.He is getting grey around the ankles and does'Nt show much age. He is still a good servise horse.The breeding of this horse is mainly steel dust.

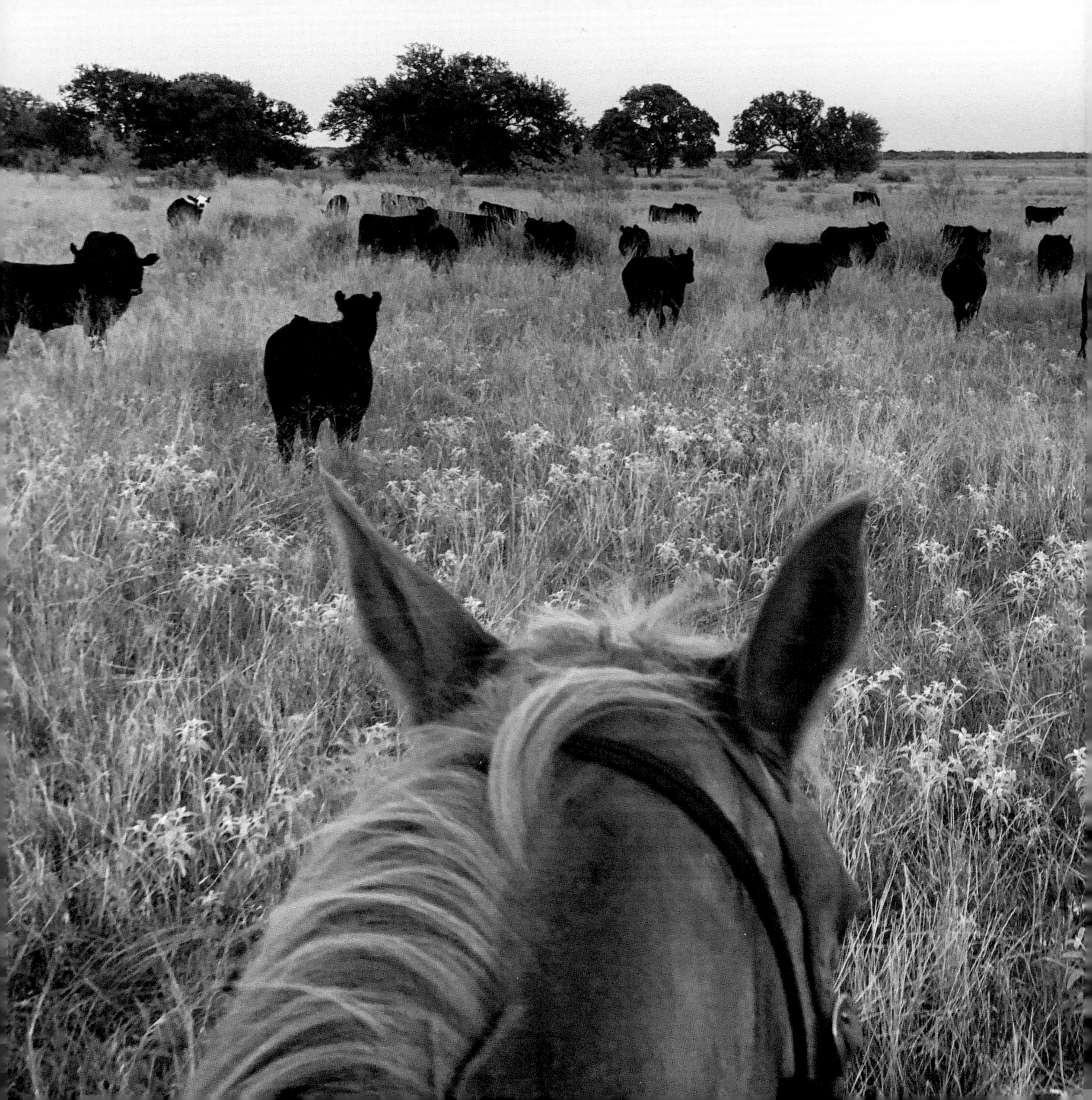

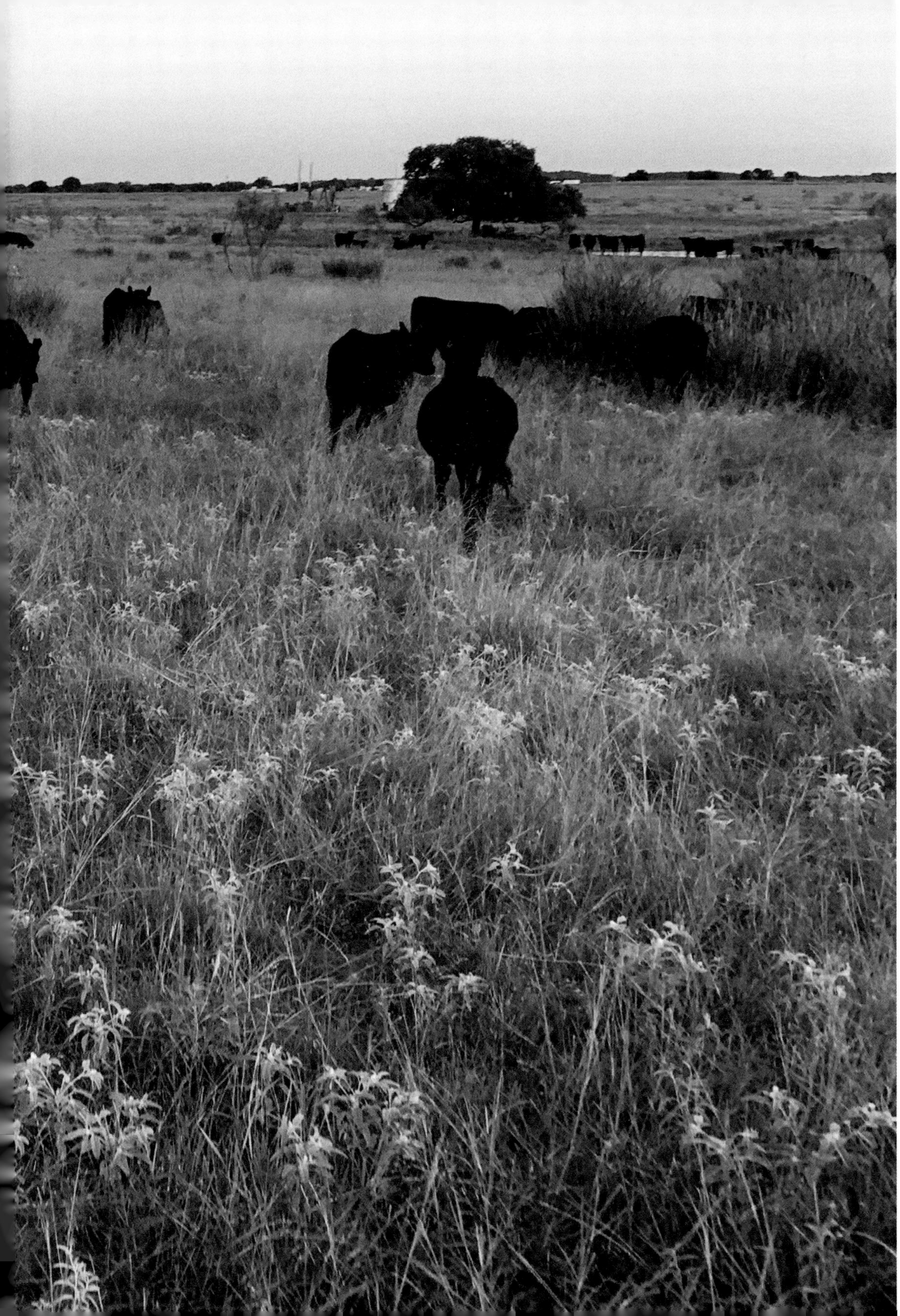

"Move 'em out," 2019.
Photo by Jeremy Enlow.